INDIAN IN THE CABINET

Also by Jody Wilson-Raybould

*From Where I Stand: Rebuilding Indigenous Nations
for a Stronger Canada*

INDIAN IN THE CABINET

SPEAKING TRUTH TO POWER

JODY WILSON-RAYBOULD

HarperCollins*Publishers*Ltd

Published by HarperCollins Publishers Ltd

First edition

HarperCollins books may be purchased for educational, business or sales promotional use through our Special Markets Department.

HarperCollins Publishers Ltd
Bay Adelaide Centre, East Tower
22 Adelaide Street West, 41st Floor
Toronto, Ontario, Canada
M5H 4E3

www.harpercollins.ca

Library and Archives Canada Cataloguing in Publication information

Title: Indian in the cabinet : speaking truth to power / Jody Wilson-Raybould.
Names: Wilson-Raybould, Jody, 1971- author.
Description: First edition.
Identifiers: Canadiana (print) 20210259876 | Canadiana (ebook) 20210259884
ISBN 9781443465366 (hardcover) | ISBN 9781443465373 (ebook)
Subjects: LCSH: Wilson-Raybould, Jody, 1971- | LCSH: Legislators—Canada—Biography. | CSH: Indigenous legislators—Canada—Biography. | CSH: Cabinet ministers—Canada—Biography. | LCSH: Attorneys general—Canada—Biography. | LCSH: Justice ministers—Canada—Biography. | CSH: Canada—Politics and government—2015- | LCGFT: Autobiographies.
Classification: LCC FC656.W55 A3 2021 | DDC 971.07/4092—dc23

Printed and bound in the United States of America
LSC/H 10 9 8 7 6 5

For Kaija, Kaylene, and Kadence—
you make all sacrifices worthwhile

CONTENTS

INDIAN IN THE CABINET

Vancouver, February 10 and 11, 2019

The sun was flooding through the third-floor windows of the Signature private plane terminal at Vancouver International Airport as I sat waiting for the prime minister to arrive. The terminal is distant and isolated, far from the bustling main terminal and the eyes of the public and the media. My husband, Tim, had dropped me off and then parked to wait for me among the cars of the prime minister's motorcade. The PM was late. Building in me was a creeping realization that this was the beginning of the end. It was here. The time had come.

It had been three days since Robert Fife's front-page story in the *Globe and Mail* set off a series of ongoing convulsions over the Liberal government's attempts to "pressure" me on the prosecution of SNC-Lavalin. As soon as the story broke, the prime minister said that "the allegations in the *Globe* story this morning are false. Neither the current nor the previous attorney general was ever directed by me or by anyone in my office to take a decision in this matter." The government's response over the next seventy-two hours had been a case study in hubris—at once both surprised that they had been caught and offended that anyone could think they would ever do anything wrong. In the Indigenous political world I had come from, we always talked about how government practice, for generations, was to deny, delay, and distract when it came to Indigenous issues. I had heard that phrase—deny, delay, and distract—since I was a kid. The past three years had shown me that governments use that strategy far beyond their dealings with Indigenous peoples. Sometimes all Canadians are treated contemptuously. On SNC-Lavalin, few were buying it. And they were right to be skeptical.

I wished it had not come to this. I felt a familiar conflict inside of me that had been there my whole life: A deep desire to believe in people. To expect the best out of them. To want them to do the right thing. Almost a protective desire to see them do right. And yet simultaneously knowing that sometimes this does not happen. That when people act a certain way time and again, they are likely to repeat it, whatever my hopes and wishes may be.

As I sat there in that room—a big room, all by myself—waiting for Prime Minister Justin Trudeau to arrive, I asked myself why I felt that I had to try to help him out of this mess, to protect him. Especially when his government had been digging a deeper and deeper hole by the hour by not coming clean on how I was pushed to take over the prosecution of SNC-Lavalin to enable them to enter into a deferred prosecution agreement, or DPA. Especially when his office had been telling their MPs to repeat lines they knew were not accurate.

I was anxious as I sat there. I could feel my lingering hope that I would be proven wrong and that everything was not as terrible as it seemed. I wished that the government would just admit their wrongdoing and deal with it openly and transparently. I knew the only way to deal with it was to tell the truth. Full transparency. It was as clear to me as sunlight. The prime minister had to simply acknowledge that the attempts to apply pressure were not proper and take concrete steps to address the wrong actions. Deep down I think I knew better than to expect him to own up. However, at that moment, I still wanted to give him the benefit of the doubt.

I saw the Canadian Armed Forces Challenger land and pull up to the private terminal. As the prime minister walked up the stairs, I could hear him talking to someone moments before he entered the room. He greeted me in his typically physical and warm way, with a hug and expressions of appreciation. "I so want you to keep being part of this government," he said.

As always, from the first time I met him in Whitehorse in 2013, he reflected on the good we can do for the country. This is so Justin Trudeau. Taking control and setting the tone. Trying to remind everyone in the room—in this case me—who is in charge. "I don't think that you leaked the story [to the *Globe*]," he said. Unless I told him otherwise, he added. A power play. He was trying to push the ball into my court.

Looking back, I do not think the prime minister had a clue what I was going to say in this meeting. As it turned out, this was the first of three private meetings with the PM over the next thirty-six hours, before I eventually resigned from his Cabinet. That resignation—and everything that led to it—would lead to him tossing me out of the Liberal caucus and then removing me as the confirmed Liberal candidate for Vancouver Granville in the 2019 general election.

The prime minister and I had not communicated since the *Globe* story broke—not even by phone—but the world had exploded around me. The public and media barrage was unlike anything I had ever experienced or could ever have anticipated. And it was a similar firestorm for the prime minister and his office. Intrusive, relentless, and everywhere.

I know the prime minister had always considered me a bit of a challenge—not political enough, too independent-minded, and ultimately not part of the inner Liberal crowd. I think I was foreign and incomprehensible to him. After all, I was from the other side of the tracks. I was an Indigenous girl from a small fishing village—Cape Mudge, on the southern tip of Quadra Island just off Vancouver Island. I am Kwakwaka'wakw. The PM did not grow up in my neighbourhoods, with the kids I grew up with. None of his family went to residential schools. My childhood memories are closer to Comox and Cape Mudge than Rockcliffe. My political point of reference was the Big House, not the House of Commons. To be fair, he did not choose how and where he grew up or who his parents were. But Liberals? Political parties? Not my world.

With the ice cracked but not broken, I started softly, reminding the prime minister where I had always stood. "I got into politics because there are issues that I am seriously committed to helping resolve." I recalled for him then one of our first conversations when he was recruiting me for the party. We were in Whitehorse, and we had talked about our visions of the country and how we seemed to have similar views. I got involved with the Liberal Party largely because I believed we shared those views, and because I thought he would be a good prime minister and create a good team. I had believed all that I'd said to him five and a half years earlier. As I repeated it in that big airport room, I found myself wondering exactly when I first realized I had been wrong.

I got to the heart of the matter. "Since you brought it up, I did not leak the story, and it is absurd and offensive you would suggest that." I wondered if he knew that I had warned Gerry Butts, his principal secretary, that I had been cornered by Robert Fife after Cabinet on February 5 as I came out of the elevator on the ground floor of West Block. Fife's questions had been so detailed they indicated something explosive was coming. I rhetorically asked the PM about the leak: "Why would I ever do that?" There was so much I had come to Ottawa to accomplish. For Indigenous peoples and all Canadians. I had traded my life as I knew it to enter federal politics, just as I knew 337 other people had. Taking myself down, which in any scenario was the most likely outcome of the story leaking, did not advance those causes. Absurd. Like so much else that was to follow.

There is no question in my mind that the prime minister knew there were attempts to pressure me to avoid a criminal prosecution of SNC-Lavalin, and while those attempts failed, thankfully, they were wrong and he knew it. Instead of simply addressing the issue publicly and accurately, the government was sending out talking heads—the new attorney general, David Lametti; Marco Mendicino; Arif Virani—to make comments that evidence has now shown were not accurate or right. I told him that he should be telling Canadians the truth.

The prime minister seemed to be listening intently. "I never directed," he said, referring to interfering in my role as the attorney general in relation to the SNC-Lavalin prosecution. His public lines started coming, which were designed to deny responsibility and culpability. There are differences between pressure and direction, he emphasized. We talked about our soon to be infamous meeting with the clerk of the Privy Council on September 17, 2018, where I had asked him directly, when SNC-Lavalin was raised, "Are you politically interfering with my role, my decision as the attorney general? I would strongly advise against it." He repeated in that airport room that I was not shuffled from being minister of justice and attorney general because of SNC-Lavalin. To which I thought to myself, *Oh yes, I remember Scott Brison resigned from Treasury,* so, of course, you then had to move the attorney general and two other ministers and elevate two MPs to fill one spot. Good grief.

As he went on, I suddenly blurted out, "I don't want you to say anything further about what happened after September 17." To this day, I am still surprised I said that. I know why I did it and why I wanted him to stop talking—I was trying to leave space open for a constructive solution to the mess the PM and his office had created and that, in my overly optimistic opinion, could still be found. Either the prime minister knew everything that had happened and did not care and was clearly lying to me and the country, or he did not know what had been happening during the months after September 17 to try to exert pressure on me and was not in control of his office. He was either complicit or incompetent. If it was the former, and the prime minister admitted it to me, there was nothing I could do to help address this matter. It was over. Either for him or me. Or even potentially the government. If it was the latter, lord help the country, there still would have been a way to admit everything publicly, address the wrongs, and do better—much better; there still would have been a way to preserve the credibility of our system and respect the rule of law.

As I had in the past, I gave the prime minister the benefit of the doubt—for what would be the last time. I made it very clear I did not trust the people around him and that he was being badly advised in this situation. He made it equally clear to me that he would never fire some of them. So I laid out the only other options that existed: The Prime Minister's Office (PMO) stuck with its current approach of changing its story over and over again, which would only make things worse. In which case I would resign. Or he came out and came clean, and we placed our trust in the truth and in Canadians.

I pushed this second option. He said he would think about it and that we would talk again.

✦

I left the meeting feeling hopeful—in hindsight, too hopeful. I believed the prime minister had actually heard what I had to say and would genuinely think about it. "I am feeling positive," I told Tim as we drove back home to our condo.

That feeling of optimism was short-lived. That evening, while we were out for dinner with my sister and our nieces, a second meeting was arranged for the prime minister and me at 7:30 the next morning at the Fairmont Pacific Rim in Vancouver, where he was staying. I am pretty sure I did not get a wink of sleep that night.

As the sun rose across Vancouver on February 11, I was still optimistic that the PM might take my best advice and come clean.

When we arrived at the hotel, Tim dropped me off out front. I saw Gerry across the lobby as I entered. He did not acknowledge me, and I felt my positive feelings floating away. The prime minister again greeted me casually and kindly at the door of his top-floor suite. But I got the sense that not all was going to go well. He mentioned that his friend owned the hotel as he gave me a quick tour of his suite. It was just the two of us. The North Shore mountains were glistening beyond the picture windows. There was a large sectional sofa and a coffee table with an odd, huge sculpture in the middle that looked as if it was made of glass. The prime minister walked over to it and kind of chopped and punched it with his hand, like he was going to break it. It was rubber. He laughed. I was on edge and uncomfortable, so seeing the PM joking around was very disconcerting. Perhaps it was his way of trying to break the tension—although I am not sure he felt any. It kind of made things worse. This all seemed like a game for him.

The prime minister launched the conversation by saying he had thought a lot about what I had said the day before, and then gave me his version of the "Shawcross" doctrine. The doctrine is the principle that states the attorney general must act with a "judicial mind" and not a "political mind" in exercising responsibilities with respect to criminal matters; it is, of course, something the PM and I had talked about before. Honestly, I cannot tell you how many people have told me they are experts on this doctrine since this SNC-Lavalin story broke. What has always been crystal clear to me—at that moment and throughout—is exactly what my role was as the attorney general. In the PM's description and questioning it was clear he had talked to others. I remarked, "You have been talking to a lawyer."

We then proceeded to cover the same ground as the day before. I recounted, again, the incidents where pressure was attempted, and he again had excuses or answers for everything. He repeated that he would not clean house or fire anyone, and then he offered up, "If we did, we would not be government in October." I replied, "I would be surprised if we were in government if you did not clean at least some of the house in some way and call some type of investigation." I added, "After all, if you are confident you did nothing wrong, then why would you not want to do this?" This was about the maintenance of the rule of law and the fundamental tenets of our democracy. Surely this was worthy of our attention. He again insisted that no one would be fired.

At this point, I could feel the conversation beginning to turn. It was going to get personal, and with that, a bit more heated. He asked if I trusted him. He also asked if I trusted his judgment to build a team. Ugh. Such questions. "I want to believe in you and trust in you," I replied. "But it is hard to separate the two questions. I do not trust the people around you any longer."

I could see the agitation visibly building in the prime minister. His mood was shifting. I remember seeing it. I remember feeling it. I had seen and felt this before on a few occasions, when he would get frustrated and angry. But this was different. He became strident and disputed everything I had said. He made it clear that everyone in his office was telling the truth and that I, and by extension Jessica Prince, my chief of staff, and others, were not. He told me I had not experienced what I said I did. He used the line that would later become public, that I had "experienced things differently."

I knew what he was really asking. What he was saying. In that moment, I knew he wanted me to lie—to attest that what had occurred had not occurred. For me, this was just more evidence that he did not know me, did not know who I was or where I was from. Me—lie to protect a Crown government acting badly; a political party; a leader who was not taking responsibility. He must be delusional.

As he went on, I stared out the window over to the North Shore. I did not say anything for a while; I was struck with an overwhelming feeling of sadness and loss, and of deep disappointment. I knew then that the path that had led me to being the "Indian" in the Cabinet had veered in a different direction. The work was not over, certainly, but this man was not the leader I had thought him to be. It was clear. Now, it was clear.

I eventually told the prime minister that I was feeling uncomfortable and that I wanted to go. I told him the only option he had left me with was to consider whether I could stay in my position or whether I needed to resign, but that I needed to think more.

Before I could leave, he started to talk in his aggressive and condescending way about how much work we had done and still had to do. I cut him off and countered, "Don't blame me for this. This is not my fault." I was laser angry in that moment. I felt him turning on me even more—I could see it in his face, his eyes, and in his mannerisms—because he wasn't getting his way.

I told him I had serious concerns and that my belief in him was very shaken. At some point, he asked me what he should say to the media. He had a media availability ostensibly on housing later that morning. He mentioned a line they were thinking of using: "Her presence in Cabinet speaks for itself . . ." Can you believe it? I told him I was not going to give him communications advice. How ridiculous. In my opinion, there is no spin on dishonesty.

I got up and left. I had to think.

◆

Tim and I drove home.

My mind was swirling. I had gone to that meeting open-minded, ready to discuss and address the prime minister's comments and questions. But it had gone too far when he got angry because I would not acquiesce to what he wanted, and when he made it clear that he was convinced he and his staff had done nothing wrong. He clearly believed others were giving him better advice. And he trusted them more. He would not listen to me. My opinion, and the reality of what had happened, did not matter. I did not matter.

As Tim and I talked in the car—and as I had talked with Minister Jane Philpott, my closest friend in government, and Jessica Prince, to whom all of this was no surprise—I knew in my heart what I had to do. Knowing all that I knew as the former attorney general, and now knowing the prime minister was not going to come clean, I had no choice. There was now no trust. I had lost any belief I had in the prime minister. And there is no room in Cabinet for someone who thinks the prime minister is untrustworthy. There was also no room for me in a government that would act this way on matters of core principle such as upholding the rule of law.

It was about 8:45 in the morning when we got back to the condo. We later turned on the TV to watch the PM's media availability, which we knew was going to be late. The first question he took was, inevitably, about me and SNC-Lavalin. He replied, "In our system of government, of course, her presence in cabinet should actually speak for itself." I turned to Tim and said I had to resign.

I called Jessica to set up another meeting with the prime minister so I could tell him I was resigning as a member of Cabinet. That meeting—our third in thirty-six hours—was set for seven that evening. My intent was to resign at 1 p.m. Eastern Standard Time the next day.

Not everyone around me was sure about my decision. I could tell Jessica was uncertain that I would actually end up resigning, but she began making plans for our staff regardless. Tim was angry. Angry at the prime minister. Angry at the whole situation. And he did not want to see me resign, but he also knew it was time. That too many lines had been crossed.

◆

I started the conversation that evening. No pleasantries and no hugs. "You once said to me that if ever I was going to resign that I must tell you directly. I agreed when you asked me to do that. So that is why I am here. I intend to resign from Cabinet tomorrow at 1 p.m. Ottawa time."

The prime minister did not react. At all. I thought to myself that he must have already known it was coming. He did not really ask for an explanation or seek to understand.

Then, like a broken record, he began repeating his lines about SNC-Lavalin. Casual comments were not pressure. Pressure was not direction.

I think at one point I might have actually laughed. Admittedly, it would have been disdainful if I did. But the only thing I could do was laugh. There had been few times in my life when I could actually feel anger building up inside me. This was one of them.

Suddenly I just wanted to be away from this man.

As he went on about the Shawcross doctrine, I thought I heard a strange noise in the suite. I looked down the hall to see who was there. The prime minister noticed and quipped, "No one is there."

As I had earlier in the day, I started to feel very uncomfortable. I told him so. I let him know I was not comfortable being there, in that room. And that I thought someone was listening. He said nothing to this. I can't recall the exact words I spoke next, but it was something along these lines: I am not going to have legal debate with you. I told you my views in September. We went over it yesterday and again this morning. My views have not changed. You are wrong, Prime Minister, and you are on a dangerous path. The truth will come out. It always does. And I will not lie for you.

As we went back and forth, the prime minister started acting in ways I had seen him act with others, but never before with me. He cut me off, and in one of his signature moves, he flipped up his hand to indicate I should stop talking. He rolled his eyes and did his own disdainful laughing at my responses to his questions. He did not seem to understand why I had come or to care that I was resigning.

We went around and around. He was increasingly exasperated and angry. September. December. Why he had not heard from me directly. He emphatically told me that SNC-Lavalin was not the reason I had been shuffled. He also said that from September 17, 2018, to the *Globe* article published on February 7, 2019, he had not heard anything about the matter and did not know it was an issue. This was an amazing admission—if it was true. At one point, he even speculated that the leak to the *Globe* was from the Privy Council Office.

Again, I just wanted it to end. The condescension. The belittlement. The lack of seriousness. The lack of commitment to the truth. I felt he was trying to put me back into my place. What did I know? Why was I there? In the prime minister's version of the SNC-Lavalin affair, I did not know what I was talking about. I was wrong. The so-called experts in the PMO were right. It was all in my head. In his view, I was just hurt.

"We have all tried to help you," he said. "We have all tried so much to help you be successful." *Thank you, great white father*, I thought to myself.

We were both totally exasperated at this point.

"I do not believe in you anymore," I said.

"I still do not know why you are resigning," he said.

"I do not trust you anymore," I replied.

With that our conversation ended. The prime minister, as was his way, asked for one last hug.

I felt sick. And sad. I cannot remember if we hugged. I left.

I went to the airport and boarded a plane back to Ottawa, where I would resign the next day. I slept the whole flight. Go figure.

ONE

Recruitment

Why did I write this book? Good question. Honestly, I am not sure. No doubt, I wanted to make sense of things I experienced while in federal government—including how I ended up resigning from Cabinet and becoming an Independent MP. That explains why this book is not a memoir of my entire life. I cannot imagine writing (or someone reading) such a thing. Another reason is that I felt and continue to feel that I have a duty to share some reflections on the particular circumstance in which I found myself—of being the first Indigenous person to be minister of justice and attorney general of Canada. Fulfilling that role was not what I expected. Writing has helped me explore this reality, and perhaps it will be of interest to some of you. I think it may also provide a perspective on this moment in the life of Canada and some of the challenges that we face.

Of course, no one's life unfolds in structured chapters. We all emerge from layers of peoples, places, cultures, and experiences.

Histories shape our stories. So, I can only speak of today—and yesterday, and tomorrow, as this book does—from a place that starts with the obvious but most important facts that have determined my life. I am Indigenous. And Canadian.

I come from the Musgamagw Tsawataineuk and Laich-Kwil-Tach peoples of northern Vancouver Island, who are part of the Kwakwaka'wakw, also known as the Kwak'wala-speaking peoples. I was raised in a family of Indigenous leaders. My grandmother's name was Pugladee—the highest-ranking name in our Clan—the Eagle Clan. Her name means "a good host." My father's name is Hemas Kla-Lee-Lee-Kla, which means "number one amongst the eagles, the Chief who is always there to help." He is our Clan's hereditary Chief—and maybe I was just destined to carry on their work. My name, Puglaas, means "woman born to noble people." Our culture, worldview, spirituality, and way of life are integrally related to the natural world around us—the land, air, and waters that have always sustained us; this is our religion. My society, in important ways, is a matrilineal one. This means that descent is traced and property is inherited through the female line. We are potlatching peoples. The Potlatch is the core of how we govern ourselves. It is here that our names are passed down or given from generation to generation. It is where laws are made, disputes are settled, people are married, and wealth is redistributed.

I was born on March 23, 1971, at Vancouver General Hospital. My mum is Sandy, whom I have lovingly called "Oldboot" since she moved in a few doors down from me on our reserve at Cape Mudge in 2007. Indigenous people tend to give nicknames to others, particularly those they love. Oldboot has reminded me over the years that I was not the prettiest baby. I was born jaundiced, and with a purple birthmark in the middle of my forehead.

I was named Jody for no particular reason except that it was a popular name at the time. Puglaas was given to me by my grandmother in her Potlatch at Gilford Island when I was five. I was given that name because of the roles and responsibilities, including around leadership, that I was expected to play and accept. As you will see, striving to embody my name is a big part of my story, and the story told in this book.

My dad, William Lane Wilson (Billy to my mum and his mum), was not at my birth. As was common for him in those days, he was away for work. My parents were married in 1966, after being high school sweethearts in Courtenay, British Columbia. While they did not divorce until 1980, I have no memories of being at home with both mum and dad, as they separated not long after I was born. My sister, Kory, who is fourteen months older than me, also does not have memories of us living as a family.

My family is, in many ways, typical of a First Nations person growing up in Canada. I have an Indigenous father and my mum is of English and German descent. My dad, mum, sister (and her kids), and I are all registered as status Indians by the federal government and are members of the We Wai Kai community at Cape Mudge. My identity and reality were, and are, as an Indigenous person. In addition to my sister Kory, I have two half-brothers: William (Jumbo, as we call him) and Cory. We didn't know of Cory until recent years. My extended family is large and sprawling, a web of endless aunties, uncles, and cousins. Many live on Indian reserves on or around Vancouver Island, while others live close by—in places such as Campbell River, Comox, and Courtenay—or have headed to the bigger cities of Victoria or Vancouver. Some also live south, in Washington State. Many of my older relatives attended residential schools. My dad managed to be protected from them (more on that later), and the possibility of attending a residential school was never a threat to Kory and me.

I did not grow up on reserve, though I have had a house on my reserve in Cape Mudge since 2006 and have spent as much time as I can living there.

My early childhood was somewhat nomadic. Mum, Kory, and I had lived in Vancouver, Calgary, Victoria, and Port Hardy all by the time I was ten. After that we settled in Comox, where I lived for the next eight years and graduated from Highland Senior Secondary School in 1989.

While, evidently, I may have been an ugly kid, I was headstrong and determined, without fear, from my first days. My mum describes this as my having "personality." I guess these traits explain why I'd had more than two hundred stitches by the age of twelve. This pattern has continued into adulthood—such as when I impaled my right arm on a wrought-iron fence when I was in my twenties and had to be hospitalized. I come by it honestly; my mum, a teacher, is pretty fierce and determined herself. When I was in grade three, she was my teacher, and one day during the first week of school my work (apparently) was not acceptable. When Mum asked me to correct it, I stomped off. Mum, in front of all the other kids, marched me down to the principal's office. Definitely a win for her, as the other kids were now scared. If she could punish me in this way, what might she do to them?

When I was a teenager, I was a teenager. I tried all of the stereo-typical teen stunts. One time I snuck out at night only to find Mum in my bed waiting for me when I returned in the wee hours of the morning. Mum likes to say I was "full of it." She calls me a "rat" for all the mischief I got into in those years, though she gives me credit for being a good student, a good athlete—going to the BC Summer Games twice for swimming and track and field—and, more impor-tantly, for always being "very caring towards Elders." Tim McKinnon, one of my favourite teachers from those days, describes me as an unusual kid who sat back and watched a lot, was reticent in revealing her full self, and also acted out a fair bit—though he is kind in saying my acting out was "bright and full." He says I always thought about things before I spoke. I like to think that is still true.

Growing up we would see Dad regularly, but it was a reality that he was travelling much of the time for his work as an Indigenous political leader. When I was younger, my dad would send me a plant on my birthday every year, and flowers to Kory on hers. I think he felt the need to send us something living, something that needed care, almost as a reminder of his deep love and care for us and his pride in how we were growing up. There were some periods of time when we would see him more. Kory and I lived with him—and his second wife, Shirley, and our younger brother Jumbo—in Comox for my grade five year, which is the longest stretch we were with him. During that year, he was travelling as usual, which was really hard. But it did mean we spent a lot of time with his mother, my grandmother Ethel (Pugladee). We called her "Granny" and she also lived in Comox—about a twenty-minute walk from my dad's house. Kory and I would walk there often.

Our granny was a force. She has been a profound figure in my life, in some ways a shaper of the person I am as much or more than anyone else. I know it is hard to understand what I mean when I say this, but in many ways the story I tell in this book—entering into Indigenous politics, moving into Canadian politics, becoming a minister of the Crown, and then speaking truth to power and being kicked out of the Liberal caucus because of it—is partially her story. I think by the end of the book it will be clear what I mean when I say this. I hope so anyway.

But don't mistake me. Many things my granny experienced feel worlds apart from the reality of my life—and she, like so many others, endured things I can barely imagine. We do not know exactly when my grandmother was born, but we guess it was around 1910. The only records of her birth were destroyed because of fires over the years. She was the oldest of seven kids. At age nine, she was sent to residential school with her younger sister, Alice, who was eight. At the time in our territory, it was typical for Indian agents to just show up in a boat and take the kids away. Her father wanted to avoid that, so he brought his children to Alert Bay himself, where he bought them some clothes and then dropped them off at St. Michael's Indian Residential School; they were going to be forced to go one way or another. In 1990, my granny was recorded by Kory telling stories of many aspects of her life, including her first day in residential school. Of course, many generations of Indigenous peoples from across the country have stories of their experiences in these schools, many of which were heard by Canadians through the Truth and Reconciliation Commission report. My granny passed away before the commission did its work, and I am grateful to have her recollections recorded in this way:

> *I will never forget the day we went there. There was a little Japanese lady in Alert Bay that made clothes and I don't know whether my parents had seen her but anyway we didn't go to school until towards evening when the little dresses she sewed for us were made. And mine was pink and my sister's was blue. And they were the nicest things we ever had up to then. Funny what you remember. We went to school and we must have went there in the evening because it was time to go to bed. You had to be there August 1—and that is still summer up there—that is when the good weather starts. We would go to bed at seven o'clock and we could hear the kids playing and all the noise outside. And I thought it was so cruel, but I guess they were doing their best for these little dumb ignorant Indian people—didn't know anything.*
>
> *It was a great big dormitory—I forget whether there were fifty-two beds in this dorm. Forty or fifty and there were two big porches, glassed-in porches where they put the kids that they suspected of having TB. They were segregated at night and they had to watch them for the symptoms whatever the symptoms were. But seems like whatever they did unconsciously they always seemed to separate you, so they put me at one end of this great big dorm and they put my sister in one corner and I in the other corner. And there was no electric lights. When they went out the place seemed so dark. It was a*

great big dungeon—all these metal beds, row on row like you were in a jail—not a jail . . . jails are in little cubicles, aren't they. Anyway, it looked like an institution—well it was . . . it was an institution. So I couldn't sleep. I had never gone to bed that early in my entire life because I was like a little gypsy at home. You know . . . we just did exactly what we wanted to do . . . playing . . . it was a great life.

So, I could hear my sister sobbing. You could still see cause the summer nights don't seem to get very dark—I said come on . . . they put me in a double—why I don't know . . . I think they did everything to torture me . . . I was on a double . . . like bunkbeds only they were metal ones—army cots, I was on the top one and instead of putting my sister down below me they put her in a regular little bed. She said, I can't get up to your bed, you better come into mine. I crawled in bed with her and we cried ourselves to sleep that first night. And quite a few nights after that.

When I listen to my granny say those words now, I hear some of the sorrow and pain in her voice, but what comes through far more is the indomitable fortitude of this woman. The unrelenting strength. She had that strength as a child. In terms of being at residential school, she said, "Something told me then that you were put here to learn how to talk English so you could talk for your people." Another story she tells about the school was when they were threatening to send her to "reform school" in Vancouver unless she ratted on what some of the other kids were up to. My granny had never been to Vancouver, so she told them to go ahead and send her. Instead, they decided to strap her, which my grandmother said was almost a daily occurrence. On recounting that occasion, she said, "They said the first time we cried they would stop but I was too stubborn, I didn't care if they beat me till I was dead. I just bit my teeth together so I would not cry. They just gave up strapping me, but I could feel the blood running down my legs. That is what we learned from the Christian." My grandmother was eventually kicked out of the residential school. A blessing.

Her first marriage (she had three) was an arranged marriage at the age of fourteen, primarily for the purpose of bearing children to join families. As she would often say, "The first marriage was for duty, the second was for children and comfort, and the third was for love." My dad was from the second.

But when I think of my granny—I am pretty sure when anyone thinks of my granny—I think of none of these darker and sometimes horrific things. Rather, I think of her indomitable spirit and certainly of her role in our culture. As a keeper of knowledge. Her place in the Potlatch. Her leadership. It is how she brought our teachings into my life, demonstrated them in her life, and how she guided us. Granny lived in an old green house at the end of Centennial Avenue in Comox, with a little alcove off the front door with four chairs around a table. For countless hours, we would sit there listening as she talked, shared, and schooled us. Just as I cannot imagine my life without her guiding me along the way, I cannot reflect on the truth of my story without discovering and sharing more of hers.

In my speeches and interviews I often talk about addressing Canada's legacy of colonialism. My granny lived that legacy—like so many have and still do—of being an "Indian" in Canada. She also revealed so much of what we need to know to address that legacy and live fully as an Indigenous person in Canada. Somehow, my Canadian journey as an Indigenous woman led me to Cabinet. And in some ways, that experience deepened my experience of being an "Indian." It is that story that I try to tell.

•

Long before I entered federal politics, I was involved in Indigenous leadership. On November 27, 2012, I was re-elected by the Chiefs of BC as the Assembly of First Nations (AFN) Regional Chief of

British Columbia. In Canada, the "Indians" are politically divided up into approximately six hundred bands under the Indian Act. A small number of these bands have transitioned to self-government; currently there are twenty-five recognized self-governing nations in Canada, representing forty-three Indigenous communities. They collectively belong to a political organization called the Assembly of First Nations. There are ten Regional Chiefs representing regions of Canada, as well as a National Chief.

At the time, I was the only female Regional Chief in Canada, as I had been since first being elected in 2009. I was also chair of the First Nations Finance Authority, a board member of the First Nations Lands Advisory Board, and a Councillor for We Wai Kai, my community. We Wai Kai is like a lot of communities. It is small and part of a larger Indigenous language group and nation that was divided up by the Indian Act. We, along with other communities that are part of a broader nation, have long tried to negotiate a proper relationship with the federal and provincial governments. Like most such efforts across the country, this has never gotten far.

When re-elected as Regional Chief, it never crossed my mind that I would not finish my second three-year term. It would have been unfathomable that the reason I ultimately did not was because I would end up running to be a member of Parliament for the Liberal Party of Canada. And that I would become a minister? In fact, the minister of justice and attorney general in a country that had colonized Indigenous peoples for 150 years? Ludicrous.

My only political preoccupations in 2009 as a newly elected Regional Chief were about the increasingly complicated and sometimes dysfunctional reality of national Indigenous politics. When Shawn Atleo—who is from the community of Ahousaht off Vancouver Island and was Regional Chief of BC before me—arrived on the scene as National Chief of the Assembly of First Nations earlier that same year, he was confronted with the many ongoing realities. These included the lack of respect for Indigenous rights by governments, of course, but also a lack of appreciation on the part of a number of long-time Regional Chiefs from across the country of his BC roots and his skills and focus on building bridges with all Canadians. Shawn had been elected in the AFN national election by a razor-thin margin against Perry Bellegarde, who is from Little Black Bear in Saskatchewan.

There has always been a challenging relationship between the Indigenous leaders from British Columbia and those from parts of the rest of the country. I suspect other regions would say the same thing. One of the main reasons for this divide is treaties. Historic treaties are in place over most of Canada—the numbered treaties entered into between 1871 and 1921—but not in British Columbia. These treaties were understood by Indigenous peoples as a proper recognition of their title, rights, and government, and as documents that secured particular lands to them as part of the treaty settlement. Canada has viewed these treaties as land surrender agreements and, even then, has utterly failed to honour them. Other than part of Treaty 8 in the northeast of BC and the pre-Confederation treaties on parts of Vancouver Island, there were no historic treaties entered into in British Columbia. This is a significant issue. While all First Nations peoples have experienced colonialism in the same way in terms of the imposition of the Indian Act and residential schools and being governed over by a separate department of "Indian Affairs," some of the areas of political and legal focus have been distinct. And sometimes that results in different priorities.

In those early AFN executive meetings the tension was often intense, and little concrete work was getting done. Shawn and I were natural allies in terms of policy objectives and strategy as well as in trying to change the way the AFN operated. We were both interested in mitigating some of the long-time tensions that existed between and among regions.

However, the executive was basically split down the middle on regional and generational lines. There was also the challenge that not everyone on the AFN executive was as prepared or ready to work as hard as others. This was not so dissimilar from federal Cabinet, as I would learn later. Some Regional Chiefs would not come prepared for the meetings. This drove me crazy, as there was so much work to do and so little time. It was here where I became more aware of the fact that, in some cases, people may get into politics primarily to achieve office. They do not necessarily aspire to use that office to do something to better the world and the lives of people. It still upsets me that I met some who I perceived to be passive seat warmers—both in national Indigenous politics and in federal politics—who listen to others and let them do the "work" without contributing much to what needs to be done.

Dialogue at the AFN executive often followed typical patterns, rehashing the same themes and lines and getting off topic. Decisions were often foreordained and not always debated in principled terms. Shawn worked, in ways that I supported and often led, to overcome this pattern. But change was slow, as is often the case in organizational cultures.

And then there was the fact I was a woman in a boys' club. This was also not dissimilar from the culture of Parliament Hill. There had never been a female National Chief and only a handful of female Regional Chiefs. Sexist remarks were regular. In one heated meeting on Indigenous health, an older male Regional Chief said, "Don't worry, little lady, I will protect you," and patted me on my knee. Gah! "I can protect myself," I replied loudly.

In such circumstances, I know that to keep quiet is enabling. Even where it is difficult to speak up, one must—not with aggression or malice but with conviction and strength and with a kindness that says, *The world is changing and people need to change as well.* I know that people need to understand that they may be part of the problem they are trying to fix. I do not know if this individual at the meeting really ever understood what he was doing, but he never said anything to me quite like it again at the executive, and I hope he thought twice before speaking in such ways in other contexts.

During my time as a political leader in the Indigenous community, I gained a reputation for speaking my mind. I remember one of the first meetings I had with the Union of British Columbia Indian Chiefs (UBCIC)—an organization that historically has represented the perspective of those First Nations in the province that do not support the BC treaty-making process—when I challenged the orthodoxy on sovereignty and rights recognition. If the sovereignty some leaders supported was followed to its logical conclusion, it would mean splitting up Canada. I rejected the idea of sovereignty as meaning the end of Canada. But I do support sovereignty in the sense of structuring proper nation-to-nation relationships between Crown governments and Indigenous governments that recognize Indigenous Nationhood, title, rights, jurisdictions, and laws.

I do not think any leader had ever spoken about this issue in the way I did during that first meeting. I think I may have challenged people. But I always supported rights recognition and rebuilding our nations as part of a strong Canada. Back during the constitutional negotiations in the 1970s and 1980s, the goal for my father and other leaders was a Constitution that included recognition of the history, place, Nationhood, government, laws, rights, and territories of Indigenous peoples in Canada. I have always said that bringing Indigenous peoples into Confederation—finishing this unfinished business so that Indigenous peoples can see their faces in the mirror of our Constitution—is the best approach for ultimately improving the quality of life for Indigenous peoples and in Canada as a whole. I still believe this.

On top of the internal challenges at the AFN, we were dealing, at best, with an indifferent Stephen Harper Conservative government in Ottawa that was not sympathetic to true reconciliation. A "hostile government" is probably a more accurate description. And partially as a result of this, the dynamics in the Indigenous world were changing. Restlessness among Indigenous peoples was spilling over into the streets and onto the headlines. For the first time in a long while,

Indigenous matters were a preoccupation of the country as a whole. Indeed, I think 2012 and 2013 will be looked upon as a time when a permanent shift about Indigenous realities in this country took place in the Canadian consciousness. This is vitally important, as it is only with increased, and increasing, awareness of the truth of our history and present circumstances that real change can take place.

Idle No More, of course, was in the forefront, along with hunger strikes. For a time, this movement galvanized work at the national level. Idle No More started in late 2012, established by a number of women who were protesting the dismantling of environmental protection laws and calling for a real "nation-to-nation" relationship with the Crown, a relationship based on respect. Protest movements under the Idle No More banner sprouted up very rapidly across Canada and beyond. This led to several hunger strikes, including one by Chief Theresa Spence from Attawapiskat. The push for tangible change was growing fast on every issue you can imagine, from upholding Indigenous rights to dealing with the housing crisis on reserves.

I believe Idle No More was a cry for us all to do better. In the wake of the protests, Shawn, along with a few Indigenous representatives from across the country, including myself, met with Prime Minister Harper in January 2013. As we sat in the meeting, the sound of drums could be heard outside the Langevin Block (renamed the Office of the Prime Minister and Privy Council in 2017). While not making too many commitments, Prime Minister Harper did at least agree that he needed to establish a high-level mechanism to oversee reform of the way Canada negotiates modern treaties and how it implements historic ones. Senior Oversight Committees were formed that included representatives from the Prime Minister's Office, Privy Council Office, Indian and Northern Affairs Canada (INAC), as the department was called at the time, and the AFN. The prime minister also agreed we needed to get rid of the Indian Act and said he wanted solutions. We, of course, told him we had solutions.

But ultimately the challenges of renewing the relationship between First Nations and the Crown overtook the AFN. When Shawn was accused somewhat unfairly by some Chiefs of cutting a backroom deal on education reform with the Harper government, it was clear the end was coming for him. Shawn began to recede until he ultimately resigned in May 2014.

And for me, all this turmoil meant I was extremely busy—which I have always liked. Driving my hard work was my continuing passion to see change happen and to build on the work of the leaders before me, now fuelled by the renewed and increasing energy of Indigenous youth and women from across the country. But my frustration was also growing. Work in BC was fine; we had completed most of the major initiatives we had set out to do, including progress on First Nations rebuilding strong and appropriate governance, which had been my primary focus. And, as was often the case at that time, it seemed easier for BC leaders to make progress compared to much of the rest of the country. In BC, we were able to move work forward at a provincial level through the combination of our three province-wide organizations—the First Nations Summit, the British Columbia Assembly of First Nations (BCAFN), and the UBCIC, collectively known as the First Nations Leadership Council. This progress was evidenced by the formation of a province-wide health council and authority and an education steering committee, as well as by the support given to nations leading the charge to advance rights recognition in the courts.

Ultimately, like Indigenous people across the country, I was getting restless. While I appreciate that true change takes time and some progress was being made, the pace of change was too slow and inconsistent. We had to do more. Change takes courage, including the courage to break away from old ways of doing things that are not achieving the needed results. The groundwork had been laid. We had experience and we knew what was working and what was not in improving the lives of our peoples. But the change was not deep enough or as widespread as it could have been. And while I was working harder than I ever had, my anxiety to get more done was also increasing. Deep inside I knew that to help drive that necessary change, I was going to end up adjusting my political direction. But I did not have any idea what that might look like.

◆

A recurring theme in my life is that almost imperceptibly, out of nowhere, I come to realize my path has shifted. This is especially true in relation to the leadership roles I have been guided towards and fortunate enough to play. Fate seems to intervene. Without my instigation, person after person and event after event send me on my way towards a realization of where I need to focus my energy.

Given this theme in my life, I am not surprised that going to Whitehorse to attend the 34th Annual General Assembly of the AFN in July 2013 ended up marking the beginning of my life in federal politics. It was there that I first met Justin Trudeau. But as I think back and try to remember what was going through my mind in the lead-up to that moment—how I felt, what I wanted, and what (if anything) I anticipated—little is clear.

The one obvious and relatively constant force in my non-Indigenous political life then was former prime minister Paul Martin. We first met in person in 2012 when he slipped into the back of the room at the BCAFN AGM I was hosting at the Westin Wall Centre in Richmond. He appeared when we were presenting financial statements, so from the stage we cracked the inevitable jokes about having a former federal minister of finance evaluate the statements. Prior to that we had talked on the phone a few times. Our first-ever conversation took place when I was on the ferry between Prince Rupert and Digby Island (Tsimshian Territory). I was impressed that the former prime minister would be calling me as I visited Indigenous communities on the northwest coast.

At the time I had no real idea what was motivating him to connect with me regularly. I suspected, and he later confirmed, it was because of his interest in the Indigenous governance work we were doing. Ever since his time as prime minister, when he had tried valiantly to drive a transformational breakthrough in Crown-Indigenous relations through the Kelowna Accord, Indigenous governance had been one of his passions. He recognized that addressing Canada's legacy of colonialism required Indigenous governments to rebuild, and he wanted to be a part of that, including through the Indigenous education work he was spearheading at his foundation.

But beyond Prime Minister Martin becoming a friend and mentor, there had been little fostering of a connection to the Liberal Party or a potential role in federal politics. We never discussed that he was also sizing me up for the Liberal Party. I realize now that he must have called Justin Trudeau, Gerry Butts, and/or Carolyn Bennett, who was the Liberal Aboriginal affairs critic at the time, saying I was someone they should meet or talk to. This became more obvious in the lead up to the Whitehorse AGA. Trudeau's office reached out to mine and asked to set up a meeting in Whitehorse. We were told Trudeau, then leader of the third party, would be hanging about to watch some of the Assembly, meet the Chiefs, and learn more about the relationship with Indigenous peoples. I found out later a primary reason he came up to Whitehorse was to meet and try to recruit me to run for the Liberal Party.

The first time I saw Justin Trudeau was when he walked into the back of the assembly room while I was up on the stage. He listened to my report on the Senior Oversight Committees and the tensions with the Harper government and also sat in on a workshop I was facilitating on some of the government's policies, including those that guide the government in how they negotiate treaties (often referred to as the "comprehensive claims policy") and self-government. He mostly just listened.

Later in the afternoon, I headed to the small room in the Coast Hotel next door for the private meeting that had been arranged for Justin and me. By that point I knew I would not be surprised if the issue of my running for the Liberal Party came up. But going into the meeting I truly did not know if that was something I would consider if asked. I had questions. Concerns. I wanted to see what this son of a former prime minister was like. Was he down to earth? Was he kind? Was he interesting? Did he share any of the same visions and values as me? Was he authentic? Or was he just another typical politician in the mould that has historically, at best, put many Canadians off politics, and at worst removed their trust in politicians and governments?

I did not know the answers to these questions or what to expect. I was aware he was a bit of a "celebrity." I was a little nervous—not about meeting him or being star-struck. More about being sized up, and the growing feeling that was building inside me that I was being courted. It felt a little overwhelming. Why me? Why now? And . . . just . . . why? Yes, we needed a transformation in federal politics, but Indigenous leaders almost never crossed over into that world. Why would I be the one to do it? Should I be?

Justin opened by saying he was happy to be in Whitehorse and to listen in on the Assembly. He did not waste any time. He was organized. And, I guess you could say, charming. He talked about his vision for politics and the next election. He said he wanted me to run for the Liberal Party. It was not a job interview; it was a job offer.

I did not answer him. I steered the conversation to my questions around a vision for the country and values. And I conveyed my frustration, my restlessness, at the lack of coherent and tangible change regarding the place of Indigenous peoples and beyond. I gave him examples. I told him of our meeting with Prime Minister Harper, the work of the Senior Oversight Committees, and the importance of rights recognition and self-government.

I liked him. Yes, he was a smooth talker, but at that time it did not come across as an act. We even talked about our fathers, how they had gone toe-to-toe years before, and how we were now talking. He seemed genuine, and I believed him to be so.

As the meeting started drawing to a close, I told him I would think about running. I was committed to my role as Regional Chief and the work we were doing. But I also knew in my gut that that work would not be supported further with the Harper government in power and given the existing legislation and policy respecting Indigenous peoples. "We will keep in touch," Justin said, "and Gerry will be calling." And so it would be that on that day in Whitehorse, my relationship began with both Justin Trudeau and Gerry Butts, the two most powerful people in Canada for all of the years I was a minister in government.

◆

I think, like many people, I often know I am going to end up doing something even as I am telling myself, and others, that I have not yet made up my mind. The voice in the back of my head has already spoken, and is preparing for or coming to terms with the change ahead.

This was the case coming out of that meeting with Justin Trudeau. As much as I might have tried to deny it, I had pretty much made up my mind. I was going to do it. I already knew that getting something serious done for Indigenous peoples was going to require stepping up in new ways.

With the ongoing challenges at the AFN, that organization was going to struggle to lead that change. In some respects, this remains true today. As Tim and I talked about it as we left Whitehorse, we could feel ourselves getting excited, and we became increasingly so over the weeks and months that followed. I had first met Tim when I was at the British Columbia Treaty Commission (BCTC). Tim was the chief negotiator for the Westbank First Nation, negotiated the Westbank Self-Government Agreement, and had been deeply involved over decades in development of legislation creating First Nations fiscal institutions and land management regimes. I had been immediately taken with Tim. Not only was he one of the smartest people I had ever met, he was deeply passionate, thoughtful, and caring (and funny)—and remains so. A wonderful partner in work and in life. We got married on November 29, 2008, in Cape Mudge. His counsel was invaluable as I moved towards this life-changing decision.

The full-court press from the Liberals was on. Paul Martin and Gerry were in touch a fair bit. Encouraging me.

I started talking to a broader group about the possibility of running. There were many Indigenous voices who would have preferred I run for National Chief. Shawn was one of those. We met in Gastown in Vancouver—he was still National Chief at the time. He pressed hard that by being the first woman National Chief I could breathe new life into the work and the organization—help with the needed institutional reform and to re-envision it. To make it less Indian Act focused. I thought hard afterwards about his words. I valued them. They also echoed in some ways the voice of my grandmother that I could hear in my head. "Nasty white politics?!" I could imagine her saying.

Some of my Indigenous friends' and colleagues' observations reinforced in me a nagging fear about whether I should run or not. Would people think of me and treat me as a "token" or a "box-ticker" candidate? As a woman, as an Indigenous person, and most certainly as an Indigenous woman? At some level, I knew this would be true, but I felt this was just the cost of politics when people like me had been excluded for so long. There would be many costs, I imagined. So it would be.

And at the same time, I was buoyed by the fact that there was a difference between mainstream Canadian politics and Indigenous politics around tokenism. Despite the bad behaviour of certain leaders, in Indigenous politics there was no place for tokens. I knew my Chiefs, and the vast majority of Indigenous peoples, would never think of or treat me this way. In many Indigenous cultures in Canada, through our families, communities, and Clan Systems, people are raised to be leaders from birth. In my Nation, the values, roles, and responsibilities of leaders—and names and ceremonies that reinforce those—are integrated in the rhythms and realities of life. For these reasons, position, rank, and commitment matter. Hard work matters. Fulfilling one's roles and responsibilities matter. There is no space or time or place for tokens. And, of course, we—all Indigenous leaders—feel such an urgency for change. There is little time for unseriousness or focusing on appearances. If I was asked and chose to run for National Chief, or to go into federal politics, it would be expected that I would lever every possibility to make a real and tangible impact and to bring my values to the political space. To push in ways that had not been pushed before.

My developing relationship with the Liberal Party did not become public until the Liberal biennial convention held in Montreal in February of 2014. Tim and I travelled down to Montreal from Ottawa, where I had been for meetings as Regional Chief. I had, in fact, spent most of that day meeting with Harper government officials and political staffers who were not aware I was going to be co-chairing the convention that week or that I was thinking about running. I knew everyone would figure it out soon enough, and whether or not I said publicly I was running, the rumour mill would assume I was.

Tim and I did not have any idea what to expect when we headed to Montreal, as neither of us had attended anything like a political convention before. Although we both had been involved in politics for years, we were still political neophytes when it came to this sort of partisan politics in Canada. It was not our world.

In the Palais des congrès de Montréal, there was palpable excitement in the air. We could feel it. At times I wonder if I was just naive, but I know that was not fully the case. I understood that in Ottawa, at that time, the political world was on the edge of its seat with the idea of change in the air. There was new hope—a new generation. Trudeau epitomized this, and he was surprisingly credible. The Harper government had become embroiled in scandal and everyone knew it was likely on its last legs. The convention exuded this sense of anticipation and change in the extreme. And delegate after delegate came up to me on the convention floor, at the hotel and at the airport, to express their excitement about the future of the country. They made me feel hopeful. They made me want to run and to confirm what that voice in my head back in Whitehorse had already told me.

Like any convention, as I know now, this one was not all excitement and unity. One could see some of the fissures and tensions—ones that would continue to play themselves out in the years ahead. There were, of course, many dedicated, hopeful delegates representing their electoral districts and working to build the best country. I so love and admire these people. They are there because they want to see the full potential of Canada met. They are not there because they are seeking political favour or power for its own sake. Yes, they may be partisan, but being a Liberal or having membership in a political party does not define them. What does, and what binds us all, is being Canadian. These people continue to inspire me every day—regardless of political affiliation.

But there was also a political class that made me uncomfortable, some of whom seemed as preoccupied with self-interest and opportunities as they were with pursuing a big, bold vision of real change.

And while I was certainly feeling caught up in the energy of the convention, there were also little indications of the challenges to come. For example, as a co-chair I was given speaking points by the party leadership. These included their desire to have me use the term "middle class." I had concerns about how this term was being used, as they were not being clear about what they meant by it. I now understand that there is a standard political practice of appealing to an undefined and amorphous "middle class" to reinforce a certain perception. While I recognize this has been shown to be successful, in my mind, it remains wrong and unhelpful. A teaching instilled in me from my upbringing is that words matter because you cannot take them back. I try not to use terms or speak in slogans when their meaning is not clear and especially when those words are being conveyed publicly. This remained the case throughout my years as minister.

Yet aside from what I viewed at the time as little things, I was fully swept up in the excitement and optimism, and with the discussion around the issues being raised. I was a little surprised by this, and so was Tim. I had never really been interested in mainstream Canadian politics. Beyond voting, I was not involved much. Even given my political roles, I did not follow closely House of Commons debates or the political chattering class in the media. I studied politics and our institutions in university and, in my work life, legislation that was important to our agenda. Unlike many in that sphere, I for one would never sit down to watch question period. However, I often went to parliamentary committees as Regional Chief and knew a lot of people as a result. But I was not a political insider. I had never belonged to a political party and did not really understand the world inside the "Ottawa bubble" and the realities of the "politics" of Parliament and how it truly operates. This was a practical knowledge I lacked—for better or worse, depending on your perspective. It would be a problem for the future, as I had high expectations for people and for the institutions they were responsible to uphold. It was never a "game" to me—as it turns out it is for many.

Of course, I was and still am a politician—but an Indigenous politician. And that is not the same thing. Indigenous politics has real differences from mainstream Canadian politics, animated by the distinct worldviews and experiences of Indigenous peoples. Our worldviews are integrative. We organize our lives and realities in recognition of the interdependence of all things in existence, including all things in nature. For these reasons, community and kinship are central, and a community is only as strong as its constituent parts. Individuals have required responsibilities and roles in making the community better. This is why, for example, when someone passes away, the whole community stops, feels the loss, and uplifts each other.

This is also why Indigenous politics can look and feel so different. Every Indigenous leader typically speaks of the lineage they come from and represent. That is because they view their role as a community role, not an individual one, and the work they do as measured in generations, not electoral cycles. What we do is for the past, the present, and the future—not just to get re-elected in four years.

This was the political culture I was raised in. The main leaders in my family were my auntie Donna, my father, and my grandmother.

I always looked up to my auntie Donna Tyndall (née Cook). She was always out protesting and speaking up, and she raised my cousins to be activists. She has passed away, but she left her mark on the world by the many things she did. As an example, Auntie Donna encouraged and supported my granny adopting (in our traditional way—in the Potlatch) Leonard Peltier, who has been imprisoned since 1977 for the murders of two FBI agents in 1975 at Pine Ridge Reservation in the United States. (For those of you who are not familiar with this story, check out *Incident at Oglala*, a 1992 documentary by Michael Apted, narrated by Robert Redford.) My auntie had connections to the American Indian Movement and she, along with so many others, campaigned for clemency for Peltier. He had come up from the United States to Comox a number of times, including when I was a child, and became close with our family. I often think of the portrait Leonard painted of my grandmother in her regalia with an image of Auntie Donna behind her in front of a totem which is said to represent my father. It shows Donna's back, not her face, because she has passed on.

My father was and is the epitome of a leader; he will be until his last breath. He was raised to be, and chosen to be, our Chief. I cannot really remember my dad not being in some form of a leadership role. He was always the centre of attention and focus. Over the years we have had a very interesting relationship. We have had our ups and downs, yet I have always been proud to be his daughter and have always marvelled at watching and listening to him speak.

He taught me what it means to be authentic, to speak truth—no matter the consequence. His leadership style was uncompromising. He never bought into the mode of "hang around the fort Indians"; he has always been about storming the fort. He has a fortitude that I have not witnessed in many people. When I was young, I worshipped my father. Now, having been in many leadership roles myself, I have also gained the deepest respect for him and all that he accomplished and sought to accomplish in the face of so many challenges. While he is not a "traditional" father—he did not tuck me in at night or come to my swim meets—he always made sure I knew that he was thinking of me. And he raised me to lead.

My grandmother always had people calling on her. She was the keeper of knowledge of our Musgamagw Tsawataineuk traditions, culture, and language, and as such central to our Potlatch and our connection to the "old people." Every year she would "can" fish, and we all had to help. Kory and I spent a lot of time with my granny. Travelling to Potlatches or sitting around her as she drank tea and held court at the kitchen table—unless *Another World* was on TV. My dad depended on his mum, and he was her prized child. Many of my grandmother's other children have sadly died over the years, along with other close family. My grandmother knew suffering—more than I have ever known. And she channelled that into being a true leader while also teaching me what it meant to be Musgamagw, to be proud of who I am and where I come from, to know my rights and responsibilities, and ultimately what it means to be an Indigenous woman leader.

This understanding of leadership, and how it is embedded in our culture and community, is also why Indigenous modes of decision-making are so different. For many Indigenous peoples, decision-making is communitarian and consensus-based, though there are many differences and distinctions between peoples and nations in how decision-making operates. We are always working to build that consensus from which a decision will emerge. Individuals do not decide, nor do they have the authority to decide. The spark of truth comes from everyone contributing, sharing, and building the best decision together. Almost every Indigenous environment that I have been in—whether it was gatherings of hundreds of Chiefs, around my small Band Council table, in community halls, or at the executive of the AFN—at the end of the day, striving for consensus was the paramount ethic.

·

At the 2014 Liberal biennial convention, I heard speaker after speaker talk about "doing politics differently," which I equated to helping mainstream Canadian political culture become more consensus-based, less partisan, and less about individual power. I thought, as I said in my remarks to the convention, that there was much that could be learned from Indigenous legal orders and governance practices.

My hope that the future really would look different—and that this Liberal Party was ready to be a part of that difference—was reflected in the speech I gave. I had worked hard on it in the weeks prior and it laid out what I thought had to be the path on Indigenous issues. The message was simple: that the work of addressing our legacy of colonialism and recognizing and implementing Indigenous rights and practising better governance would make Canada better:

> *The resurgence of Aboriginal governance—based on Indigenous legal traditions—will, over the next generation, change, for the better, the way Canada is governed—not only in transforming Indigenous Nations but our country as a whole. For I believe that truly having a third order of government in Canada with real powers and real influence will be good for the federation and for creating the proper national balance.*
>
> *As Aboriginal peoples continue to take back control of our lives, so, too, will all Canadians take back control—ensuring*

we have a Canada that I think we all aspire to live in. A country based on shared values and principles that we have spent years as a Nation fostering—creating a caring and liberal society to ensure our place as a favoured Nation and one of the best countries in the world in which to live.

I laid out the plan—a plan that Indigenous peoples had built over years of tireless work—of establishing a principled, comprehensive, rights recognition framework in new legislation and policy. "What is needed is the political will," I said. It also requires, I continued, "a non-partisan approach to developing federal Aboriginal policy. In this area, as in some key others, ensuring a long-term federal strategy that lives beyond the life of a single government—that has multi-party support in its development and implementation—is prudent." In my own, but absolutely clear way, I was laying out my vision of a different politics. More independent, less partisan, and committed to working through greater consensus. The prime-minister-to-be and the party insiders knew who I was; if they ever thought I would be anything other than committed to this vision, then they were not listening, or thought I was just being "political." I guess the years ahead revealed the truth.

Reflecting on the pressures that had been building for years, I underscored that action was needed now. "I cannot overstress enough the need to proceed with urgency. Canada cannot, as a country, afford to let another generation of Aboriginal peoples down. Because in doing so we are letting Canada down . . . Our people are simply crying out for change and are taking steps to secure that change and we need partners."

The speech echoed themes and solutions I had spoken about for years as Regional Chief and was the same message I delivered as a minister in the years ahead. And as always, I reinforced that the core values that needed to guide our approach are the best of Canadian values:

Wherever we live, or whoever we are, or no matter how we are governed, as Canadians we all expect that our governments will be respectful of the principles and values upon which our country was founded as we continue to develop the very idea—the very concept—of Canada—as a beacon of hope and optimism in a world increasingly shrouded in conflict and division. For me, core Canadian values include—among others—kindness and generosity, a strong work ethic, trust, respect, and integrity.

I was very nervous when giving this speech, which was not unusual for me. I have always been nervous when speaking publicly; to this day I still do not really enjoy it. Justin was in the front row, beaming. Tim was also in the front row, wearing a classically conservative blue sweater and a tag on it that said "observer." He was sitting next to Margaret Trudeau, Justin's mother. I think Tim was being a little contrarian with his choice of attire. After I finished my speech Justin ran up on stage and, as he does, gave me a kiss on the cheek and a hug. I just felt relieved.

The speech seemed to resonate, at least as much as one could tell at such a staged event. Most important to me was the response to the message—of bold action on Indigenous issues unlike what we had seen before in Canada's history. Everyone was saying the right things, especially the future prime minister.

Carolyn Bennett was one of my barometers of the party's stance on Indigenous issues. I really liked Carolyn and considered her my friend. We had already been working together for some years. After appearing a number of times as Regional Chief before the House of Commons Standing Committee on Aboriginal Peoples and Northern Development, I started to chat more with Carolyn about issues and began to meet up with her when I was in Ottawa. She had also begun sharing with me her preparatory work for committee including the questions that were developed by the committee staff, which

I found interesting and helpful. I actually thought committees were important at this time—and an important part of the legislative process. I still feel they should be. But they simply are not right now. I will say more on that later, as there is much that needs to change with the way the House of Commons and its committees operate.

Carolyn had taken on the habit of calling me a "national treasure." I thought this a little strange, but I know she was trying to be endearing. Before the convention she had been actively encouraging me to run, and at the convention, and certainly after the speech and in the follow-up, she pushed even harder. I had a clear sense from her, and everyone else who was in a position of influence, that they agreed with the vision and plan for Indigenous policy I had laid out. At least they said they agreed with it. (And let me say again, it was not my plan; it was one that Indigenous leaders had endorsed, and it had been informed by numerous commissions, reports, and studies.) I felt there was alignment of visions and a shared sense of purpose. I was optimistic that there was a team that was ready to do the heavy lifting and the real work together. I left Montreal feeling more excited than when I had arrived. It was time.

Back in Vancouver I still felt captivated by the convention: by the people I met, by Justin, by such large numbers of people who seemed to have the same vision and desire for change as I did. It was all a bit intoxicating, and I was swept up in it all. Some close to me were a little more skeptical. Tim had never liked Justin very much, and while he fully supported me running, he was not as excited or "sold" about the seriousness of our future prime minister. Some of my staff at BCAFN were also not as keen on the likelihood of real change being afoot. Of course, for Indigenous peoples the proof would always be in the pudding. Change had to be seen to be believed. I thought I had seen it coming. I thought there was a path, and I was all in.

Over the months after the convention, I began to plan out how to move forward. I had to consider many things, including where I might run. There was a lot of wrangling, with Liberal Party brass in

BC trying to convince me to run in a number of ridings that I had no connection to, such as Esquimalt–Juan de Fuca. It seemed like people were just being moved around a map with no rhyme or reason. It started to feel a little chaotic.

In April, I went to meet Justin when he was in Vancouver. He was finishing his yoga when I walked into his hotel suite. "I am all in," I said to him, putting aside my feeling of awkwardness at the informality of the meeting, "and I want to run in the new riding of Vancouver Granville." It had been where I wanted to run ever since I'd begun contemplating the decision. I was born in what is now affectionately and simply called VanGran—at Vancouver General Hospital, to be precise—and was moving back to the riding. It was also winnable, but not a lock. At the time, Tim and I were living at Raven Woods on the Tsleil-Waututh Nation lands in North Vancouver. While it is more common than you would think for people in large urban centres to run in a riding they do not actually live in, I thought it was essential I live where I ran. I expected that I would have to compete for the nomination for VanGran. But when I told Justin that morning at the Sheraton Wall Centre that I wanted to run in VanGran, he responded, "Then that is where you will run."

And so it began.

TWO

Running

My father was the first in our immediate family to go to law school—a departure for our family and community from the more typical pursuit of fishing. My grandfather, Charlie Wilson, in addition to owning a gravel business, was among the first of the successful Cape Mudge seine-boat owners; the *Howe Sound IV* was magnificent in the day. In 1973, my dad graduated from University of British Columbia (UBC) law. He was the second Indigenous person to graduate; our cousin, the late Justice Alfred Scow, was the first. It is a well-known tale that my dad started the annual "trike race" at the law school. I imagine some of the older graduates out there know what I am referring to and are enjoying it.

When I did eventually decide to go to law school in 1996, it was not really by choice. It was by design. I was to attend my dad's alma mater. I was okay with this. Having been raised to be a leader in my world, law school—albeit to learn about the "white man's law"—was a part of the plan. Preparation, I guess, for the inevitable work ahead for my community.

At the time, law school was increasingly part of the path for young Indigenous people who wanted to help and work for their communities and nations. The courts were more and more on the front lines of the fight for Indigenous rights and justice. And, in my heart, I knew it was one of the places I would have to be. To be honest though, like many students, I was not that focused on a specific career path or really mindful of what leadership roles, if any, I might hold in the future. Yes, I knew what was expected of me, but I was also living life in the moment and taking it day by day. Still finding my way in two worlds.

Law school was a good experience for the most part. I had the good fortune to attend with my sister, Kory. We could have been twins as far as many were concerned. We went through it together. For this I was grateful. We made many friends, some of whom we remain close to today.

At UBC, as at University of Victoria for my undergrad, I did not join many clubs or societies. I certainly did not belong to any of the campus political organizations. Like my sister, I often felt like a fish out of water. The most exciting thing that happened in law school was that Kory had her first child, Kaija, two weeks prior to our graduation in 1999. This was so wonderful and I was excited to be an auntie. When we graduated it was a big deal for our family. Dad, Granny and Fred (her third husband), and so many others all came to our graduation ceremony, and Dad had a party for us at the Chateau Granville downtown. What a celebration and an amazing extended family reunion. Only Mum was missing; she was looking after baby Kaija.

After law school I articled at a medium-sized law firm in Vancouver, Connell Lightbody, and then moved on to the provincial Crown as a prosecutor. I liked being in court, regardless of the type of case. I was first hired on in traffic court and then transferred down to

222 Main Street, the central criminal courthouse in Vancouver. I eventually came to be responsible for my own courtroom, #304. As it happens, when I was a minister in April 2016 I returned to #304 and was so pleased to witness it operating as a specialized drug treatment court.

Located on the Downtown Eastside of Vancouver, 222 Main is in a neighbourhood that starkly reveals the great challenges Canada faces, including the severe disparities in wealth that exist and continue to worsen. The poverty in the area is crippling, not very different from the situation on so many Indian reserves across the country. With these disparities come high rates of drug addiction and violence. This is the neighbourhood where serial killer Robert Pickton found many of his victims; it is one of the "ground zeros" for murdered and missing Indigenous women and girls. It was my experience as an Indigenous woman, and working with people in this neighbourhood and in our communities, that made the announcement of the Missing and Murdered Indigenous Women and Girls (MMIWG) Inquiry in 2016 one of the most personally emotional and important moments for me as minister of justice. So many of the people and places in this neighbourhood are beautiful and inspiring, but by anybody's standards it is a hard, hard place. On February 14, I, along with thousands of others, join the annual Women's Memorial March that starts in the intersection at Main and Hastings, a block and a half from the courthouse. It is an empowering coming together of so many people working to remember and honour those lost and missing and to take back the streets and bring about greater justice.

The work at the courthouse was important. It was a learning experience for me, no question. But I also observed that in small ways—and within the confines of the legal reality—everyone there was trying to assist people and to advance justice. I will always remember the time I secured a peace bond (called an 810) on someone in order to protect his partner from violence. Later that night, the man who had been placed under the bond approached me when I was out at the Yale pub with friends. He pointed his finger at me and said, "You are that prosecutor . . ." I looked at my friends and said it was time to leave. We did. The next day, I was on the ferry to Victoria washing my hands at the restroom sink and a woman came in. Amazingly, it was the partner of the man from the day before. She burst into tears and said how grateful she was.

I loved doing this work. It was important. It allowed me to see first-hand how our criminal justice system is consumed by the over-representation of Indigenous people and other marginalized Canadians. It also taught me the importance of innovation and reform to make a real difference in people's lives. Lots of effort was being made to figure out ways to do justice better, more compassionately, and more humanely—concepts like the Downtown Community Court were being formed, the Native Courtworkers were operational, and various restorative justice measures were being discussed.

At the same time, I knew that I would not be long at Main Street. After about three years it become apparent that I was being pulled, and pushed, into the next chapter of my life. Miles Richardson—a Haida, and the chief commissioner of the British Columbia Treaty Commission—along with some others, had been trying to convince me for some time to join the commission, as staff.

The BC treaty process had begun in 1993 among First Nations, the federal government, and the provincial government with the intention that issues of title and rights in British Columbia would be settled within five years. The growing wave of title and rights court cases would be stemmed, there would be certainty on the land base, First Nations would be self-governing, and the lives and well-being of First Nations would be vastly improved. There would be justice.

Some ten years later, when I took a job as a process advisor at the BCTC, little or none of that had been achieved. Not one treaty had been completed, let alone the dozens and dozens that would have been required to settle the outstanding "land question" in British Columbia. About half of First Nations were not even participating in the process. One of the reasons was that they rejected the approach to negotiations taken by the federal and provincial governments. Some nations were also simply not internally ready for complex treaty-making. And the BC Liberal government at the time was openly hostile to modern treaty-making with First Nations, and particularly to the idea of self-government and the protection of constitutionally entrenched rights. They went so far as to hold a province-wide referendum about rights for Indigenous peoples in relation to the Nisga'a Final Agreement (which was the first modern treaty in the province but was negotiated outside of the BC treaty process) and fought self-government in court (and lost).

Today, almost two decades later, the same challenges remain. Only eight modern treaties, including the Nisga'a Final Agreement, have been completed, and governments continue to use the process to try to limit, alter, and even extinguish Indigenous rights, rather than uphold and honour them. I expected this—the denial of rights—would be one of the first things to go when I became minister of justice and attorney general of Canada, as these approaches were completely irreconcilable with the federal Liberal commitments made in the 2015 election. As I write this, Crown-Indigenous Relations and Northern Affairs (CIRNA) continues to largely negotiate in the same way as when I went to the commission. So disappointing.

In going to the British Columbia Treaty Commission, I did not have any illusions that this struggling process could easily undergo the transformation it needed. After all, the core of the challenges lay with Crown governments, and there was little the commission, even though established by legislation as the "keeper of the process," could do to change or control them. Mandates are set by governments and, in this area of public policy, more rigidly than in others; any change depends on the will and competence of government, and the priorities and motivation of the sitting prime minister or premier and his or her Cabinet. But as my dad had taught me, there was no merit in focusing on the obstacles. If one knows the change that is needed, then the mission is to relentlessly pursue that change in a principled and coherent manner and to look for allies. That was his example, and I had learned from it.

I had taken a one-year leave of absence from being a prosecutor to work for the commission. However, nine months into the job I was convinced, somewhat reluctantly, to run for election to one of two of the treaty commissioner positions appointed by the First Nations Summit. This was my first time—aside from student council—pursuing an elected leadership role. I remember my dear friend Jack Weisgerber, at the time the BC-appointed commissioner to the BCTC, saying to me as I ruminated about my decision, "Don't be such a chickenshit, just do it."

The first political speech I ever gave was to the Chiefs who would vote in the election. I had five minutes. My dad had helped me write it out and I rehearsed it over and over again. The all-candidates forum was being held at the Chief Joe Mathias Centre on the Squamish Nation lands in North Vancouver. It was packed. When I stood up to present, my mind went blank. I could not think of anything. For what seemed like minutes I did not speak. Imagine: a would-be Indigenous political leader, standing in front of leaders who had gone before her, done and said so much, and from whom she had learned much, having nothing to say. I looked over at my Chiefs, the Musgamagw Tsawataineuk Chiefs who always sat to the right of the front, and I saw their supportive and anticipatory faces. I started speaking, and the words finally came. Thank goodness.

It was soon after winning that first election that I became aware of being my own person in the Indigenous political world rather than how I had always been known, as "Bill Wilson's daughter." It is a strange sensation to be primarily known as someone's child. I always felt great pride in being identified this way, but it could also be a burden. For me, I realized the challenge, the burden, was to simply make the jump into leadership as I had been prepared to do. I certainly had a zeal to pursue real change for our peoples as I had been taught, but

I have never felt I had to lead in the same way, or style, as my father, or measure up to him and his accomplishments. Indeed, I think when one is driven by the desire to live up to the ideal of one's parent, it can lead to poor decisions—such as a greater preoccupation with appearances than substance.

Being a treaty commissioner was also my first direct introduction into the unique world of contemporary Indigenous politics. It is not for the faint of heart. It does not always match the ideal that I describe when I speak publicly to our values and worldviews. In part, some of the problems are a symptom of the challenges inherent in deconstructing a colonial past while still being very much a part of the colonial framework and influenced and governed by it. People can sometimes be harsh, and thick skin is a must.

Indigenous politics remain, to this day, very colonial and very male-centred, although this is changing. The Indian Act, and the institutions it supports, perpetuate this reality. The misogyny exhibited by some around the Assembly of First Nations executive table was just an example of this. Indigenous peoples are healing, and as individuals each of us is at a different place along the spectrum of decolonizing. This is true of Indigenous leaders as well, and as in human societies throughout history, women have borne the brunt of some of the hardship and inequalities this creates.

But Indigenous politics is also visceral in an important and good way. Most people in Indigenous politics, at all levels, have a stated and shared goal—a common purpose—to outrun the shadow of colonialism (whether they realize they are colonized or not and whether they may or may not be a part of the problem they are trying to fix). This includes the linked and equally important objectives of improving the basic quality of life for their people (putting food on the table and a roof over their heads), maintaining and advancing our cultures, traditions, and languages, and reclaiming the relationship with our lands and resources. To do all of this requires the institutions of governance to be strong and appropriate and, where necessary, rebuilt and recognized by other governments. Most Indigenous leaders I have worked with would agree with these basic goals. Where there is divergence is in how we pursue achieving them. But at least we have dialogue—sometimes endless, vigorous dialogue—about how we get there.

In one way, this is good and necessary. It is part of how we build consensus and move forward together. At times, however, dialogue can be weaponized to stop change and maintain the status quo. Indigenous leaders and peoples can use dialogue, and claims of the need for more dialogue, to give in to fear of real change. And many non-Indigenous politicians have learned this and use it to their advantage. These politicians make claims of being change-makers, but subtly and not so subtly push in ways that instigate endless rounds of consultation and engagement among Indigenous peoples so that nothing really has to change. This is a pattern I would see play itself out time and again after I became minister.

There has been a convergence in thinking among Indigenous peoples on what needs to be done. This growing unity of purpose and direction has made it harder for other actors, including governments, to try to divide and conquer Indigenous peoples or make excuses for inaction. It made my own experiences later in Cabinet even more disappointing, knowing how much more could have been done.

These patterns, for both Indigenous and non-Indigenous politicians, are symptoms of colonization. The effects of colonization are within each of us, as much as they are in our social realities, culture, laws, policies, and institutions. Patterns of thought and actions have been shaped, often in unseen ways, by the experience of colonization. For First Nations people, this is seen in how we have internalized aspects of being an "Indian," often feeling dissociated inside ourselves from our true identities, who we are, and the very places to which we belong.

Of course, the residential schools were a major part of this, something my father was shielded from and that were closing when Kory and I were growing up. It was my grandfather, Charlie Wilson, who himself had been at residential school, who protected my father from going, using the resources he had to move my grandmother and dad to Comox. There, my dad attended public school. He was the only Indigenous kid in the school, and though we do not know for sure, we think he may have been the first. One might say my grandfather was undertaking an act of resistance to colonization and pushing back in a way that has long been part of my family's lineage. My grandfather was able to protect my dad because he had the means as a well-off fisherman and the local connections to make it happen. Many—most—did not. We were lucky.

For non-Indigenous people, this internal colonization is seen in the ingrained, casual, often unrecognized racism and paternalism that is frequently present in interactions. I have witnessed this ever since I was a child. The expressions of amazement and surprise that an Indigenous girl would be good in school or sports. Or that her teeth were not rotten. The lack of expectations for achievement (other than from my own family and community, of course, and from some amazing teachers). The subtle and not so subtle questioning of whether one had done their work on their own or earned the position or recognition they got. Unsurprisingly, all of these patterns emerged during the time I was minister of justice and attorney general, including from some Cabinet colleagues.

♦

Deciding to run for Regional Chief was an easy choice to make. It felt like everything lined up. I was frustrated with the treaty process and saw little chance, in my role as treaty commissioner, to move negotiations in a new direction. I was restless and wanted to do more in leadership. Tim was really supportive and excited about the idea. I had a plan I wanted to advance, with self-government and nation rebuilding at the centre. And just as I was feeling all these things Shawn became National Chief and there was an opening. I went for it.

My first election for the position, in 2009, was hotly contested; I had to beat four other candidates including the venerable Grand Chief Stewart Phillip of the Syilx (Okanagan) people, who was the long-time president of the Union of BC Indian Chiefs. Stewart and I had known of each other previously, but our relationship, our friendship, was cemented during that campaign—we really got to know and respect each other. When he threw his support to me on the third ballot, with a powerful statement that we needed young Indigenous women in leadership, the die was cast. While he and I pursue justice and decolonization in somewhat different ways, I know we have always shared the same goal of a transformation in the lives of Indigenous peoples grounded in the recognition and implementation of our inherent title and rights, and we remain friends to this day. I won my second mandate in 2012 with 78 percent of the vote on the first ballot—reflecting, I believe, that the focus I had been placing on Indigenous self-government and nation rebuilding was supported and that the consensus style of leadership rooted in building trust among the Chiefs was desired and needed.

Being Regional Chief also put me on the First Nations Leadership Council with six other leaders, including Stewart. For most of the time I was the only woman, which brought with it the usual challenges.

Over the years as I played different political roles, I would find myself wondering what the conversations and dynamics were like at the tables I was not at. Was the dialogue different? Did people think and act differently? Did they pursue change in the same way? Did people use the power they had in the best way possible? I reflected on one aspect of this in a talk on Indigenous women and politics and law that I gave in October 2018. I had no idea at the time that I was soon to be shuffled out of my position as minister of justice:

In my own experience serving as the first Indigenous person to be Canada's Minister of Justice and Attorney General, I have unfortunately had it reinforced that when addressing Indigenous issues, no matter what table one sits around, or in what position, or with what title and appearance of influence and power, the experience of marginalization can still carry with you. But this does not deter me. It only makes my resolve stronger and more determined.

As the male members of the leadership council were learning about me, I was also gauging and learning to work with them. Ultimately, we worked fairly well together, my main regret being that we were not able to always get on the same page about doing bigger and bolder things. But these were great times. I was energized by the work and by my fantastic all-female staff. I doubt any regional or national Indigenous political organization had had an all-female staff before; if they had, they were far and few between. We were an amazing team of five, and like most Indigenous organizations then, we had to do much with little.

My early experiences in leadership had helped crystallize my belief—which had already been instilled in me by my dad and grandmother—that at its core, decolonization in Canada is the right to self-determination, including self-government, and that Indigenous peoples should be supported in exercising that right to rebuild their nations and governments. Governance reform was at the heart of my almost six years as BC Regional Chief, and "Building on OUR Success" was the motto.

One centrepiece of our governance work was the creation of the *BCAFN Governance Toolkit: A Guide to Nation Building*, including the second edition of *The Governance Report*—collectively three volumes totalling more than a thousand pages. It covers every topic that has to be addressed as part of rebuilding First Nations governments, drawing on Indigenous laws, protocols, and traditions, and moving beyond the Indian Act. It considers the legislative tools available as well as the impediments and highlighted what needed to be done to support the recognition of Indigenous self-government in Canada. This was a project that Tim and I had talked about for some time and had been working on prior to my election as BC Regional Chief. It was a large project for the BCAFN to undertake, but it was a true pleasure to document and recognize all of the incredible work done by our Nations in BC. In addition to the support of the Chiefs, we had the resources to get it done, including the advice of Indigenous leaders and others who had done the real work of rebuilding governance beyond the Indian Act, and a peer review group of experts against whom the ideas could be tested.

As it happened, self-government was central to my first political interactions with a federal government as Regional Chief. These interactions were sometimes testy. As Indigenous issues were heating up across the country, I was asked to give one of the speeches on behalf of the AFN at the Crown-First Nations Gathering in 2012, a speech that focused on self-governance and economic development. The event opened with Prime Minister Harper giving remarks. He spoke of the Indian Act tree and its roots, implying that the Indian Act was formidable and hard to unearth and that our Nations did not have the ability or capacity to move beyond it. It was ignorant and I was infuriated—as I would be a year later when I sat at the table with him in Langevin.

At the Gathering, I quickly rewrote part of my speech in order to rebut the prime minister's message. I used the phrase "with all due respect, Mr. Prime Minister" numerous times as I dissected, and rejected, his comments. As the Chiefs, spectacular in their regalia, applauded my remarks with standing ovations, I could see that the prime minister was not looking directly at me. John Duncan, who was the minister of Indian and northern affairs and my member of Parliament (Vancouver Island North), and with whom I was friendly, was fuming. Afterwards, he said angrily, "Jody, do you know what 'with all due respect' means? . . . it means 'fuck you.'" I was somewhat glad he had interpreted my message properly, though perhaps crudely. I felt I had said what needed to be said, and what the Chiefs—my Chiefs— had wanted me to say.

My focus on governance also did not help me much in navigating the dynamics at the national level with the AFN. The reality is that most First Nations that are far along in their self-government work do not participate regularly at the AFN. The assemblies of all of the Chiefs from across the country sometimes end up mirroring the kind of dynamics one sees in certain Indian Act Band Councils, or in the tensions that can arise as communities with hereditary and elected systems figure out their roles and responsibilities in the contemporary world. The Indian Act treats Indigenous peoples as children—it is colonial paternalism at its core, resting on the racist belief that Indigenous peoples are uncivilized and cannot govern themselves. Indian agents, INAC, and the current Indigenous Services Canada (ISC) manage a colonial piece of legislation that systematically disempowers people and creates a climate of powerlessness. In such a reality, it is natural that a disproportionate amount of time at assemblies ends up being spent on things that, in terms of the bigger picture and what needs to be done, do not matter. This is how colonialism designs it. It is also not atypical that the important things are left unattended because one is restricted in how to deal with them, and there may be costs to doing so. A degree of fear and an avoidance of pushing for real change sets in.

So, while the Assembly of First Nations has a role, and it is currently one of the means "Indians" have to push and lobby for change, we have to create the organizations that can drive the change we want to see. Or we need to look—as has been done in the past—to restructure the AFN. National Chiefs are needed who can build trust and support to transform the organization and what it stands for. This was not what the national executive was focused on doing when I was Regional Chief. And while I was being encouraged to take that on instead of moving to federal politics, ultimately I did not think it was the right time.

In April 2014, when I told Justin I was "all in," I knew it was going to be an interesting transition from Indigenous politics to mainstream Canadian politics. Not many had done it before—at least not while being an active Regional Chief—so there was no real playbook to follow. For some of the transition I knew what to expect. First, there was the need to complete the publication of the *Governance Toolkit*. Then there was a need to get clearance from the BCAFN board of directors to run and take a leave of absence. I had a great sense of loyalty and responsibility to the work that we had done and were still doing in BC and did not want to see any of it fail or slow down. So, it just meant working harder to keep things moving as I started shifting to preparation for the federal nomination campaign.

There was also some expected resistance from the Indigenous world of politics beyond BC, as well as some silliness. A few Chiefs complained about my candidacy, alleging that it was a conflict of interest to remain as Regional Chief while standing for the Liberal Party nomination. But, in the end, none of the complaints or resistance amounted to anything. There was no conflict, and the BCAFN Chiefs-in-Assembly adopted a unanimous resolution in support of my nomination and expressing full confidence that I would be able to continue to perform my duties as Regional Chief. The early resistance was just an expression of the more broken edges of Indigenous politics.

But there were surprises as I moved out of the world of Indigenous politics and into getting ready for and then mounting a federal general election campaign.

Of course, I knew well that a main distinction between these two political worlds was that in Indigenous politics there are no political parties, unlike in the federal system. Indigenous politics does not divide along partisan lines, although there can be factions. Indeed, the idea of partisanship has always felt foreign to me and continues to feel that way to this day. Part of this is simply a reflection of Indigenous integrative worldviews. To organize around difference, and then to emphasize that difference—especially a difference that is manufactured, like a political party—feels, and is, unnatural.

As the Liberal Party brought me into its world, I could feel this difference right away. It was disorienting. I was immediately struck by the mentality of being on a team or in a club that spent a lot of time talking and strategizing about how to beat others and win. In the Indigenous world of politics, we would certainly foster and encourage team building, but the dialogue was always focused on how to build momentum to achieve a social outcome, to address wrongs, and to better the lives of people. Moreover, everyone was a part of the team, not just those in your party. The team was the collective. The team on council at We Wai Kai was all of us. The team at the BCAFN was all the Chiefs and their communities. My new reality felt weird to me.

And I imagine I seemed a bit weird to them. Many of the federal Liberals I met had dedicated their adult lives—some from the age of fourteen, when they could officially become a young Liberal—to finding a way to win and to the belief that the other guys were "bad." Now they felt they were getting close to winning federally. Many had never been in power. And here I showed up, clearly as an outsider. Not a party member until after the convention. Never having contributed a dime or any of my time to their "team" or to the cause.

It was not quite like oil and water, and I do not want to exaggerate. By far and away the people were great, and we were certainly able to mix. But there were others with whom things weren't so smooth; in these cases, it felt as if we were rarely, if ever, talking in the same way about the same things. This group I saw as being Liberal first, above all else, and they identified as such. It was quite something. I knew I could never be that kind of a Liberal, a diehard partisan, as it was not a primary or core part of my identity.

Related to partisanship is, of course, power. And a different conception of power animates Indigenous and mainstream Canadian politics. In our Canadian political culture, the goal is not only to become government but to stay in government. I came to realize that this goal—to hang on to power—is the paramount objective through which every decision is filtered. Sure, one can convince oneself, as many do, that there is no distinction between staying in power and what is good for the country. That what the country needs to guide and protect it, is—above all else—you. Arrogant but necessary, as the other guys are so bad. But, of course, that is just human ego and narcissism talking. As is sometimes said, "The human capacity for self-delusion is infinite."

From the earliest days, I felt within the party this preoccupation with power and with the notion that somehow the federal Liberal Party was going to be the saviour of Canada. To me, it came across—and still does—as a recipe for closed-mindedness and not listening to divergent views, and not conducive to making the best decisions. Good ideas can come from anyone, anywhere, regardless of what party label they ascribe to themselves. We spend so much time in this world fighting against arbitrary distinctions that have been the source of discrimination—race, gender, sexual orientation, religion, disability, health—and yet here we are using the arbitrary distinction of a party label as the determinant of an idea's merit.

Of course, this Liberal Party focus on keeping power only became more pronounced when the party was in government. I believe the prime minister and those around him convinced themselves of the importance of staying in government for the good of the country, that their beliefs and approach were effectively unassailable. I think this sense of self-importance can lead people in power to do and say whatever is necessary to hold onto power, with decisions being driven by political expediency and not an authentic confrontation with the challenges we face as a country, as a world, and as humans. Power and the desire to cling to power can change people—of any political party—as they move away from core values and principles. The triumph of power and partisanship over truth and principle was a major part of my experience as a member of the Trudeau government.

I do not want to romanticize Indigenous politics. Indeed, I am probably one of the last people to do so (and Indigenous women generally are far less likely to romanticize it). In Indigenous politics, there are self-interested people and those who want to be in power positions for the sake of being in those positions. But even those people carry with them the experience and reality of a community in need, with children and families suffering, where cultural and social oppression remain, and intergenerational trauma continues to play itself out. And even those who act like typical politicians come from somewhere with a culture and tradition that speaks to what is expected in leadership and from leaders. They all have Elders. They also live knowing the reality of having rights violated. These realities are always front of mind; they ground the work, and recentre it when it goes astray. The need for true politics—the collective doing better through striving to make the best decisions together and implementing them successfully on the ground—is ever-present. These roots run far deeper than a policy convention held somewhere in the country once or twice a year, or a platform that is rolled out every four or five years to try to win an election and have power.

As harsh as it sounds, sitting today as an Independent MP in a corner of the House of Commons, looking around at the empty posturing and game playing that is unfortunately all too dominant, I feel like I am in an environment that has lost its soul. The sense of purpose that many hard-working and well-meaning members of Parliament bring to Ottawa when first elected is obscured in an environment that feels more like the worst reality show than a place where people are truly trying to effect the best change for Canadians.

On the more positive side, I did not feel any barriers to running for the Federal Liberal Party because I was a woman. This would not have been the case a few years ago, and I imagine it is still not the case for many. Even though we still have a ways to go, things are getting better for women running for political office. I may have been a fish out of water, but at least for the time of the campaign I had the support of the party, like any other candidate—perhaps even more so because some saw me as a "star" candidate. I understood this to mean that not only did I have a chance to win an important riding, but I could also potentially be helpful to the party on a national scale. Indeed, I was strategically placed to be seen whenever Justin was in town, and I even went on a trip with the leader, which was not common. Of course, part of this was tokenism—and I was well aware of that.

•

For all the disorientation that came with the transition, ultimately it felt straightforward. I knew why I was doing it. This was the next path that had unfolded. It was carrying on the leadership role I had been raised to take, just from a different venue. And the focus remained the same: to build a better Canada based on certain core values and principles. This included better governance and greater justice, equality, and inclusion, not just for Indigenous peoples but for all Canadians.

So as my nomination candidacy became official and I became more entrenched in the Liberal Party, my focus appropriately started to shift. If anything, I know that when I set my mind to something, I work hard at it. And so I threw myself into preparations for the campaign, building an organized approach much as I had in my time at the BCAFN. While my mind would creep ahead to the change I could advance if I did get to Ottawa in a position of influence, I did not think about it much. I knew it would be different, and it would be hard, but I had hope for the future and was ready to help make that hope a reality.

I did not know exactly what would happen next, when Justin said he would tell the party I was to be the candidate in Vancouver Granville. I was not part of what unfolded internally to secure the nomination for me. From media articles written over the years and from some of my own conversations with those in the know, I am aware of the names of several people who wanted to run in Vancouver Granville at the time, one of whom would end up running against me in the riding for the Liberals four years later. These people either chose not to run or were told not to run for the nomination in 2015. I am not sure. I assume they were told not to do so.

I was intent on working for my nomination, as I did not want anyone to be able to say I did not earn it. So I did what I understood you were supposed to do. I started to create a team of volunteers. We sold memberships. Met with countless local party people, including those that I knew or suspected wanted to run as well. Many on the already established electoral district association were not happy. Whatever their reasons, I respected their position and knew I had to try to build relationships with these people. I met with each of them, to hear from them and also to talk about myself, my background, and why I was running. Some were very welcoming; some not so much. And through them I also sought to learn about the Liberal Party in the riding. Vancouver Granville was a new riding in 2015, and I wanted to understand what had been done in the past and what was needed for the future.

Tim and I also moved into the riding. We bought a condo just off Cambie Street near the police station and just down the street from our iconic City Hall.

With a place to live and a growing cadre of friends and supporters, we set forth in relative ignorance to confirm the nomination and run our first federal election campaign. In the midst of this excitement and expectation of what might be accomplished with our team was some general skepticism that an Indigenous woman could win in Vancouver Granville. In fairness, I think many held this view just as a matter of pure demographics. It was not a comment on me, Indigenous peoples, or the beliefs or attitudes of people in the riding. Vancouver Granville is an incredibly diverse riding both in terms of its social-economic makeup and in terms of the so-called political party spectrum. But the average price of a single-family home in 2015 was about $2 million.

I remember talking to a prominent community leader who expressed concern to me that he did not think an Indigenous person could win in this neighbourhood. As he said that, I remember feeling my determination grow to prove him wrong. More importantly, I wanted to prove that this place where I was born was, and is, a place where if you work hard, bring forward ideas, and engage with people, it does not matter what you look like, where you come from, who you love, where you worship.

I think my confidence came from a familiarity with living in multiple worlds—one of which was not so dissimilar to VanGran. My schools in Comox could have been in Vancouver Granville: diverse, fairly privileged, and not very Indigenous. At the same time, though, I had another life away from school, with my cousins, in community, on the "Potlatch circuit," and in the summer back at Cape Mudge with my grandmother, aunts, uncles, and cousins—so many cousins. In that world I felt most at home—knowing best who I was. But having this life did not mean that I could not connect with the kids in Comox.

I think my two-worlds experience is fairly typical for many First Nations kids growing up in Canada. The reality is that First Nations people know far more about how non-Indigenous people live their lives in this country than what non-Indigenous Canadians know about life on the reserve. The reserve, and, far beyond that, our cultural ways, seem foreign to many Canadians. But the neighbourhoods and cities of Canada do not necessarily feel that foreign to many of us. I was confident that I could navigate the world of Vancouver Granville, even if the voters—at this point—did not know me or my Indigenous world.

My formal nomination meeting was held on July 31, 2014, at the Holy Trinity Anglican Church on West 12th Avenue. Gordon Gibson—a prominent Vancouver Granville resident, political columnist, author, and former politician—introduced me, and many prominent Indigenous leaders and Liberals from BC came out to support me. I felt very honoured.

Reading today the words I said that night, I cringe. The talk reflects the messages and values I had always talked about (and continue to): good governance, trust and consensus building, equality and inclusion, and justice for Indigenous peoples. But the speech also reveals how much I had begun playing into the partisan political game and projecting a belief in the image the Liberal Party wanted to construct. While I know I sincerely believed and meant every word that I spoke at the time—and, as I am reminded, everyone in that room did as well—I cringe today because I know it is, to a great degree, an imaginary and ideal image, and I guess I am surprised that I ever subscribed to it quite that much. I always felt I would never "drink the Kool-Aid." I think it shows how convincing Trudeau was—or perhaps how desperate we all were for hope in a different way of doing politics. I hear that old line about "self-delusion" ringing in my ears as I look back on my words:

> But, most of all, thanks to all of you for coming out and showing just how much support there is in our riding for Justin and Justin's team.
>
> Tonight is all about continuing to take back control of our country from those who currently govern and have demonstrated a profoundly different and divisive vision of what our Canada is, and should be . . .
>
> But with hope and hard work, as Justin says, supported by a strong plan, we can and will put Canada back on track . . .
>
> I have, in fact, been fighting for what we know as "liberal values" my whole life . . .
>
> This government [the Harper government] has been systematically tearing apart everything that is good about Canada and we have a responsibility to stop this . . .

It gets even worse:

> There is a better way—the Liberal way—based on our Liberal values, which are Canadian values—and under the demonstrated and strong leadership of Justin Trudeau.
>
> My approach has always been that when I see something wrong, when I see something that needs to be changed, I get involved.
>
> I have met, and worked with, Justin Trudeau. I like him. I trust him. He has a good mind and a great heart.
>
> I like the way he is reaching out and bringing people together in common cause.
>
> He has given me hope that, working together, we can bring a government of good people and great integrity to Ottawa, to make the changes that will make all of our lives, and our country, better.
>
> That is why I have put my name forward for Justin and the Liberal Party.

And some of my words that night ring true today in ways that I never imagined at the time:

> Unfortunately—and it is of great concern to me—far too many Canadians—including many here in our riding—have become disillusioned with politics, and disengaged from our politicians.
>
> This is one of the greatest threats to our democracy.
>
> When our voices are lost, our opportunities are diminished.

Four days after I secured the nomination, Trudeau was in town. The day of my nomination was planned around the leader being in Vancouver to attend the Vancouver Pride Parade along with all of his BC candidates. On August 5, we had a picnic at Douglas Park, in the centre of Vancouver Granville. Throngs of people showed up. Justin was the rock star, and he was there in part, I know, to show me off and springboard my campaign. All of the other confirmed Liberal candidates in the area were strongly encouraged to come to the picnic; this would become the pattern to follow—all of us were expected to attend any event where the leader was to be. I introduced him to a raucous crowd and had my first introduction to political selfies. That has never stopped; indeed, ever since the SNC-Lavalin affair, the attention, including requests for selfies, has only intensified—exponentially so after being kicked off Team Trudeau.

After the picnic, Justin and I flew north to the pristine Great Bear Rainforest, Prince Rupert, and Hartley Bay, ostensibly to meet First Nations peoples in the area and to view the route that the proposed Enbridge Northern Gateway Pipeline would take. The pipeline had long been controversial, and later would be killed by the government while others were approved in a compromise decision that pleased almost no one. This was the most time I had ever spent with Justin so far. We met with Indigenous and local leaders. We flew into Hartley Bay to visit the Gitga'at First Nation, a Tsimshian community at the mouth of the Douglas Channel. Elderly women waved through their windows as we walked around the community. We gathered in their band office with some of their leaders, all of whom I knew. There was a sense of excitement and hope. I was happy to have been able to travel into this community with Justin—to be with him as he heard directly from these Indigenous leaders. The trip was also magical as we were immersed in the beauty of the natural world. We saw humpback whales bubble-net feeding as we made our way back to the airport. It was an extraordinary sight.

The trip was also one big photo-op. Adam Scotti, Justin's accomplished photographer, was with us, and took endless photos. A shot of Justin and me talking on a rocky beach on Digby Island near Prince Rupert ended up adorning the environmental page of the platform. This was certainly helpful for my campaign, and other candidates were not so lucky. I ticked the boxes for the party that needed ticking. This is obvious.

After this trip, I started getting involved more nationally in platform development, especially on the environment and on Indigenous issues. I was glad to do this—to contribute some of my experience and expertise on the issues on which I wanted to see bold action. I was pleasantly surprised how open the party was to accepting language regarding the recognition of Indigenous rights—which was how Indigenous peoples had talked about the transformative change that was needed for decades. I realize in hindsight that the Liberal Party did not understand what this really meant, or did not care, but at the time the inclusion only reinforced my belief that I was doing the right thing. Later, it became clearer that what was in the platform did not really matter that much. The platform was simply to get elected. The about-face on electoral reform in 2016 was the first big public indication of this for me.

◆

While I was excited to get campaigning, I also knew it would feel awkward for me. After all, I am really an introvert—or at least I recognize that I have increasingly become so over the years. I know that is not how people see me or experience my public persona. But I am not a big fan of crowds, and I do not seek out opportunities to speak in public or with the media. I like my privacy. But I do love people— meeting people and talking with them about their lives or their issue of importance. I feel most comfortable one on one, or in very small groups. As Tim always liked to remind me when we were campaigning, for a politician I am very perplexing and it drove him crazy (in a good way). I do not think about where to stand or finding the mic or getting in the shot, and I do not give easy sound bites. I have had communications directors whom I have made equally frustrated— they are always encouraging me to do more of the "political" or media stuff because it is necessary and they think I am good at it. But I do not enjoy that stuff at all.

When I was young, I was quite outgoing, always curious and always up to mischief. I remember being happy as a child, even though there were many challenging times, including periods when Kory and I were away from our parents. As I get older, and with taking on the responsibility of leadership roles, I can see now how I was protective of myself when I was younger and continue today to recede from many social connections. As an adult I think this is also a survival mechanism, to manage the scale and scope of the expectations of being in leadership and the massive amount of energy and time—the work—it requires. This was especially so when I was a minister. To self-preserve I think I have become even a little more closed off, and spend more and more time on introspection as part of coping with the stresses and sleepless nights that build up.

By the time my journey into federal politics had begun I intimately realized that a life of leadership meant a life of sacrifice, and that sometimes these costs can be very personal. I had seen this firsthand, in how leadership had taken its toll on leaders in my family and community, including on their health and well-being and that of those around them. Indeed, this toll is seen in leaders from all walks of life and many backgrounds.

As part of coming to understand what leadership may involve, I had to come to terms with the reality that for me the leadership roles contributed to our not having children. I desperately wanted children, as did Tim. We tried in all ways possible and suffered many losses along the way. But if I am honest, there is part of me that knows that the health impacts of the work I was doing made it much harder for me to get pregnant, and stay pregnant. In my quiet, darker moments this haunts me, and I know it always will. And so I often find myself looking for calm, inside myself and in the world I create around me. For most Canadians, the WE Charity and WE Day are now just names in another Liberal scandal. For Tim and me they are much more. It was while speaking at the 2011 WE Day event in Vancouver, at Rogers Arena, and in front of thousands of kids, that I started to have a miscarriage. Literally, while on the stage. I could feel it. After I finished my welcoming remarks, I left the stage, found a toilet, and cleaned myself up. And then I went to meet Mikhail Gorbachev, who was also speaking that day. Then I went to the hospital.

Increasingly turning inward and greater self-reflection has helped me, I think, to try to maintain balance and stay focused on the most important things, even as I performed leadership roles. I had not closed off at this point, but I was certainly no longer revealing myself as I did when I was younger. And it did not mean I was not open to other people and their needs and views. Or empathetic. Quite the contrary. But it did mean that some of the dynamics of campaigning would not be my happy place. And I would need help.

There was never any question that I would ask Lea Nicholas-MacKenzie to manage my campaign. Lea is an Indigenous woman from Tobique, New Brunswick, and it's often remarked that we are kind of doppelgängers, or that we are like sisters. Apparently, we share many mannerisms and styles of laughter. Lea and I met many years ago; she is the type of kind, caring, and fierce person that anyone would be fortunate to meet, let alone call a friend. She really is my best friend. Writing about her makes me emotional, as I am so grateful to have her and her husband, Rick, in my life. Tim feels the same way.

Lea has taken her own remarkable journey. She has been, among other things, chief of staff to National Chief Phil Fontaine, sous chef to Prime Minister Paul Martin at 24 Sussex Drive, and a consultant for the 2010 Vancouver Olympics. There was no way I was going to take this step without Lea helping to lead the way. And I also knew that if I made it to Ottawa, I would need to have Lea there with me to make things move along smoothly. She was, and still is, a confidante.

As Lea, Tim, and I began plotting out the campaign, people started coming out of the woodwork to help. Reflecting my idea of what it meant to be a leader, the campaign was a collaborative effort from the start. A few of the people who joined us were campaigners from within the Liberal Party apparatus. With them, they brought considerable knowledge and experience that was helpful. And we were fast learners. But by far the most wonderful part of the campaign, and its absolute backbone, were the volunteers—those people who came out on a daily basis.

Every volunteer has their own story for being involved. An early team of people, most of whom had volunteered on some type of political campaign before, felt that something special was happening, that somehow this was different than the campaigns they had been involved with in the past. I wasn't sure exactly what was different— having never been involved in one myself—but the optimism and excitement was palpable, and I am glad this was the case. It was fun. We had purpose and we became friends for life. While victory was not assured—the polls went back and forth—we knew we could win if we worked hard and got the vote out.

It was a gruelling eleven-week official campaign, running from August 2 to Election Day, which was October 19, 2015. That amounted to seventy-eight days—the longest federal election campaign in recent history. When I think of it, my mind often goes to door-knocking. So much door-knocking. I had not knocked on doors for many things in my life. Indeed, in Indigenous communities such a sight would not be commonplace, and certainly federal and provincial political candidates rarely venture onto the reserve. I do not remember ever seeing a candidate back home at Cape Mudge—let alone one knocking on our doors.

Another dynamic on the campaign was the reality of being what the party considered a high-profile candidate. This had its benefits. The party certainly was supportive. We knew this, as polling was shared with us in ways that few other candidates got to see. It also meant a lot of calls from Gerry and others. Of course, these calls may have been because Lea and I were somewhat eager, and often reached out to them to ask for things or advice. As novice campaigners, we wanted to understand everything as best we could.

But being high-profile also came with challenges. The party was convinced from the start of the campaign that Vancouver Granville was going to be a victory, much like the ridings of Vancouver Quadra and Vancouver Centre. Following Lea's lead, and with all of our tremendous volunteers, we ended up with one of the highest-performing ridings in the country in terms of contacts with voters as well as fundraising. By the midpoint of the campaign we became a model for the Liberal Party's field team program in BC, which also meant that the party was trying to take some of our best people to help out in other ridings. This was understandable. But our volunteers were really dedicated and did not want to leave. And, of course, Lea and I did not want them to. We were not taking anything for granted, and we worked all-out until the last minute. Never count your chickens before the eggs have hatched, as they say.

Perhaps one of the most upsetting aspects of the campaign was dealing with racist comments from within the Liberal Party. One Liberal MP and candidate put an ad in an Indigenous paper congratulating Indigenous grads with the tagline "Sobriety, education and hard work lead to success." The candidate did apologize and blamed a staffer for approving the ad. I was not pleased. Who are these people? Of course, the party went into damage control mode and asked me to help. I certainly did not realize at the time that this challenge trickled down from the top.

Throughout the campaign—and as would be the case during my time in Ottawa—when challenges arose or things upset me I turned to those closest to me to confirm the facts, test my interpretations of what was going on, and challenge my assumptions. Tim has always been unrelenting in telling me the truth, whether about political realities or how I might be thinking or acting. He is my greatest champion but also my hardest critic. Lea is the same. Both of them call it like it is and check me when I might be getting out of line, having fanciful illusions, or becoming overly hopeful. On the campaign this loving support was indispensable.

•

On election night we watched the results on TV in our condo: my mum, Tim, Lea, Kory, and my three nieces (Kaija, Kaylene, and Kadence). We were all waiting for that tick to appear at some point next to my name and photo. We had heard from our volunteers at polling stations that the numbers showed that we had won comfortably, but we were waiting for the media to call the race. We were nervous. And while Tim and I have long been a supportive and loving team of two, we can have a tendency to feed each other's nerves. My mother has the opposite effect on me and I needed her there. She has always been a constant support, bringing consistency, strictness, and love to our relationship. Her whole life has been dedicated to the well-being of Kory and me, and she has always kept us stable even when other support was missing.

And as has always been the case in the big moments of our lives, Kory and I were together on election night. In my first memories, Kory is always there. Like any sisters there are times we poke each other, but we are each other's foundation in life. Our lives have always been together and they always will be. And her daughters are like mine and Tim's.

When the tick appeared on the TV screen next to my name, it was done. The forty-second Canadian general election saw the Liberal Party win 184 seats (17 seats in British Columbia), enabling it to form a majority government with Justin Trudeau as the next prime minister of Canada.

We finally made it to our victory party at the Diamond Ballroom on West 8th Street near Granville Street. Our team showed up gradually. Vancouver Granville was a late riding to be called, and many of our team were still at the polling stations. We had not really planned a victory party. We didn't have music picked out, so the same three songs played over and over. Nobody seemed to care. I gave a speech, though some of the media seemed annoyed at how late the speech came. Afterwards, many of us headed over to the large Liberal victory party on 2nd Avenue in Olympic Village, at a brewpub called the Steel Toad. It was packed. When we all arrived there was huge applause and I was guided up onto the stage to make a speech. The room was electric. Everyone wanted to take a photo, buy me a drink, or chat. We had won a majority. Sunny days were here. Canada was back.

We broke away from the crowded party to spend some much-needed time with our amazing team at the campaign office, and then Tim, Lea, Rick, and I had our own quiet celebration. I was so tired. We all were. We went back to our condo and had some champagne and reflected on the reality that after this night life was going to change dramatically. We were Ottawa bound—whatever that meant.

THREE

Sworn In

Sometimes I ask myself: If I were Gwyneth Paltrow in the 1998 romantic comedy *Sliding Doors*, which scenario would I be in? Gwyneth takes one train, discovers the truth of betrayal, and gradually improves her life. On the other train, she does not see the truth and grows increasingly miserable. I guess I have been on the first train, and for that I am grateful. I feel sad for those riding along glumly on the train in the second scenario.

But couldn't I have missed the train altogether? Wouldn't that have been better?

◆

There is a photograph of me looking up at the prime minister on the day he officially became prime minister, with my hands on his shoulders and his on mine. It is November 4, 2015, the day I was sworn in as the fifty-first minister of justice and attorney general of Canada.

The picture, which was taken right after I said the oaths, conveys what I felt at that moment—joy, excitement, the weight of an extraordinary responsibility, and, yes, a belief we were going to make real change. There are similar photos taken with many other Cabinet ministers from this day, all of whom I am sure felt the same way. There was great optimism.

I do not remember the prime minister or me saying anything in particular as we stood there looking at each other. Being sworn in was a little overwhelming—because of the impending and important responsibilities being placed on me; because I was the first Indigenous person to be minister of justice and attorney general of Canada; and because of being in such a spotlight. *This is real*, I thought to myself. *I am part of a government that is committed to doing the work to create the change I was raised to help make.*

The sixteen days from election night to being sworn in were a whirlwind. Even today, they are a blur. Things were happening on so many fronts that there was little chance to stop and think, let alone take it all in and reflect on what was happening. Closing up campaign operations, preparing to move, responding to the countless emails, texts, and calls, and continuing to meet with people throughout the riding who were soon to be my constituents. But, of course, the issue of who is going to be in Cabinet was looming in the mind of every member of Parliament belonging to the party that won. As it happens, I did not have to think about this for long.

Within days of the election I got a call from Peter Harder, who was assisting with Cabinet selection as part of the transition team and who would later be appointed a senator and the government leader in the Senate. When I was minister, he and I spent a great deal of time together working to pass government bills. I was driving north on Cambie Street very near our campaign office when he called. I pulled the car over to answer and, after he identified himself, Peter said, "You are being considered for a possible Cabinet position." He added that Tim and I would have to fill out a number of screening forms but did not say more than that, other than to emphasize that this had to be kept in the strictest confidence.

This was the first confirmation I had that Cabinet was a possibility. But it was not the first indication this might occur. Justin and I had an indirect conversation—at least I thought it was—about it when we were flying back from Prince Rupert during our campaign trip to the Great Bear Rainforest. He raised it, asking what areas I might be interested in while dancing around the word *Cabinet*. He talked about immigration and the environment. I expressed interest in those areas without mentioning any others. Of course, we had spoken a fair bit about Indigenous and broader social justice issues already.

Not too long after the Harder call, it became apparent to me that a game of "telephone" was beginning among the newly elected Liberal MPs in BC, who were trying to mine information about Cabinet selection. I knew, as Gerry had hinted at it in the past, that Justin did not like being approached and asked about Cabinet positions. I had never thought about doing so, but realized many others did. The rumour I heard was that some candidates they had been considering might have been dropped because of their efforts to seek a post.

The security forms were detailed, and included questions about all my relatives—particularly my immediate family members. It has always been my tendency in such matters to err on the side of caution and go beyond what is required. I am also a bit of a detail freak, as is Tim, so we dug into the task and revealed all. Someone somewhere has paper evidence that I was caught shoplifting hair elastics with my sister at the Campbell River Kmart when I was nine. My dad met us at the police station. So much mischief as a child.

It was also during this time, as Cabinet possibilities were starting to be rumoured, that I resolved to myself that I would carry on the practice that I had long held of always having little black notebooks with me and writing everything down. I had begun this in earnest when I became Regional Chief, because I knew I would want to remember clearly what was said, and by whom. To have a record of my experience, yes, but also a record of the unfolding of this history, of change. If it was appropriate and possible to write my notes during meetings I always would. If not, I would often do so immediately after when I could, sometimes writing down thoughts on a day as it came to an end. I am fairly certain everyone who worked with me in Ottawa remembers seeing me with a notebook, jotting stuff down, whether the meeting was large or small, with public servants or politicians.

Gerry Butts once said to me, sometime during my early years as minister, that they had always planned that I was going to be the minister of justice and attorney general. That it was never a question, right from the beginning, even during the campaign. The prime minister and Gerry also told me many times that I would be the minister of justice and attorney general of Canada for as long as the prime minister was the prime minister. There are lots of such comments in my Moleskine notebooks. I did not put much stock in such comments, whatever the motivation. And, of course, the latter turned out to be false. Who knows if the former was just flattery. What I do know is that I never thought about becoming the minister of justice, or even considered that it was among the possibilities, until it was hinted to me late in the transition.

Tim and I headed out to Ottawa on October 27, 2015. This was the beginning of many trips back and forth to Ottawa with and without Tim. At this point, while not having been told anything specific, I knew I was going to be in Cabinet but not in which portfolio. Peter had told me to get on a plane and get out there. So we did.

On October 28, I met with Peter Harder and Marc-André Blanchard on Slater Street at the transition offices. It felt like a bit of an interrogation combined with an indoctrination about the possibilities of being in Cabinet. Two questions from that meeting have always stuck in my mind. "Is there anything in your background that would bring embarrassment to the PM, the government, or the

Party?" That one was easy to answer. No. The second: "Is there any position in the Cabinet that you feel you would not be able to fill for reasons of conflict or otherwise?" Also easy for me to answer, although I took much more time in answering this one, as there was a ministry I knew I could never lead.

I told them unequivocally that I would be unable to accept the job of minister of Indian and northern affairs (as it was then called). There were many reasons for this. I could not, in good conscience, be the minister responsible for overseeing the suffering of my own people through administering the Indian Act. I had spent my life— and generations of my family had spent their lives—advocating and fighting to move beyond the Indian Act and the paternalistic role that the minister and the department play in the lives of Indigenous peoples. I could not become the "head Indian agent," ministering to the suffering of my own people. This would be an impossible situation for me. Additionally, of course, it would create a situation where Indigenous peoples would have high expectations—expectations they should have. But those are expectations that cannot be met through the minister administering the Indian Act. The way to change the system was not by being legally responsible, literally, for administering the system that had to change. More than anything, the colonial laws themselves and the systems they create are what need to be transformed. This change would need to be enacted by the government as a whole and led from the highest offices. They understood and clearly agreed with me on how this would be an impossible role for me to play.

Peter and Marc-André both confirmed that I certainly would be in Cabinet and in a very high-profile position. They talked about there being lots of stakeholders, and that the position would be very busy and central to the government. As the conversation went on, I got the clear impression that it would be a dual role of some sort, and that is when I first sensed I would be minister of justice and attorney general of Canada. I remained calm, and I realize now that I had not really processed what this would mean to me both personally and more broadly. The scale and scope of the work and the life changes it would entail. Oh my. But also, the fact that an Indigenous woman would now be the Crown's chief law officer.

I left the meeting that afternoon and went back to the Sheraton Hotel where Tim and I were staying. Tim was waiting in our room. Before I even got in the door I said, "I think the prime minister is going to ask me to be the minister of justice and attorney general." "Why you?" Tim immediately replied. Ha! His incredulity matched mine. It was at this point that I began to see the possibilities—more so than at any time during the campaign. And it was becoming very real. What a night of mind-racing and not much sleep.

The next day it became official—at least for Tim and me and those in the know at the PMO. I again went to Slater Street, this time to meet with the prime minister-designate, Gerry (who was now principal secretary), and Katie Telford, the head campaign advisor who was to be the PM's chief of staff. I arrived and was taken into a room. Trudeau was sitting behind a desk, there was a chair for me facing him, and Gerry and Katie were off to the side by the window. Right from the beginning Adam Scotti began snapping photos.

After minor pleasantries, Justin simply leaned across the desk towards me and said, in his soft and charming way, "I would like you to be my minister of justice and attorney general." Despite my intuitions from the day before, I was overwhelmed. I instantly teared up, and the prime minister did too. He reached across the table with his hands to grab mine. Justin Trudeau and I had this way of being caught looking into each other's eyes in photos, as was the case with many others, too. This scene was no exception. "I would be honoured to serve in this capacity, and I will work hard and to the best of my ability . . . Thank you."

Sitting across from me, the soon-to-be-PM remarked that "this is a role [minister of justice and attorney general of Canada] my father had and it means a great deal to me to have you in the same role." He said he thought it would mean a great deal to the country. He spoke about Indigenous peoples, and the future.

This was a meeting for which I did not take contemporaneous notes. But as I immerse myself back into that moment, as I have many times over the years, I recall a million thoughts, emotions, and reactions running through me all at once. I did not keep them all inside. My first policy thought was "OMG I am going to have to legislate medical assistance in dying," which I ended up saying out loud. We touched on that and also on being an Indigenous minister of justice—what this meant for Indigenous peoples (this reality did take my breath away) and for the country—as well as the dual roles I would fill. He said I would do a good job and that this was the right thing for me, the government, and Canada.

He seemed very happy, gave me a hug, as did Gerry and Katie. Gerry was happy, all smiles. Katie and I did not know each other, really, but we hugged awkwardly as well. The meeting did not take too long.

I left the Slater Street office. It was a Thursday, and I knew that come the following Wednesday, November 4, all would be different. They'd indicated I could tell Tim, confidentially, so I raced back to the hotel where he was waiting. He gave me a big hug. He was so proud, and we were both stunned. There were a few swear words spoken, and then we kind of just stared at each other for a bit and set in for another night of imagining the possibilities. I so wanted to tell others. I imagined telling my parents. I suspected my dad would make a joke, but that I would see in his face immense pride as he did. As for my mum, she would grin from ear to ear while tearing up. In addition to family, I really wanted to let Carolyn know, as I assumed she would be the minister of Indigenous affairs and that we would have to do so much together. But I did not tell her or anyone else. No one did, as far as I know.

We went back to Vancouver for the weekend to continue getting organized. Although I wasn't permitted to speak about my position,

I was allowed to invite a few people in addition to Tim to the swearing-in at Rideau Hall. My mum was too ill to fly at the time, but Kory and Lea would be there.

Arriving back in Ottawa a few days later was a different experience. Indeed, things had changed. As we descended the escalator to the arrivals hall at the airport, I could see many cameras and many journalists, some of whom I recognized. I remember media asking if I was in Cabinet, and me responding with the standard deflection about being happy to have been elected as the member of Parliament for Vancouver Granville. I could feel the sense of anticipation (like at the Montreal convention) that I was told later had been building in Ottawa for months if not years—about a new government, a new generation, a new era. There was electricity in the air throughout the city.

The night before the swearing-in, Kory, Lea, and I went for a walk up to Parliament Hill. It was a cool, crystal-clear night. The Peace Tower loomed above, stars glimmering in the sky around it. It was magical, with the Centennial Flame warming us as we stood there taking it all in. I've always found Parliament beautifully imposing, particularly at night. I felt its full majesty that evening, along with the awesomeness of the responsibility I would be taking on in that building on behalf of Canadians. I felt proud standing there. Three Indigenous women, one from the East Coast, two from the West. Never in our wildest dreams had we imagined our paths would lead any of us here. It was unfathomable. I remembered some of the biggest adventures Kory and I had as kids. Taking the six-hour bus ride alone from Port Hardy to Victoria in the summer to see Grandma and Grandpa, or the time we went to Disneyland. Feeling totally carefree. Yet here I was, standing on the shoulders of those who had come before me, about to assume responsibility for justice as part of a government system that my family and others had spent generations demanding justice from.

I look at the picture of the three of us I took that night—the Peace Tower lit up in the background—and I see at once the past, present, and future of this country. All we have been and all that is yet to be.

The greatness that still lies ahead if we can keep confronting some of the legacies that remain with us. And I see in my face a look of joyful hope and anticipation.

◆

November 4, 2015. Swearing-in day. In the morning I was a member of Parliament; by afternoon I was the minister of justice and attorney general of Canada. And then the madness set in—for the rest of that day and for the many days to come.

The soon-to-be ministers were all told to meet that morning at the Delta Ottawa. This was the first time we were to know who our Cabinet colleagues would be. Perhaps some had been told who else was in; if so, I was not one of them. I had never met most of the others, but I did see some familiar faces, including Carolyn and Harjit Sajjan, who was a friend and someone I had worked closely with during the campaign. Everyone was excitedly saying hi and trying to figure out who was in what portfolio. The only exception was Stéphane Dion, who said he was not going to say anything until the ceremony. And he did not.

As I met my Cabinet colleagues for the first time, I realized something that would be talked about at length by the media. This Cabinet was not only diverse and representative of Canadians, but it also was filled with individuals with real-life experience and knowledge about the ministries they would lead. A doctor as minister of health. A soldier as minister of defence. An astronaut in Transport.

We were bussed to 24 Sussex Drive and were then to walk up to Rideau Hall together. We were told our positions: where to stand and walk alongside or after the prime minister. It was a nice, brisk sunny day—the dreamed-of weather for the return of sunny days. The crowd was pretty big and lined up along our pathway, and there were people cheering and crying. As we approached Rideau Hall, throngs of media greeted us. This was certainly not a scene I had ever experienced in Indigenous politics. To see people's faces, hear people screaming out names of politicians: it was surreal.

As I walked into the packed ballroom where the ceremony was being held I saw William F. (Bill) Pentney, who I knew was going to be my deputy minister (I'd been given a briefing note and photograph of him the day before). I briefly paused to say hello. I do not know why, but I assumed he knew that I was to be his minister. From the look of surprise on his face, I realized immediately I was wrong. I then turned and said hello to Michael Wernick, who was then deputy minister of INAC, who was sitting beside Bill and whom I had known for years. I also acknowledged the Indigenous leaders attending.

The ceremony got underway. I was sitting in the front row between two old Liberal warhorses, Lawrence MacAulay and Stéphane Dion. When my name was called and I was introduced as the minister of justice and attorney general of Canada—or MOJAG, as I and others came to call me—there was a collective intake of breath in the room and then an audible gasp. And then applause. I thought about my dad, mum, and many others. I knew my mum was watching on TV, bawling away. Later, Mumma told me she stood up, pumped her fist, and yelled, "Holy F@#k." As I rose to accept my new position in that room in Rideau Hall, with all eyes on me, I looked to see the faces of Tim, Kory, and Lea. Where was I? How had I gotten here, to this moment, with these people? It seemed, in a way, unreal.

As I took the oaths I could feel my legs shaking.

Oath of Allegiance

I, Jody Wilson-Raybould, do declare that I will be faithful and bear true allegiance to Her Majesty Queen Elizabeth the Second, Queen of Canada, Her Heirs and Successors.

Oath of the Members of the Privy Council

I, Jody Wilson-Raybould, do solemnly and sincerely declare that I shall be a true and faithful servant to Her Majesty

Queen Elizabeth the Second, as a member of Her Majesty's Privy Council for Canada. I will in all things to be treated, debated and resolved in Privy Council, faithfully, honestly and truly declare my mind and my opinion. I shall keep secret all matters committed and revealed to me in this capacity, or that shall be secretly treated of in Council. Generally, in all things I shall do as a faithful and true servant ought to do for Her Majesty.

Oath of Office

I, Jody Wilson-Raybould, do solemnly and sincerely promise and declare that I will truly and faithfully, and to the best of my skill and knowledge, execute the powers and trusts reposed in me as the Minister of Justice and Attorney General of Canada.

I remember thinking I hoped people could not tell I was nervous and feeling overwhelmed. I hoped my voice would not crack. The prime minister was beaming, as were his mother, Margaret, and his wife, Sophie. That photograph was taken.

After the ceremony, the official photos were taken of Governor General David Johnston with the 29th Canadian Ministry under Prime Minister Justin Trudeau—I was seated in the front row, three seats to the right of the prime minister between Minister Stéphane Dion (Foreign Affairs) and Minister Ralph Goodale (Public Safety). And, of course, we had the press conference. We all stood with the prime minister in front of Rideau Hall, sun streaming down on us as if on cue. When asked about the gender parity in Cabinet, the prime minister responded with his now famous—and we know now very planned—line, "because it's 2015." The crowd loved it. We were happy. Very happy.

A short reception followed in the Tent Room, or the "Circus Room," as my sister calls it because of its distinct pink-and-white décor. There were a lot of people wanting to meet the new ministers.

Tim, Lea, Kory, and I took a whack of photos. When it was over, all the newly minted ministers got on the buses once again and were driven to Parliament Hill for our first meeting as a Cabinet. Ralph Goodale and I were in the back of the last bus with Minister Kent Hehr (Veterans Affairs), who was in the very back in his wheelchair. As we turned the corner by the Château Laurier, the back doors of the bus swung open. The wheels of Kent's chair were locked, but as the bus made its way up the slight incline of the road, the chair began to tip back toward those open doors, putting Kent in danger of a fall—out of the chair and out of the bus. The moment played out almost in slow motion. *Oh God,* I thought, *his chair is not secure and we are going to lose him.* Ralph and I frantically grabbed on to him. Kent nervously laughed, taking it all in stride, and we continued on. I do not even know how many people on the bus realized it had happened.

Once on the Hill, we all made another orchestrated and well-photographed walk up to Centre Block and were led to the Cabinet room. Seats had been assigned to us around the large oval table. I was seated across from the prime minister, between Ralph and Navdeep Bains. The prime minister sat down.

"Holy shit," he said. Everyone erupted in laughter and applause. For me, it was out of a sense of relief. I imagine that was the case for many.

◆

Early in my tenure as a member of the government, including this first day, the messages I was receiving reinforced the core ideals and values that we'd campaigned on. The message was of service and openness—that we needed to be committed to transparency, ethical government, and leading by example. The prime minister spoke of how we were "open to differences." He told us we needed to bring our expertise, research, and policy options to Cabinet, and bring our best practices for collaboration and working together to Cabinet, to caucus, and to our relationships with all politicians. This included making Parliament positive, respected, and effective.

It was a message of good governance not unlike the one I had delivered for years to Indigenous leaders. It was truly what I believed in and what I felt, frankly, the country needed. I thought to myself, *I wish Canadians could hear this.* I was pumped. Looking back now, I realize this kind of message was also reflected in my election campaign in 2019, when I ran as a results-focused, values-based Independent who leads by example. Not partisan.

Was this a performance by the PM? Did he believe it? Which of Gwyneth's trains was I on?

I have no idea what the correct answers were at that moment. I do know I believed it, and frankly I think everyone else who had been appointed a minister that day did as well. It felt like anything—and all good things—were possible, and the prime minister was a leader who would listen, learn, and make decisions collaboratively and in the best interests of Canadians. The early conversations around the first bits of policy all positively reinforced the hope that real change was on the agenda and on the way. We were going to move forward to accept twenty-five thousand Syrian refugees, and it was emphasized that a "whole of government" approach would be needed. Not only would we be helping individuals and families who would contribute greatly to Canada, as refugees have over generations, but we would also be challenging and changing attitudes domestically and abroad.

In addition to the pep talks and words of inspiration and hope, we were, as new ministers, also given some strong messages in terms of our roles and responsibilities. This was intended, I think, to instill a bit of fear and caution. About ethics, conflict of interest, Cabinet secrecy, Cabinet solidarity, expectations of preparedness and working hard, and the role of the public service. These were important messages and absolutely necessary.

What I did not realize then, but came to appreciate more and more over time, was that all of these messages—whether inspirational or

intimidating—were expected to be interpreted through the thick filter of partisanship and the desire to retain power. I think the more
experienced ministers knew this and simply took it for granted. But
some of us newbies (especially me, who had no prior connections to
a political party) took these messages at face value. This was clearly a
mistake. Partisanship comes first, then everything else. I just did not
know it at the time.

Later that afternoon there was media mayhem, and I ended up
being one of the key faces of the day. This was truly jumping in
headfirst. I had never done much media. I had done interviews and
been in stories while Regional Chief but rarely nationally—with the
exceptions of the time around the two meetings with Prime Minister
Harper and little bits of coverage during the campaign. But I had
certainly never been at the centre of public attention. Now all eyes
were on us. I know as newbies we were given some slack, a chance to
get our feet wet before the Hill reporters—some good, some not so
good (as I would come to learn)—got to work and performed what is
a necessary and critical function in our democracy as the fifth estate.

Sometime during the day of the swearing-in, presumably after
people realized I was minister of justice and attorney general of Canada, a video had resurfaced of my dad and Prime Minister Pierre
Elliott Trudeau having a stand-off during the constitutional talks in
1983. The media ran with it.

The clip was from a critical moment in the debate over whether
amendments to the now repatriated Constitution would clarify the
protections for the rights of Indigenous peoples, specifically the
inherent right of self-government. Canada, and most provincial governments, had come to the constitutional conference in 1983 with
no real intention of reaching a deal to describe further the now recognized and affirmed rights of Indigenous peoples in section 35.
Indigenous peoples who have a historic relationship with the British
Crown, including through treaties across much of the country, were
worried about what repatriation might mean.

Ultimately, after tremendous advocacy by Indigenous peoples—including my father's own integral work—section 35 was amended to address future treaties and agreements, among other things, but progress on the recognition of self-government was left as unfinished business. It was Canada's first amendment to the Constitution Act, 1982.

I know the federal and provincial governments did not understand at the time how important section 35 was and what it meant. Thirty-five-plus years of court cases and ongoing negotiations have begun to tell us much. As Indigenous peoples have used section 35 in the courts, it has increased the general understanding that reconciliation is a fundamental imperative of our Constitution, that historic treaties must be upheld, that Aboriginal (Indigenous) rights, including title, continue to exist to our territories, and that duty to consult and accommodate must be affirmed.

What the first Prime Minister Trudeau and my dad were debating—the protection of Indigenous rights in the Constitution—has, in the decades since, fundamentally changed this country. The fact that I was now in Cabinet and working with the first Prime Minister Trudeau's son, and was MOJAG to boot, was important. Not so much for me personally but symbolically for the country and practically for what might come next in terms of policy development and approach on Indigenous issues. A full circle. Justin Trudeau and I had talked about this in Whitehorse. Now it was public. From many angles, it was a great story.

Over the course of that day, I had been told how the video was popping up in the mainstream media and on social media. I remember being in my grade-six class at Comox Elementary watching my dad and Justin's dad when it was happening live on TV. I had also watched the National Film Board documentary *Dancing Around the Table*, in which the clip is featured, many times. But it had been years since I had seen it.

What struck me most about rewatching it was not the debate on Indigenous issues. In the clip my dad is sitting across from the prime minister, pushing him, challenging him. This was after it was obvious that progress on self-government was not going to be made. My dad—great and spontaneous orator that he is—speaks in his eloquent way:

> **DAD:** *I have two children in Vancouver Island, both of whom for some misguided reason say they want to be a lawyer. [pause] Both of whom want to be the prime minister. [Pause] Both of whom, Mr. Prime Minister, are women. [Laughter]*

> **TRUDEAU:** *Tell them I'll stick around until they are ready. [Laughter]*

> **DAD:** *Mr. Chairman, I'm informed by the government of British Columbia that one of them could be out on a plane this evening. [Laughter]*

Many people comment to me today about how the men in the video, including the prime minister, are laughing at the exchange. Not about the fact we are Indigenous. No. It was that we are women. The sexism of it. And certainly, that is noteworthy.

But when I look back at that video I focus on my father, not on the laughter. Perhaps I do this in recognition of how our loving but complicated relationship has evolved over the years. My dad was not joking. He was not really laughing. He was making a serious point. While I realize that there were some political tactics in what he did, I also know that in that moment, with everything else that had happened during those constitutional talks, my dad was proud. He was strong. He was proud of how far Indigenous peoples had come, what had been accomplished, and that now he was sitting across from the prime minister. And he saw the change that was possible. I know he was also proud of my sister and me and that he always believed we could, and perhaps would, do anything and everything we set our minds and hearts to. I think about how he must have felt—that the world was shifting in that moment—and I feel how much love he must have had in that exact moment when he thought of my sister and me and spoke of his hopes for our future.

So I was not totally surprised that when the video clip was played during my first formal interview as minister, on CBC's *Power and Politics*, I almost broke down. When I was asked how I felt seeing the clip, I made a joke about my dad looking young to stem my emotions. In front of thousands of television viewers, I was having an intimate moment with my dad, seeing him express his love and hopes for me. I thought of him sitting back at home, with his TV on, realizing that the world was still shifting as he had felt in that moment decades earlier. He was right.

My emotion behind the reaction? It was not nostalgia or the symmetry of my dad and a Prime Minister Trudeau with myself and another Prime Minister Trudeau that got to me. It was knowing what he had lived through and what he had accomplished. It was also the reality that in certain moments you are struck with the belief that a better way really is possible. There was poetry in that moment for me. A feeling that optimism, hope, and hard work can bring change. My dad always had that hope. Despite so many challenges, he has seen some of the fruits of that hope. And this one was particularly personal for him, as a father.

The next day we had our first national caucus meeting. The prime minister walked up to me and said, "I hear you want my job." I stared at him, and then he laughed.

◆

Do I still believe what I thought in those early days? That with optimism, hope, and hard work real change can occur? Or did the train ride I ended up taking change that?

I know, deep down, that I do still believe it. I wish, however, I could say that from November 4 onward that belief was reinforced in clear and steady ways. That the values and ideals spoken of at the outset were upheld and honoured. That they were believed by everyone around that table. I wish I could say to Canadians that the state of our government is that of a good government, ready for the challenges we face today. But I cannot.

I think if I were in his shoes I would want to impart similar words to the ones spoken by the prime minister early on—about responsibility. But I know that I would make sure that everyone, including me, lived up to my words. I would ask that those around me warn me if I was not following my own advice. These ideals are consistent with how I was taught to understand leadership. Leadership as distinct from power and office.

Moving forward from that day, yes, much of what the Trudeau government has done and is still doing is good. Yes, there are many good people within the government and its support offices who work hard every day. But there is a lot that is wrong and that requires bold change and new thinking. Our mode of governance, as successful as it has been compared to other countries, is not designed for or functioning in the ways that are needed at this moment as we evolve as a country. The fundamental reality of our time is the complexity brought on by the integrative nature of our complex world. From climate change to social media to economic imperatives to diversity, inclusion, and justice, to govern means to be able to respond, adapt, and lead on both a local and global scale. And then there is the COVID-19 pandemic that is still, as I write, teaching us the lessons of integration in even more intense ways.

What I have come to realize is that some of my optimism and hope was invested in an illusion regarding how we govern, no matter who is in power. Parties over ideas, leaders over parliamentarians, secrecy over transparency, centralization of power in the unelected over deliberation and consensus decision-making, blind loyalty over independence, and self-interest over the collective good. On all of these equations we are tilting in the wrong way. We can tilt in other directions, and indeed we must if we are to rise to the challenges of the world. It took me a few years to fully realize this, but once I started seeing more clearly what was going on, the learning was fast and furious. Much of what follows here is about how it worked and did not work in the areas of law and policy that I was either entrusted to lead or inserted myself into because they were important.

In the first days after being sworn in, there were warning signs of what was to come. And there was so much that was great. I see that now.

My deputy minister, an extraordinarily kind, thoughtful, and talented man, spent most of my second day as MOJAG with me. He introduced me to officials and provided essential briefings, and together we strolled through the department. People were very welcoming and clearly excited. Some were even in tears.

Over the years I spent as minister I would occasionally get reactions like that—people moved and hopeful by what they felt I represented or stood for. After the SNC-Lavalin affair, it happened even more; it still happens to this day, and it continues to amaze me. I think it says something about our country and our collective psyche. It is not about reactions to me personally but about what we aspire to, about the idea that we are good people. And that we care. I realize how much we need hope and belief that things can be better. For Indigenous peoples, this has had to be the case in order for us to push through and sustain our families and communities in the face of tremendous difficulties. But it is the case for all of us. We are all suffering in various ways that challenge who we are and our well-being. We all feel the drive to make the world better for ourselves, our families, and those around us. We all need to believe it can happen. I believe it has and that it will continue to. Our collective job is to ensure it does.

Soon after the swearing-in, government continued to reinforce how positive this moment could be. The mandate letters were being finalized, and that was exciting. It was the first time that such letters—which detail what the prime minister is expecting of his ministers—would be made public. Much of the talk around the letters was great, and many of the orientation messages were music to my ears: "Politics is a secondary role we play"; "Science and the rule of law and the Constitution must be woven through everything we do"; "We must demonstrate the impact of how we spend taxpayer money"; "We must be open-minded about all different perspectives"; "Restoring Cabinet government, making decisions that reflect a team effort, will lead to better decisions"; "With politics we need to learn humility." This was great stuff. I remember one day when we left a meeting, public servants were lined up clapping and cheering. They seemed so excited and relieved.

In these early days, a senior PMO official made a statement in front of the prime minister, members of the government, and public servants that has always stuck with me. It would come to mind many times during my years as minister. "The prime minister is your brand. You each serve at his pleasure. You each have a duty to country—and will need to at some point speak truth to power."

I took this to heart. I wrote it in my notebook with quotation marks around it. What I did not realize at the time is that I was not expected to take the last sentence seriously.

FOUR

MOJAG

When contemplating writing this book, I asked a few people close to me what they thought I should write about, what people would want to read. They had many excellent ideas, and these are reflected throughout. One idea I heard from many was that I should write about the day-to-day life of a minister and how I went about and enjoyed my work. These people encouraged me to describe a day in the life of being a minister—what I loved about it, what I hated about it, how I understood the role I was playing. I was not so sure about this; I was skeptical readers would be all that interested. To my surprise—though I should not be surprised, because my friends' and family's ideas are usually more on the mark than mine on these things—when I started talking to editors and publishers about the book they had the same idea. "It will be so interesting for the readers . . . to talk about 'doing the job as a team' . . . and what the interactions were like." That's how this chapter came about.

I admit I am still not fully convinced. Many people spend their days doing things just as or far more interesting than being a minister of the Crown. My ministerial days were long, seemingly endless, filled with countless piles of paper, and crammed with so many meetings that they truly blurred together. As I became more accustomed to my role, the days only got longer, and it felt like sleep disappeared altogether. While there were little joys every day, the work was sometimes interspersed with moments of true exhilaration and sometimes with utter disappointment. But ultimately, for me, it was simply the kind of work where one could never do enough. And still, I felt compelled to do even more all the time, because of how it could impact people's lives. You always know your time to serve is finite. The old adage that there is never enough time in the day could not have been more true.

My role, of course, was also dual—as the minister of justice and the attorney general. The fact of these dual roles, and how they are different, would come into the spotlight during the SNC-Lavalin affair. In Canada, these dual roles have existed ever since the department was created in 1868. Sir John A. Macdonald was the first minister of justice and attorney general of Canada.

As minister of justice, one is responsible for a number of legal policy areas, such as criminal justice (including youth criminal justice), family law, access to justice, Indigenous justice, public law, and private international law. The minister has to provide policy advice to Cabinet, and has responsibility for dozens upon dozens of federal statutes. As attorney general, one is the chief law officer of the Crown—basically the government's lawyer. The AG protects the interests of the Crown by litigating on behalf of the Crown and by providing legal advice to the government, departments, and agencies of government. In this role, one has some unique responsibilities, some of which require a degree of independence, to ensure the rule of law is upheld. Most prosecution functions of the attorney general have been assigned to an independent organization, the Public

Prosecution Service of Canada, which was established through legislation in 2006. The attorney general is supported in this role by the director of public prosecutions (DPP). As such, on a day-to-day basis, on both hugely impactful prosecutions and minor ones, the attorney general plays no active role, gives no direction, and generally receives very little information from the DPP. When they do, the AG rarely shares it with ministers or the PM.

As I struggled with this chapter, trying to convince myself of its merit, I began to think about what I thought the life of a minister was like before I actually became one, and how I played my dual roles while I was in government. Even though I had been in many meetings with ministers as a Treaty Commissioner and as Regional Chief, I am not sure if I ever really thought about what their daily life was like. But I do know I thought about what I wanted them to be like, what I thought they did, and how I thought they could act in their roles. I certainly also thought about how decisions were made and what kind of processes would take place within government—both within a minister's office and within Cabinet. And then I realized: this is what my friends and editors were really talking about. How do the assumptions and perceptions we carry of ministers, assuming we care or have any interest, match the reality of how they work, and how our government makes decisions? Does the life of a minister match what our hopes and aspirations are for how our government functions? And how might my daily life differ when acting in my roles as minister of justice or attorney general?

She's got the power. Legislating doctor-assisted suicide, legalizing marijuana and undoing key parts of the Conservative legacy—from court challenges over banning the niqab at citizenship ceremonies to criminal justice—are among the priorities for Jody Wilson-Raybould, a former Crown prosecutor. But the member of the We Wai Kai Nation and former regional chief of the Assembly of First Nations will also have a powerful voice in indigenous issues, a centerpiece for the Liberal government, as one of two indigenous cabinet ministers. Ms. Wilson-Raybould will play a lead role in establishing an inquiry into murdered and missing indigenous women and girls, as well as in amending anti-terrorism Bill C-51 and modernizing the Access to Information Act. She also sits on six cabinet committees—more than any other minister— including Agenda and Results, and she's vice-chair of the committees for public security and intelligence.

That is how the Winter 2016 issue of the Hill Times' *Power & Influence* magazine described me and my role in its feature on the one hundred most powerful and influential people in government and politics. They put me at number eleven on the list. Erin Anderssen, writing for the *Globe and Mail*, called me "The justice minister without precedent."

Well, if I had that kind of power (and as I will share later, ministerial power is not what most people think it is), it does not mean that the work life of a minister is not stretched by relatively mundane tasks, and a lot of them.

Now, please do not get me wrong. The days were long and often hard, with highs and lows, but there is no question that as a minister you are treated differently. People want to be around you. I understand this. Everyone (in the Ottawa bubble, at least) knows you or of you, and they want you to know them. And more Canadians generally know of you—although as ministers we were often told by the PMO that we needed to raise our profile. Fair enough. In the beginning I also came to appreciate just how much some people—okay, many people—sought proximity to power in order to gain something from it.

What I did find difficult personally was how some people I had known for a long time changed the way they interacted with me. I was the same person I was before November 4, 2015, but in their perception I was living in a different world. They seemed unable to separate the person and the office. Truthfully, there were only a few people who remained the same with me both before and after I was minister. I was so grateful for them.

Some people were also visibly nervous to talk to me. I found this so strange, and I certainly tried to make people feel less nervous or, as best I could, more comfortable. I remember speaking to Jessica Prince soon after she was newly installed in her role as my senior policy advisor; she was clearly a little nervous. I tried to make her more relaxed by talking about how we were "two gals from Vancouver Island." Many people looked at the floor or seemed to feel that they should not speak to me. And I lost my name. Everyone was told they had to call me "Minister." Even when I said to please call me Jody I would get a "Yes, Minister" in response. With the exception of my mum, sister, close friends and community on Cape Mudge, I do not think anyone called me Jody after I was sworn in. And Tim, of course. He never called me Minister, but he did buy the British political satire sitcom *Yes Minister* for me to watch; it was his way of poking a little fun at me and trying to help me get comfortable. Tim was a constant, necessary, and at times harsh barometer of what was real and what was not. Thinking back, I was, and am, so grateful for him and the way he played this role.

There are perks to being a minister. Offices, drivers, money, staff, security. You get more of everything—but mostly work. And indeed, if you want, ministers can have someone to do everything for them. Even think for them, if they let them. And some did. Sometimes ministers are criticized—particularly when it appears the "perks" are being abused. But in truth I think these additional resources are not unreasonable; in most cases, they enable you to do your job efficiently and safely. I hope they are provided with the expectation that a minister is focused as much as humanly possible on their work.

On cars and drivers: this was new to me. Before becoming a minister, I had never had a company car, let alone a driver. I appreciated this "perk." What I can say is that the work done in the vehicle on the way to this meeting or that one, the prep, the urgent signing of documents, the cursing and the telephone calls—in my safe place—was important to me. It was helpful to the work. Kathy was my driver for the majority of my time as MOJAG, and we had a saying: *What is said in the car stays in the car.* I remember so many times racing out of a meeting on the Hill or out of the House at night to get into my car. Kathy always waiting in what we called the "pole position" for our quick escape. She had never been a driver before I hired her, but she was amazing—funny, tough (a bit of a badass, really), and loyal. She undertook a really hard job—drivers have to be on call at all hours—with amazing skill and professionalism. And I might add that she was the only female driver in the ministerial fleet at that time. She remains a dear friend to this day.

At one of our early working dinners as a government, the prime minister spent a bit of time focused on "work/life" balance. He gave us all something like a pop quiz about work/life balance:

Raise your hand if you get eight hours of sleep a night.
Raise your hand if you eat well and are healthy.
Raise your hand if you get exercise regularly.
Raise your hand if you regularly spend time with family and loved ones.
Raise your hand if you have time to play and spend with friends.

The PM, to my surprise (and a little to my dismay), raised his hand after all of the statements. A number of Cabinet ministers raised their hands to a few. Many of us never raised our hands at all. I have to say, there is little work/life balance for ministers in major portfolios, and it should not be expected that there could be.

The reality for me is that in all the years I was minister I never had a spare moment. My life was scheduled to the minute. Being MOJAG is a huge job. The department has almost five thousand public servants, about half of whom are lawyers. It is the biggest law firm in Canada, with offices in every part of the country. I will never forget the first in-person department-wide meeting I had with public servants in Ottawa, with other offices across the country joining virtually. It was being held in the atrium in the centre of the building, and on my way down with my deputy minister, Lea, and other senior officials, the elevator got stuck. I am a little claustrophobic, as was another person in the elevator, so some panic set in. After a few minutes we did start moving again. The "town hall" itself was exciting and full of energy. People were packed in everywhere. It was hot. After some speeches everyone lined up to shake hands and take pictures. They seemed happy and nervous, and so was I. There was an incident—I think someone fainted—so the event was a little shorter than it might have been. But I was so happy to be meeting these people. I knew how much I would rely upon them in the work that needed to be done. I wanted to have them work with me on achieving so many things, so I tried to impress upon them very early how much I valued their work, and that I would come to depend on them for their fearless advice and loyal implementation. No one was too junior to bring forward a good idea, and so I encouraged that and worked with my deputy to help that happen.

There was never-ending reading. Each night I was given a suitcase, or suitcases, of "night reading." Some were so large a human could fit in them. I know because we tried—one staff member climbed in while another took a photo. Truly, no normal human could read everything that was sent a minister's way—at least this minister— but I tried. I would also look down the list of who had handled a file. Each person who touches it signs it. Once, early on, I called the first person—the initial drafter—whose name appeared on the briefing note to ask them a question. I learned that this was not necessarily the best thing to do—they were so nervous to talk to me and apparently it was not how things worked.

The other never-ending reality was that as a minister everyone comes to you. You are the decision-maker. I understood this. There is a need to have someone as the final line decision-maker. That was me. Ministers are always surrounded by their staff. This reality is most visible outside Cabinet meetings. Everyone waits in Centre Block— political staffers and public servants alike—in the "horseshoe" on the third floor outside the PM's office and the Cabinet room. It was always busy there, cordoned off, as reams of people would wait for their turn to be called in.

But the waves of people went far beyond Cabinet, the Minister's Office (MO), and the DOJ. It was endless.

Also endless was the overwhelming volume of correspondence I received. There was a huge branch within the Department of Justice public service—the Ministerial Correspondence Unit—that did nothing but work on answers to this correspondence. For some of the letters and emails there were templates that I had to approve, and that we would continue to adapt and develop as issues changed and actions evolved. There was also the "arm"—a machine that looked like an arm and was kept in a locked room—that would sign my signature on correspondence when I was not able to do it in person. Of course, they always had to have my express approval to use the "arm," and the person responsible guarded the "arm" diligently.

There was, not surprisingly, considerable correspondence from Indigenous peoples. We were told this was coming in at a far higher volume than for any previous minister of justice. This proved to be a challenge for my political staff and the Ministerial Correspondence Unit because I insisted on directly seeing it, and often directly editing or replying to it. I did this for lots of other correspondence also, but Indigenous issues was an area I gave particular personal attention to. My reason for doing this was straightforward. For much of Canada's history Indigenous peoples had not been treated by our governments as if they mattered. That reality is reflected in how many governments over many generations have either ignored or talked about our people but rarely truly talked *with* them. I certainly was going to do whatever I could to break that pattern and to demonstrate to the civil service that this was important. Also, I knew so many of the people who wrote to me, and it would have been obvious to them if I had not had some part in replying. Ultimately, there was so much correspondence from Indigenous peoples that this approach was not sustainable. We had to create lenses to determine which pieces of Indigenous correspondence I would weigh in on directly.

Then there was the challenge of the "Berlin Wall" that exists between the department and the minister and political staff. The Minister's Office at department headquarters is located in the East Memorial Building on Wellington Street, across from the Supreme Court of Canada. It is on a secure portion of a floor behind heavy glass doors—locked, of course—and very few people are allowed or able to access it. This is for safety but it is also a cultural and operational issue. I was a new minister, in a new government, and my leadership style had always been very hands-on. From day one, it was clear that I was asking to see and weigh in on far more, I suspect, than some previous ministers. I sought to ensure that what I wanted and needed to see I saw directly, and to be confident that what I delegated to others would be handled appropriately. Over time I knew that what I would be delegating would increase; however, from the outset I reviewed all the delegated authorities that were in place, revoked some, and continued to review them on a regular basis. I also instituted practices to ensure the most complete analysis and information for briefings, both within the department and the MO.

For some, these cracks in the Berlin Wall were hard to handle. Some were not used to getting such direct input from the minister. I expected both my deputy minister and chief of staff to work more openly and co-operatively than may have been the previous practice. And they did. But it was not without the challenges one would expect.

As for a typical day, they all blur. For me, early morning, when I was fresh, was decision-making time. I love the mornings. My night reading would inevitably require a list of approvals the next day, even if it was not humanly possible to weigh all the options in that time frame, or even if more information was required. Everything was always presented as urgent, and much of it truly was. But over time the department learned that the level of involvement I expected to have, and the level of information that was required for my due diligence, meant that decisions sometimes had to be presented earlier, or in stages, so that they could be properly made.

This morning decision time usually lasted around three hours before I would head to the office at about 8 or 8:30 a.m. I would get into my waiting car and there would be my driver, my assistant, my coffee, often more files, and my daily schedule, which we would run through usually as we headed straight to meetings—either of Cabinet or a Cabinet committee on the Hill, or with officials or stakeholders at my Parliament Hill office. From the moment I left home, every minute of the day was scheduled, typically until seven or eight at night, though work would continue until late in the evening. In addition to meetings, which took up the majority of the time, my day might include giving speeches, dealing with urgent or sudden matters that came up, scheduling time with my constituency office, and, of course, being in the House of Commons during question period, when introducing a bill, when giving a speech, or when I was on "house duty" as a minister. Thank goodness that every night there would be a binder full of briefings for each of the following day's activities. Reviewing it in the morning was like reading an essential roadmap; I could not have lived without it. Public servants and political staff worked so hard to ensure I had all of these documents.

Of course, I was rarely alone during these grinding days. Lots of great people, both political staff and public servants, helped non-stop. Because of their support I was, for the most part, always prepared. If I needed assistance during a meeting, I had no trouble deferring to my deputy or other senior officials who might be there. I did, however, sometimes take meetings by myself. This too was a bit of a culture change that initially caused some alarm in the department and among some political staffers, but they got used to it over time.

I know many ministers past, present, and future can identify with much about these typical days, and with many of the experiences of being a minister. One minister whose days I knew enough about to fully compare to mine was Jane; she was every bit as busy as I was. I know many others—most—were really busy also. But some ministers in smaller portfolios had shared with me that they were not so busy and sometimes had little to do.

I guess there were also differences because I was a minister who is Indigenous. Some of these differences were quite funny. Like all ministers, I had to have a four-hundred-pound safe installed in my residences to store secret documents, and also needed to install the hardware required to encrypt communications. The DOJ would send security officials out to set up the safe and the "secure fax" (that's a little antiquated, isn't it?). Well, I do not think they had set up many of these on a house on-reserve. The government did not send enough people to lift the safe down into the basement of our tiny house on Cape Mudge. We were not home at the time, but our neighbour Howard and his brothers, all of them commercial fishermen, were having their regular morning coffee when they saw the commotion and came over to help. And they did. Now everyone in the village knew I had a safe, and they knew where it was too. I could not have been "safer." When the DOJ and the movers came back to pick up the safe, they brought enough people—though I am sure Howard and the guys would have been ready to do their part.

◆

What was never mundane about the job in any context was the human part of being a minister: building a staff, working as a team, working with the public service, working with other ministers and stakeholders, and navigating the endless complexity of human relationships. Indeed, it was around the dynamics of relationships that

I had some of my greatest joys and fondest memories. It was also where I received some of the clearest warning signs that the government was not committed to some of the high ideals it had preached and that had been demanded of each of us.

I lovingly took to calling my deputy, Bill Pentney, "Feather" when talking to Lea because of his flowy, wispy hair. I am not sure if he ever knew this, and I hope he does not take offence now. I very much appreciated Feather from day one. I know I would never have been able to get the running start I did without him. He was calm. He was obviously incredibly smart. He was kind and he was patient. He was also seasoned in the ways of Ottawa. He, like so many public servants I have met, cared passionately and deeply about Canada.

When we met the first day, he gave me a gold DOJ pin with the scales of justice on it and a handwritten note saying, among other things, that I would do well. He gave me another letter a few days later—one written by a deputy past with advice to his minister. That letter was long, and a little cheeky, and full of pointers; for example, a minister should not buy a ministerial car too quickly or in the first number of months (oops).

I came to really rely on Feather. To trust his opinion and his advice, including when we disagreed. He also learned how to read when I had made my decision, and he knew instantly how to support me in the right ways. On one occasion, we were at Justice Committee, where I was presenting, when a Conservative MP started railing at me for destroying the country's "social and moral fabric" through our massive legislative agenda. I was incensed. While he was continuing on and on, my deputy could tell I was about to light him up. Wisely, and somewhat courageously, Bill tapped his knee against mine and whispered out of the side of his mouth something like *be calm but take him down.* So that is exactly what I did. Afterwards, I went back and watched our appearance on CPAC. I remarked to Bill how his face never changed or showed any emotion. I loved and respected him even more when again we went to committee, this time in the Senate on Bill C-16: Gender Identity and Expression, and he spoke about how the history of human rights protection in Canada had been a history of evolution. He was passionate and emotional, demonstrating great empathy for people and their well-being—for human rights.

One of the hardest days for me as minister was the day he and I were alone in my office so I could tell him he was being moved. We had such a good working relationship, and I was devastated that he was being moved from my ministry. Without going into too much detail, we both knew it was coming and were as prepared as we could be. I had no choice in the matter. Senior PMO staff had disliked him and not trusted him from day one, and I can only presume this was a matter of pure partisanship. Bill had been at Justice through the Harper years. I do not know what his personal politics were. Why would I care? He was talented, dedicated, and did his job the way a public servant should. I fought the decision to move him for months and months. This was one of a number of battles with the PMO on human resource issues. I knew, though, that in our system the decision as to who the deputy minister would be was ultimately not my call. As I told Bill that day about what the PMO was forcing to happen, we both started to tear up—me from utter sadness, him from what I can only imagine was pure frustration. It seemed the filter of partisanship was guiding everything, right down to determining who was competent at their jobs.

Geoff Bickert was another tremendous public servant who I came to love and admire. He was the assistant deputy attorney general and the head of litigation. A tremendous lawyer and great human being. Our relationship of trust grew steadily from day one. He could tell I was serious about making changes in litigation, including with respect to litigation concerning Indigenous peoples.

Historically, the response of governments to section 35 in the Constitution, which recognizes and affirms Indigenous rights, was to treat it as an "empty box." Basically, the legal strategy of successive Liberal and Conservative governments was to say to Indigenous peoples that if they thought any existing rights could be found in section 35, they needed to first prove them in court. Only then would the government talk to them. Maybe. Of course, this is not what protecting rights should be all about. A government would never tell Canadians that the rights to free speech, or assembly, or religion, or legal counsel are empty boxes, that those rights need to be proven to exist before the government will respect or implement them. On the contrary, after 1982, when the Charter of Rights and Freedoms was adopted to uphold rights, government took steps to implement them, including through legislation, policies, and practices. And yet, the specific rights protection under section 35 of the Constitution was denied, and Indigenous peoples were forced into the courts for endless, long, expensive trials (the majority of which Indigenous peoples subsequently won).

As my team and I pushed hard on rights recognition and related issues throughout government, Geoff became a wise and trusted partner. He would steer those who worked in litigation in ways that started to support the directions I was fighting to advance. Towards the end of 2018, when so many difficult issues were raging, Geoff and I had one of our talks about the barriers being faced, this time with Deputy Nathalie Drouin (who would end up testifying publicly to the Justice Committee during the SNC-Lavalin hearing) and with some other officials and staff present. A lot of the issues at the time were around the government not following through on the promised recognition and implementation of Indigenous rights, as well as what I perceived as the endless blocking of the directive I intended to put out on litigation involving section 35. I was fed up with the intransigence I felt from across government, including by the PMO—an office that to me was laced with privileged paternalism. It would be fair to call much of what was transpiring systemic racism.

During that talk Geoff presented me with a handmade sign coloured by his daughter: *Illegitimi non carborundum*—"Don't let the bastards grind you down." I loved it. So loved it. And that he had given it to me in front of the deputy and others made me smile even more. He told me simply to remember the message in tough times. And that if I ever felt like giving up or giving in, or questioning whether it was all worth it, to remember how far we had come. I knew many believed in what we were trying to accomplish, and people like Geoff helped make change happen. To this day, that sign sits on my desk.

I could tell so many other stories of great people, great relationships, and great interactions. I worked on a daily basis with some senior women in the DOJ who were true quiet dynamos and real experts in their field. Carole Morency, Laurie Wright, and Michelle Douglas were three of them. Carole and Laurie are unflappable lawyers, so incredibly competent and always ready with an answer and some solid advice. Truly lovely women. And Michelle, in addition to being a great soldier, public servant, and Canadian hero, was also responsible for planning the minister's travels, which meant I ended up travelling the world with her. All of these women offered true demonstrations of dedication, love, and kindness. If Canadians got a chance to know them like I did, there is no doubt that they would be proud and would know beyond a doubt that these women are working on their behalf.

But there were maddening and saddening realities as well. A lot of this was around the hiring of my political staff, who were not part of the public service but rather hired to provide political support to the minister. Given the size of the department and the complex role of MOJAG, my political staff would be one of the largest in government, with about twenty to twenty-five members.

As soon as I was appointed, I set out to build a strong political staff. As I had when holding my previous elected roles, I knew what I needed—competent, dedicated, hard-working people I could trust, who treated people with respect even when disagreeing, and who shared a set of values about good governance. To my surprise, from the outset this created tensions with the PMO that continued throughout my time as MOJAG.

Without even talking to me, Gerry and Katie had determined who my first chief of staff would be before I was even sworn in. My first chief was a long-time, well-connected Liberal who had held senior roles in the Kathleen Wynne government in Ontario. I did not know this person, so did not have any reason to doubt them. But I had expected to be part of the decision around who my chief of staff would be, and I knew from my years in leadership the importance of having someone I could work seamlessly with in the role, especially given the scale and scope of work that was to be taken on. My plan was to appoint Lea.

Gerry worked hard to convince me that their choice was the right person for the job. He made it clear he did not like the idea of Lea in the position, and gave the reason that she was not a lawyer. Ultimately, on a phone call after some back and forth, Gerry said "trust me"; he added that I needed to "take a leap of faith." Even though it went against my instincts and better judgment, I agreed and decided to try to make it work. Indeed, that was one of two times early on that the PMO pushed me into a decision that I was uncomfortable with but that was based on what the party wanted or needed. The second was to attend a fundraiser at Torys (a Bay Street law firm in Toronto). I had pulled out of the fundraiser because I had learned that some people who were expected to attend might have submitted applications to be appointed judges and also because of certain expectations that the party had about supporting important donors and allies. The PMO basically ordered me to attend.

Neither of these decisions turned out well. My first chief and I were not a good fit. After two short months she was moved to another position. And the fundraiser became a minor negative media story. Both experiences reinforced the importance of trusting my own instincts while in Ottawa.

After my first chief left, Lea did end up as my chief of staff (she had been working in my Minister's Office in various capacities since day one). The PMO was still not happy, and even though Lea was de facto doing the job they delayed her official appointment for nine months while trying to get someone else in the role. And even after she formally became my chief of staff, they continued to make her life difficult. She was, after all, an outsider like me. She did not come up through the party and was not blindly loyal or beholden to individuals in the PMO. She was every inch the professional, and so incredibly competent, but she did not fit the political dynamic of having chiefs of staff who would focus on trying to control their ministers and serving the exercise of power by the unelected in the PMO. She was also the only Indigenous chief of staff at the time.

Lea was undermined continually, blamed for things she did not do. There was a whisper campaign among staffers outside of our MO that she was "difficult" (sound familiar?). The line also continued to be shared, mostly by Katie Telford, that Lea wasn't up to the job because she wasn't a lawyer. Lea also had to bear the brunt of the reality that some ministers were annoyed that I got the chief of staff I wanted and that I was able to keep her for as long as I did.

Lea was a fantastic chief of staff (COSMO-JAG, as I nicknamed her). Everyone in the MO worked hard for her, respected her, and followed her leadership. The team we built during that time was effective, hard-working, and got stuff done. Sure, there were individuals who were a little more focused on party-climbing, but there were many more who were real experts and go-getters. We were an impactful office, a well-oiled machine, and Lea was leading the charge. She did what I needed and more.

But the reality was that for the entire period of time she was my chief of staff, I felt Gerry and Katie would never be happy with her in that role and would find a reason to undermine and remove her. Ultimately, it became untenable. This broke my heart, as Lea was a trailblazer—an Indigenous woman with strength and capacity—and doing a great job. Ottawa did not seem to want people like that in their world. After some time, she ended up as special advisor for Indigenous issues, based at the Permanent Mission of Canada to the

United Nations in New York. Lea officially left my Minister's Office in November 2017.

I believed that by forcing Lea out, Gerry and Katie were hoping, once again, to increase their control over my office. Jessica Prince had been my senior policy advisor from January 2016 to September 2017 before moving back to Toronto. Jessica had roots in the Liberal Party and I knew her to be a person of profound talent and integrity. I knew she was, above all else, her own person. I was relieved when she became my next chief of staff in April 2018. As it turned out, she was also the person who was needed in the role. She stood up to internal pressure and toxicity for many months, and though she endured much suffering during the SNC-Lavalin affair, she stood by and stated the truth.

Simply put, I was focused on finding the best people I could, not the best Liberals. I was focused on being the best minister, not the best Liberal minister. But this seemed to be a sore point for the PMO. These struggles were not just about chiefs of staff. Ministers were expected and told to travel around the country to continue to rally support and raise money. I know I did not do that. Loyalty to party was not first and foremost in my mind. I chose to focus on my responsibilities as MOJAG. This was my priority. I also hated that my political staff—all of them—were told they had to donate to the party and do phone-banking during by-elections, and that every chief of staff was expected to become a member of the Laurier Club, which is what the party call their top financial donors. Some staff expressed concern to me about having to make donations, and I told them they did not have to do it. My team was there for their brains and their empathy, not because of their Liberal Party connections or donations.

Not unrelated, but still shocking to me, were the barriers to meeting with my ministerial colleagues. I liked meeting with ministers one on one or in small groups, especially on shared matters where we all had a responsibility. This seemed like common sense. However, it was frowned upon by the PMO. In fact, the PMO insisted that no ministers meet with each other unless their chiefs of staff were present, which was an effort at control. Some chiefs of staff even actively worked to prevent ministers from meeting if they were not present. In one instance, the PMO was outraged when Jane, Ralph Goodale, and I insisted on meeting alone to hammer out some details regarding the legalization and regulation of cannabis.

This was ridiculous, and such a blatant effort to try to control and manage ministers. It is frankly one of the most undemocratic aspects of how our government functions, and the antithesis of many of the values preached in those early orientation meetings. Transparency, teamwork, restoring confidence in democracy and government. Nope. This was just about making sure power was centralized in a Prime Minister's Office staffed by partisans and not those elected by Canadians. Foolishness.

Over time these patterns of marginalizing and trying to control ministers became worse. In real ways, a minister can be hindered from doing important things because others—unelected others—are pulling the levers. Of course, the prime minister is the boss, and that has to be respected. But direction from this prime minister rarely came directly from him, if it came at all, and it rarely came to me. His office would try to use my office or department to ensure a certain decision was made, or, to the same effect, exclude my office or department from a decision.

It was also obvious when the prime minister was just delivering lines given to him by staffers about my direction or what a decision would be. The prime minister behaved differently in these situations: he was less articulate, more repetitive, and less responsive to questions. He would repeat, whether in public or within government meetings, the points from the lines and get frustrated if there was questioning, debate, or—God forbid—pushback. I experienced this all too often and on numerous issues, particularly around the recognition and implementation of Indigenous rights and criminal justice reform, and specifically on getting rid of mandatory minimum penalties (MMPs). And, of course, on aspects of the SNC-Lavalin matter.

Early on in the mandate, other ministers and I were in fact left somewhat alone and could actually get things done. But as time went on, power became more centralized while ministers were marginalized. Eventually, ministers were treated more and more as afterthoughts. Government decision-making became increasingly sporadic, with reliance on unelected officials or some expert of the day brought in by the PMO, replacing the work of the ministers or the public service. It started to feel arbitrary—as if decisions were being made without sufficient forethought or planning ahead, and more in reaction to polling or what the media was saying than anything else. While the prime minister loved to say this was a "government by Cabinet," this was simply less and less true as days went by.

Of course, any prime minister needs a well-functioning PMO with faithful and talented people, and with a culture that reinforces good governance. However, I so wished the prime minister and the PMO would have let ministers do their work and allowed ministers to work together. I have said previously that this prime minister's mode of functioning is in some ways worse than what I knew of and heard about former prime minister Harper's. Harper was at least transparent about the fact that he and the PMO controlled everything; he let everyone know it. Prime Minister Justin Trudeau's office controlled the workings of government while creating a different public perception. For me, this is not good leadership or good government. Our country deserves a better way of making decisions.

These dynamics around decision-making, ministers, staff, and control would, of course, be at the heart of the SNC-Lavalin drama that would ultimately drive me out of government. I did not let them make that decision about a deferred prosecution—of course, as attorney general I could not and would not. But for them, the act of doing my job—which in relation to criminal prosecutions is different than any other ministerial role—was viewed as insubordinate, difficult, and not adhering to norms of government by the PMO. They were dead wrong on that count, and I am not surprised it caught up to them. I just wish it had also led to real change in how they functioned as a government. I did not (and do not) see any evidence of that.

Despite all of this I hope it is clear that there was much I loved about being a minister, especially early on. Prime Minister Paul Martin once told me that you can accomplish more in five minutes being a minister than most people accomplish in five years or even a lifetime outside of government. For the first while we got a ton done, including medical assistance in dying (MAID), cleaning up the Criminal Code for compliance with the Charter of Rights and Freedoms, and establishing a new process for judicial appointments. There were people who had worked hard at the department for decades to make progress on certain things, such as long overdue changes to the Divorce Act (which was not in my mandate letter, but we did it anyway). We set our minds to it and got it done. I know of officials who delayed their retirement to stay on to see their years of work completed. This made me very happy and even more determined.

I took the specific dual role of the minister of justice and attorney general very seriously, and I loved these roles. I had two hats, both of which are vitally important in our system of laws. This was something that many Canadians would come to learn more about during the SNC-Lavalin affair.

I was always very transparent with my Cabinet colleagues about which role I was playing and when. In Cabinet I would specifically say "speaking as attorney general" or "speaking as the minister of justice" depending on the nature of the issue and discussion taking place.

When your role includes upholding the rule of law you are a watcher over government, including the prime minister. Part of this involves protecting the government from itself—and the prime minister from himself and his staff—as the law is paramount. As such, and appropriately, on some issues discussed around the Cabinet table a question would be raised near the end: "What does Jody think . . . ?"

This made complete sense, of course, when the issue involved the role of attorney general. It was often the case that, in my role as minister of justice, this question would arise on Indigenous issues as well as those related to human rights and social justice. This changed over time as power shifted away from ministers and the tenor and direction of discussions began to change, but I think it is good practice in any government for the minister of justice and attorney general to be one barometer for the appropriateness of a government's direction.

◆

What I have described above captures, in a nutshell, my experience of being a minister in this government. Being a member of Parliament is another story altogether.

My only real contact with members of Parliament before being elected was through advocacy efforts to get rid of the Indian Act. As Regional Chief, I would appear at parliamentary committee meetings and would also have meetings with individual MPs while pushing for change.

After making the decision to run, there were a number of Liberal "campaign colleges" that other candidates and I could attend to learn how to run a campaign, but there were no real opportunities to learn about what it means to be an MP. I thought this was odd, and I was not the only one. I remember a few other BC candidates who are now MPs also having a healthy skepticism and caution about the process, and about what we should and should not be learning.

As the opening of the forty-second Parliament drew closer, there were orientation sessions for new MPs. We had our separate Liberal Party sessions, and I was already weighed down by the new responsibilities of being a minister. I believe the well-known phrase to describe this overwhelming situation was "drinking from a fire hose." I could not attend much of what was on offer. There seemed to be a lot of receptions and socializing opportunities, which are things I never have really been into. So maybe I was just avoiding them. One thing I remember Tim and Lea telling me (they attended some of the sessions) was that a strong warning was given about the high level of alcohol consumption and high divorce rates among MPs.

For most MPs—all government MPs except ministers—national caucus meetings are a central venue for your work and expressing your perspective on issues. Caucus was a weekly occasion in which the prime minister would give big rousing speeches about teamwork and provide updates on what the government was considering and how Canada was back. Early on, MPs ate it up; I did as well, to a certain degree. Things change, sometimes dramatically. In 2019, the Liberal Party would hold a caucus meeting in public—a rare occurrence—to make a show of kicking Jane and me out. A little show trial run by those progressives to illustrate how Canada was back. I watched as so many colleagues—including ones I had considered close friends—stood and applauded.

Caucus in my time was always attended by Gerry and Katie, along with many other PMO staffers. I always thought it was a bit strange that staffers were allowed into caucus (I know many of my MP colleagues did too), which ideally should be where those who are elected debate issues. As well, there were always leaks about what happened in or was discussed at caucus. I suspect this sometimes may have come from the PMO, to fit their needs, or from disgruntled caucus members (of which there were many) who wanted to secretly push against some of what the government was or was not doing. Yet at the very least, caucus was a place where backbench MPs could get up to the mic and have their say. I found this instructive. It showed me that most MPs run for the right reasons. They have a desire to serve, to advance an issue and to contribute to our democracy, and they have a genuine belief in the responsibility to represent their ridings. I think—I hope—that all new MPs, in all parties, come to Ottawa thinking that their individual voices matter and that the voices of their constituents matter.

It is also a reality that MP disillusionment sets in for many, and often pretty quickly. The reality is not what you imagined it would be and that is a hard pill to swallow, especially when one sacrifices much and works so hard to get into politics and to actually get elected. This disillusionment can be clearly seen in the difference between the old guard—those who have been MPs and even ministers for a long time—and the newbies.

I remember one long-time MP who was really helpful early on; we became quite close and would talk about lots of different things. I will always appreciate the help they offered. One evening we were having a conversation, along with some others, about why they had once run for party leader. I expected an answer that would convey a specific vision or passion—a set of ideas or ideals to be advanced. Instead, the explanation was along the lines of "it was time," "it was expected," "we needed others in the race," and "why not?" I was baffled, so I pushed for a clearer reason. The explanation I got was "I didn't really have a reason." *We are not all like you* was the underlying implication of their comment. I suddenly realized that whatever passion and drive had brought this person to Ottawa in the first place was gone. It made me sad and confused. It made me wonder if this is what happens to everyone in this town. Does that commitment to service and ideas get replaced by hollowness, lack of motivation, and self-interest—by the idea that the "best public policy is the government getting re-elected"?

As the months and years passed, I saw more and more people like this. For them, political life was just about being in a position or a career, or simply something to be pursued for its own sake and no other purpose. I also saw other unappealing dynamics: MPs who are blindly loyal to the party and spend a lot of time focused on how some other MPs are not raising enough money or doing enough. And, of course, there are those who are looking to advance, trying to impress the PM or PMO in order to move up the ranks.

In some ways, I do not blame those who are trying to advance. The current reality in Ottawa is that Cabinet is treated like an exclusive club in a pyramid of power. At the top, with all of the power, are the PM and his staffers. Far below that—so far they can barely glimpse the top—is where caucus and everyday MPs sit. People likely will deny this; that is their choice but it is not reality. This system does not get the most and best out of its parliamentarians.

In spite of this reality, there are great MPs—many of them. Solid, hard workers who are dedicated to their constituents. You can spot them a mile away. In caucus they talk about real issues and don't spend their time grandstanding or sucking up. When they meet with a minister they raise issues that actual people are facing in their riding and ask for help to solve them. I loved meeting with these MPs, from any party.

•

On the wall of the Cabinet room in Centre Block a carved inscription reads:

> Aimez la Justice, vous qui jugez la terre.
> *Love Justice, you that are the rulers of the earth.*

These words are adapted from Solomon in the Book of Wisdom. The first time I walked into that room, on November 4, 2015, I did not notice it. But I recall seeing it the second time, and I started a practice of writing it down on the inside covers of my black notebooks.

Over time I realized that when I was bored or frustrated or even angry I would fixate on the sign, on the words, even more than usual. I would never claim to be well-versed in the Bible or Christianity— my spirituality is different—and would not try to speak to its biblical meaning. But sitting there in meeting after meeting, with my mind wandering to these words, a message was conveyed to me over and over again. This is a message about the Creator, and about taking care of the gifts from the Creator. I understand that to care for those gifts, to nurture them, we must draw on the highest aspects of ourselves. Understanding. Communicating. Knowing. Loving. We need to make decisions, wield power, in ways that are wise, meaningful, true, and caring.

It is a statement about the inextricable relationship between love, power, and justice. They cannot ever be separated. *Love* and *Justice* are inscribed on the wall of the Cabinet room as a reminder of how to act when power is being wielded. I still wonder how many of my colleagues noticed those words. None of them ever mentioned them to me. Did they contemplate them like I did as the meetings wandered? Did they feel the awesome responsibility those words conveyed?

I like to think that most Canadians, as I did before coming into government, want to imagine their government is grappling with the meaning of those words from Solomon as they make decisions that impact the lives of us all. Not naively, as if Cabinet is some book club of biblical scholars. But that at its core, practically, in real terms, Cabinet is always asking questions like: "Is this the best decision?"; "Is it based on the best evidence?"; "Is it being made in the best way?"; "Who does it help?"; "Who might it hurt?"; "Is it just?"; "Is it compassionate?"; "Does it look ahead to building a better future while learning the lessons of the past?"

As my days as minister passed, the reality that set in was increasingly far from ideal. While working hard each day—long days and sleepless nights—and as we moved to address the big issues that we had been elected to address, the reality of partisanship and power took prominence over truth, love, and justice.

FIVE

Making Decisions

One of the lessons I learned growing up was that relentless-ness is needed to get things done. I learned this by observing my parents. My dad was always pushing for justice for Indigenous peoples, never letting up. My childhood years were spent watching him give speeches, attend meetings, and lead rallies—all committed to making change. I remember us travelling around the province with my father, particularly during the summers, always being in and around Indigenous political gatherings, which at the time were very large. I remember wanting to play outside with my friends but being told to sit in the meetings, to be quiet and listen.

Relentlessness has always been part of the Indigenous reality in this country. The struggles, the trauma, the social realities that include suicide, addiction, and poverty. They are everywhere. But this relentlessness is also channelled into the work of making change. You do not meet many Indigenous leaders who are in it halfway. For sure, some leaders are good and some less so. Some should not be leaders at all. But the vast majority are relentless when it comes to trying to make things better. There really is no other way. That is the ethic.

My mum is an example of relentlessness as well, in her own way. She protected Kory and me as children from a lot of hard realities raging around us. While there are ideals we strive for in rebuilding our communities, the fact is that as a result of colonialism and dispossession, life for Indigenous peoples and on many Indian reserves includes cycles of dysfunction and dependency, drug and alcohol abuse, and sexual assault and domestic violence. In the face of her own experiences with some of the darker aspects of life, including violence and poverty, my mum, as a single and hard-working woman, built a cocoon of love around us that allowed Kory and me to see how one endures and withstands whatever struggles life may bring. Whether on-reserve or off.

It is not surprising, then, that as I started to tackle the big issues before me as MOJAG I did so relentlessly. This is how I was raised, and it is the only way I know. It was also a good match for how government works in this country. With a majority government, there is a short window of eighteen to twenty-four months in which to get big things done. As time goes by, the focus turns more and more to re-election, partisan games increase, people get tired, and visions of and ambition to do good things wane in the face of the obstacles and hard work that is required. So you'd better come out of the gate in a sprint.

I knew this in the back of my mind, but I did not really know how true this pattern was until I began to experience it first-hand. Thankfully, I started strong. I was going to get things done come hell or high water. I liked to jest that my mandate letter was as long as I am tall, and I was ready to tackle it all. But priorities had to be set, and two of them were already well established publicly—legislating medical assistance in dying and the legalization and regulation of cannabis. There were many priority justice issues: the need for human rights legislation that added gender identity and expression as a prohibited ground for discrimination under the Canadian Humans Rights Act and to the definition of "identifiable group" in the Criminal Code; updating laws about sexual assault for the first time in more than twenty-five years; undertaking the first substantial update to Canada's federal family laws in more than twenty years; working with Indigenous peoples and other ministers to design and launch the National Inquiry into Missing and Murdered Indigenous Women and Girls in Canada; changing course from the previous government on certain litigation matters, such as abandoning the Zunera Ishaq appeal, in which Canada had relentlessly tried to stop a young teacher from taking her citizenship oath while wearing a niqab, a partial face-covering; and undertaking a broad review of how the Charter of Rights and Freedoms is upheld by government, including in litigation and in new legislation.

Death and drugs. In some lighter moments I would joke that it might have helped people if we had legalized drugs first and death second. I also admit I have wondered over the years about whether it dawned on anyone that the first major public policy issues Canada's first-ever Indigenous justice minister would tackle were related to death and drugs—issues that in certain ways have a particular significance to Indigenous peoples.

These were important issues, for sure—especially MAID for me. I was honoured to be tasked to deal with them. I could not wait. While they were not necessarily the priorities I would have chosen to start with, they were the ones that had to be tackled. And so, as was my style, I dove in headfirst.

•

As MAID and cannabis both involved amendments to the Criminal Code, I was the lead minister. My name would be on both bills—in all, I was responsible for and saw thirteen bills receive royal assent as MOJAG—and I would in many ways be a public face of the decisions being made.

In its landmark *Carter v. Canada* decision, the Supreme Court had set a time limit for MAID. On February 6, 2015, the Court ruled that sections of the Criminal Code were unconstitutional because they prohibited physicians from assisting in the consensual death of another person. In its unanimous decision, the Court held that the criminal laws prohibiting assistance in dying limited the rights to life, liberty, and security of the person under section 7 of the Canadian Charter of Rights and Freedoms. A permissive regime, with properly designed and administered safeguards that were capable of protecting vulnerable people from abuse and error, had to be established. This was Parliament's "difficult task" of balancing the competing interests of those who would seek access to physician-assisted dying and those who could potentially be put at risk by its legalization. This incredibly important case had been brought by Kay Carter, a woman suffering from degenerative spinal stenosis, and Gloria Taylor, a woman suffering from amyotrophic lateral sclerosis, among others. In 1993, Sue Rodriguez had raised similar issues, and the Court had upheld the Criminal Code provisions. The change in the Court's decision illustrates how our common law system works to adapt and change over time and how our Charter operates to protect the essential rights of Canadians.

The Court suspended the effect of its decision for one year to give governments time to respond. Our work was set. By the time I was sworn in, it was already November 2015—which essentially gave us only three months to complete the work. Upon my request, the Court gave us four more months (we asked for six), so we ended up having until June 6, 2016. That gave us about seven months. This was rocket speed by Ottawa standards, especially for such a major rights issue (though as COVID-19 has shown us, Ottawa can do big things faster, and needs to learn to do better and bigger things differently and faster still).

Cannabis had been a centrepiece of the 2015 general election campaign for the Liberals and was a personal priority for the prime minister. And, frankly, legalization and regulation is good. It is a first step towards the possible decriminalization of other drugs for personal use; a critical step in addressing the rising and tragic opioid public health crisis through harm reduction and treatment services; and one small but important part of the broader criminal justice reform that is needed. This reform included one of my personal priorities: getting rid of mandatory minimum penalties.

My partner on both MAID and cannabis was the minister of health, Dr. Jane Philpott. I had not really known Jane before working on these two files. We had met around the Cabinet table and at a few functions—including a dinner at our first Cabinet retreat in St. Andrews, New Brunswick, in January 2016—but we had never really chatted and certainly never worked together. How quickly this changed. Jane is truly an amazing person in all ways. Such a model of resilience, strength, intelligence, and service. She has experienced all life has to offer, including the hardest of personal tragedies. She channels all that wisdom and experience into finding ways to serve others with a grace and empathy that gets results, and she does so with a quiet, fun, introspective, humble, and thoughtful demeanour. It did not take long before I gave her the nickname "MOC," or "Mother of the Country"; for me she was calm, loving, always providing support and advice, and she did her job that way as well. We became fast friends and remain so to this day.

For all our work, Jane was a godsend. We had so much to do, and we really did fit together to form a high-functioning team. While the work at times seemed insurmountable, it all felt manageable and easier with her alongside. Following our lead, our respective deputies and the teams from Health and Justice worked well together.

The ways in which we approach dying and death as both individuals and a society reveal our commitments to and understandings of life, its purpose, and how far we must still travel to be a loving, compassionate, and just society. On MAID, I set out to immediately read everything I could, all the court cases and countless analyses, but also about the work and regimes developed in other countries. Most importantly, I had to know what Canadians were saying, so I wanted to read as much of the mountain of correspondence my department received on MAID as I could. This became an impossible task, so I came to rely on detailed summaries.

I was told we received around fifteen thousand emails and letters in February 2016 alone. We had established a Special Joint Parliamentary Committee for MAID, made up of MPs and senators, that was hearing from witnesses. At the same time, MPs from all parties were organizing and conducting their own town halls across the country. There was extensive expert and stakeholder engagement, and we also took it upon ourselves to meet as many MPs and senators as we could to have a conversation about our proposals before and after the legislation was introduced. I learned more about Parliament, the system, my colleagues, and how I expected governance to work during these six months than at any other time as a minister. To have this experience through an issue so sensitive and non-partisan—an issue that touches the lives of every single Canadian in some way or another—so early in my parliamentary tenure was incredibly real and impactful, both personally and professionally. And to have Jane with me . . . well, that was a bonus.

It was such an emotional time. Jane and I bonded even more over the tears we shared with each other and with people we talked to. For me, meeting the family of Kay Carter was particularly emotional, as was meeting with members of the disability rights community, whose stories would keep you up at night. Also impactful was meeting with leaders and passionate Canadians such as Dr. Jocelyn Downie, representatives from Dying With Dignity Canada, and the late Joe Arvay, to name but a few.

Everyone had an opinion on MAID. We were going too far or we were not going far enough. Almost no one held the opinion we were getting it exactly right, which is often the case on big issues. When I held my own MP town hall and when our legislation received royal assent, I remarked that everyone was unhappy with us to some degree, which must mean we got the balance right. We knew the legislation would need to be amended over time, as society's views evolve and we gain more experience as a country living with MAID; basically, it can be adjusted as we grow into a collective comfort with a regime. I still believe we got the balance right for the time, though Parliament amended the legislation in March 2021.

I described in the House and in many other places how we designed the legislation and safeguards at the time. Our intent was to: "recognize individual choice of medically assisted death for adults who are suffering intolerably and for whom death is reasonably foreseeable; affirm the inherent and equal value of every person's life; avoid encouraging negative perceptions of the quality of life of persons who are elderly, ill or disabled; protect vulnerable people from being encouraged to die in moments of weakness; re-affirm society's goals with regard to preventing suicide; and, encourage a consistent approach to medical assistance in dying across Canada."

MAID felt like the first real and critically important presentation to Cabinet that I made, and I was so glad Jane was by my side for it. Michael Wernick, then clerk of the Privy Council, sat in all of our Cabinet meetings. I remember him saying to me afterwards that he could tell I was a bit tense and seemed uncharacteristically nervous. Well, that was true. It was a big deal for the country, and we treated it as such. After we presented—and although I am, of course, not allowed to talk about the substantive conversation due to Cabinet confidences—most everyone around the table had something to say or something to reflect on in terms of personal experience or a perspective on the legislative stance we should take. It was not common that everyone in Cabinet felt so personally invested in a decision. And Cabinet was great on MAID: solid, thoughtful, and cautious, with a shared view that was clear after the presentation and dialogue. We pretty much had a consensus around the Cabinet table throughout. This was so important. It was how I thought it was supposed to work, and it became a standard by which I judged subsequent deliberations.

On cannabis, I had no knowledge or experience. At all. Jane and I were partners again, along with Ralph Goodale, who was then minister of public safety and emergency preparedness, and Bill Blair, one of my two parliamentary secretaries. This was another great team and a good experience. Cannabis was not nearly as emotionally intense for me, but I took it just as seriously. It was also an extraordinary amount of work. I did not, however, want to be the public face of this file. It was not a matter I was personally invested in beyond, of course, the public policy objectives. Indeed, all of us in the lead were similar in this regard. Just prior to a press announcement, Jane, Bill, Ralph, and I had a conversation in the Queen's Room (a circular room with a fireplace and a huge portrait of—who else?—the Queen, next door to the Cabinet room in Centre Block) about the fact that none of us had ever used cannabis. So funny that we were the ones in charge of this matter.

But as noted above, this had been a paramount issue for the prime minister. I believe that his initial public commitment to legalize cannabis, made in July 2013 when he was leader of the party but not yet PM, was almost certainly improvised on the spot. Sure, there had been resolutions at Liberal conventions, but Justin and Gerry no doubt saw this as a political winner and a way to engage a broader audience, particularly a younger crowd. Certainly it was effective, and it led to many more people supporting the party in the election and, more importantly, actually coming out to vote. I had a lot of cannabis shops in my corner during the campaign.

As we set about legislating this issue, we formed the Task Force on Cannabis Legalization and Regulation. The task force produced a report along with recommendations that would assist us in developing a framework for the legalization and the policy rationale behind Bill C-45. They did a good job.

The cannabis bill had a companion piece of legislation (Bill C-46) that would strengthen existing alcohol- and drug-impaired driving laws and create an impaired-driving regime that would be among the strongest and strictest in the world. The ultimate goal of this legislation was to reduce the significant number of deaths and injuries caused by impaired driving, a crime that continues to claim innocent lives and wreak havoc and devastation on Canadian families. I know there are many criminal defence lawyers out there who condemn me for the severity of this legislation. Let them. Frankly, I wanted to lower the blood alcohol concentration (BAC) in the Criminal Code even further, from 80 mg of alcohol per 100 ml of blood (commonly referred to as the "over 80" offence) to 50 mg, but this was going too far for some around me, which I accepted. I personally advocated for this legislation, though it was not specifically called for in my mandate letter. But it was necessary; there is no excuse for driving while impaired by alcohol, cannabis, or any other drug. Impaired driving remains the leading criminal cause of death in Canada. This is unacceptable. Driving is a privilege, and if you drive while under the influence you should and will be punished if caught and convicted. A bit of my prosecutor background came out around this issue.

While the work on these early priorities was interesting, exciting, and effective, it was not without its challenges—some of which foreshadowed challenges that would become more acute in the future, and in some ways threaten the government.

For example, late in the day on cannabis legalization, a senior PMO official told Jane, Ralph, and me that, in effect, we would have to make a 180-degree policy shift. Imagine an unelected staffer dictating to three senior ministers what the decision must be. None of us believed that this was coming from the PM—and if it was, why hadn't he talked to us? If he was not happy with what we had been putting in place as our government's evolving policy, then why hadn't he said something? We also found it challenging as we knew the prime minister wanted the cannabis file to move faster and faster; he said this many times. But when PMO staff intervened in this way, which seemed arbitrary, it caused confusion and slowed things down.

We resisted this directive and demanded a meeting alone with the prime minister to discuss the matter. The meeting never happened. Gerry and Katie actually chastised us—well, our chiefs of staff—for even asking for the meeting. Really. After about ten days, a meeting was in fact held, including the PM, the three of us, our chiefs of staff, and all of the PMO's people. The prime minister confirmed we should continue on the path we were already on. Hmm. Apparently, days of backdoor conversations among all of the unelected folks had taken place to help guide the PMO's people back into line. But this sequence of events was, in hindsight, an early expression of a trend in the PMO of insisting, more and more, that ministers not meet with each other alone. As a result, a creeping question started coming to mind. Who was in charge? Who was leading whom? Whose advice to the prime minister really mattered?

A similar dynamic had emerged on MAID. During one meeting, Jane and I were in my office in Centre Block on the phone with the PMO. We were being told—at basically the eleventh hour, after we had been working round the clock—that we had to change our approach and proceed in a way that did not make sense to us for any substantive reason. Jane was crying out of sheer frustration. I started getting angry and, uncharacteristically, raised my voice and stormed out of the room. We wanted none of what they were saying; we thought it was ill-informed, superficial, political, and mostly just a series of ideas disengaged from the very serious and real issues at hand. Honestly, we just wanted these unaccountable folks to go away and let us do our jobs.

In the first year or so of governing, such direction from a PMO staffer was more the exception than the norm. I could do my job—present and have Cabinet consider what I needed it to consider as the minister responsible—without too much interference from the PMO. The office was still exerting its control, just in more subtle ways, such as through the Cabinet agenda.

Cabinet time was like real estate in Vancouver—a hot commodity.

Everyone wanted it and few got it. And the PMO, via the Privy Council Office, controlled the whole thing. You really had to work to get a space on the agenda. There were always too many decisions, policy issues, and legislative pieces that needed urgent attention. There were also the ubiquitous polling numbers—so much attention was paid and weight given by the PMO to these numbers. The Prime Minister's Office made sure that matters on which the government was looking weak in the polls were getting time. The issues that were not viewed as politically important could be managed simply by not being given space on the agenda.

Getting onto the agenda at all became a game. I am not sure I was a very good player of this game. Of course, because I held responsibility for big priorities like MAID and cannabis legalization, it wasn't a challenge for me to get agenda time on these issues. But there were other critical matters on which the PMO did not share my views, such as MMPs and recognition and implementation of Indigenous rights. On these issues, things could move glacially. They might get Cabinet time, just not time that would lead to critical decision points. Things would go around and around.

Another dynamic that became more pronounced as time went on, and that I should have noticed earlier, was the way the PMO could manipulate decision-making. There were times that in spite of the conversation around the Cabinet table, or even a clear consensus forming around a decision, it would be taken another way. Early on, the prime minister would intervene if opinions diverged from his or his office's desired outcome. Later, the set-up was more crass. Sometimes certain ministers were lined up prior to decisions being made to present the same arguments for a particular position and defeat what the minister responsible had proposed. The toast was already in the toaster, and indeed had been toasted before Cabinet even met.

It seemed to me like PMO staff were trying to routinely direct ministers to do this or do that—to indicate that this was the way it was going to be and make sure what was presented to Cabinet reflected that direction. One could feel their control, and their feeling of being entitled to control, building over time. This was wrong, and I resisted the whole way. Right until my last day, if there was a major issue within my purview and authority that the PMO wanted me to go another way on, I expected to hear it from the prime minister directly—not from a proxy. And, of course, there are issues on which even a prime minister cannot tell an attorney general what to do— unless they want to break the law.

In May 2018, I was flying down to Boston for a few hours to give a talk on Indigenous rights at Harvard. It was one of the few times I ever used the Challenger, and I did so because of the limited window to get there and back and the inability to travel on commercial airlines. A few of my staff and advisors accompanied me. In a contemplative moment on our return flight, one of them, Roshan Danesh, asked me whether being in Cabinet was different than what I had expected. Roshan was a dear friend and confidante who had worked with me when I was Regional Chief; I had brought him in the year before to help support trying to get the Indigenous work on track. He was an outsider to Ottawa politics and the bubble, as I had been when I first arrived. I considered his question carefully and then replied that it was different than what I was used to in Indigenous politics, where consensus building is so central. I had thought there would be more of a search for truth and a building of consensus around the best decision at the Cabinet table. I had thought our work around that table would include genuinely caring about what each other thought and the diverse perspectives we shared, and that we would build the best decisions by drawing on all the bits of wisdom we each contributed. I reflected that it was not this way; it was not about forging consensus, and that was different for me and a surprise. A surprise that was at once sad and maddening.

So many times after Cabinet meetings ministers would groan about how everything was staged and how their opinions did not matter. Or they'd grumble about how they did not want to say anything because they knew how the PM or the PMO felt about an issue. Few have said this publicly. Few ever will. So we have a system where people at the top—despite having sworn a Privy Council oath to faithfully, honestly, and truly declare their mind and opinion—are not vocalizing what they think the best decision should be in private, at the Cabinet table, or in public to the people who elected them. That is not good enough.

•

I will always be so grateful that MAID was the first major initiative I had to make decisions on. It imprinted on me so deeply what was important, why I had decided to run as an MP, and why I was excited to be in government. MAID was not an issue I came to government with strong feelings about, but it became a barometer that would guide me throughout my time as minister. How can we alleviate human suffering, be compassionate, ensure the well-being of those that might be on the margins in our society, and do so in a principled way that builds consensus and common understanding? It was the same for Jane, I believe, and I think it was the same for the prime minister and our other Cabinet colleagues. These were the times when people spoke personally about this decision, about their family members, about religious beliefs. Over the years I have continued to hear how MAID impacted people's lives, from close personal friends and their families as well as from strangers. I will always remember one woman who came up to me in a liquor store. She was buying champagne to have with a dear friend who was preparing to die using MAID later that day, and she remarked positively that seeing me was a sign.

While I had experienced many close family members dying, Jennifer was my baseline reality throughout this time. I first met Jennifer in 2014 over the phone when I was just starting to make calls preparing for the nomination contest. She lived in Vancouver Granville and was the very first person I called from the Liberal membership lists the party had provided, and the first person I spoke to. She was lovely, very engaging and supportive. From that moment on we remained in frequent touch, always feeling connected. Eventually we became more personal in what we shared, and she told me her story.

Jennifer had multiple sclerosis (MS), and with that experienced significant ups and downs. She volunteered on our first campaign in 2015. She was there from day one with her kind and generous husband, Daniel, and they were both part of our core team all the way through to election night. I have some amazing photos of both of them from that evening. Over the years I attended MS awareness and fundraising events with her. She was a born advocate, a crusader. I found her passion intoxicating.

In 2016, as MAID was ploughing ahead, I hosted my town hall at the Seniors' Centre at Oakridge Mall in VanGran. There were many, many people there: lawyers, advocates, and citizens. No one seemed very happy, and there was a fair amount of upset in anticipation that the government might not set criteria as broad as some wanted. Some held the exact opposite view. Some people were just scared, upset, and/or angry that we were even having the conversation.

Jennifer was at the town hall. She and I had discussed MAID from time to time before the election and after, but not in much detail. We started to talk a bit more once the Special Joint Committee began meeting. At the town hall she asked me, in her characteristic way, the only real question that mattered: Would she qualify? At the time I did not know the answer, as a decision had not been made on criteria. But I immediately felt overcome with waves of pain. That Jennifer was confronting the reality of potentially ending her life, even though I knew she was in an "up" period at the time, was devastating. There was a potential, even a likelihood, that she would not qualify under many of the options being considered, which meant that this choice might be denied to her.

In those months of legislating MAID, Jennifer was always in the back of my mind. Sometimes she would flood my thoughts when things were being discussed, and I would have to suppress my tears. I have a vivid memory of crying in the bathroom in the minister's private lounge at the Ottawa airport when Jennifer came to my mind and heart as I discussed MAID issues with Jane and as we made some hard decisions over the phone about the proposed regime.

Not long after that VanGran town hall, Jennifer entered a "down" period. MAID was becoming law. She tried, but at first could not find a doctor who would say she met the "reasonable foreseeability of death" criteria—meaning it was not medically evident she was on a trajectory towards death. While she did have medical options, none of them appealed to her. She was tired, and who could blame her. She was devastated; Daniel was devastated. And whenever we spoke, it was devastating for all of us.

After being turned down a number of times, Jennifer eventually did access MAID. I learned the news while sitting in my departmental office in Ottawa. My heart broke. I could not stop the tears. I loved her and felt such loss that she was gone. I also felt some gratitude that her suffering was over, and I was overcome by the choices and realities life presents. I called in Lea, who knew Jennifer as well, and we both broke down.

It was one of those moments when the world starts to feel overwhelming. It was not being MOJAG—the scale of work and the public responsibility—that made me feel this way. It was simply that in learning of the loss of my friend, I was confronted with the question of whether I had caused her more pain. This is a reckoning we all face in life when those close to us pass on, or when we realize we are going to. Have I done good by others? Have I brought more joy than pain? Was I helping or was I a cause of the suffering of others?

Months after Jennifer passed away, I met with Daniel at their house on the east side of VanGran. We talked about her last days, her pain, how it happened. Daniel said that Jennifer loved me, did not blame me, and was not mad. This was so kind, and it reflects the beauty of Daniel and Jennifer. But one has to come to terms with one's own decisions and choices in life. I still struggle with this, and I expect I always will.

An unexpected obstacle that delayed the vote on the MAID legislation was "Elbowgate": the May 18, 2016, incident in the House of Commons where the prime minister suddenly got up from his seat and, in an effort to get the Opposition whip through a bunch of New Democrats, accidentally elbowed an NDP member of Parliament and all hell broke loose. It created a reality that delayed our vote on MAID and meant we were increasingly at risk of missing the Supreme Court of Canada deadline. The incident was also the first time many of us had seen the prime minister's temper, so it was challenging all round. Many female ministers were angry—as were so many other MPs—and a bunch of us descended on the office of the House leader and whip. Issues were raised angrily about the elbowing and how it was impacting vital work, including the passage of the bill. Finally, Bill C-14 went to third reading and a free vote on May 31, 2016. It passed with 186 voting yea and 137 voting nay. Ultimately, Bill C-14 received royal assent on June 17, 2016. We missed the court-imposed deadline by eleven days.

◆

From the perspective of getting to outcomes on big issues and making decisions, MAID and the legalization and regulation of cannabis were a success. Of course, people will have differing views about the policy decisions we made and what we did. That is always the case. But in terms of government functioning and process, of getting to results, it was pretty effective and one of the reasons I was proud of the government then. I was energized by doing this work. As hard and as much as the work could be, I felt we were changing things for the better. As for the internal dynamics, there were problems. But in this first year or so, when the hard work was done on MAID and cannabis, I thought that if this was as bad as it got we could find our way through anything.

I was even willing to put up with the casual racism and misogyny that I'd known would be present in government, and indeed was present. I'd so hoped this would not be the case. All too typically, it would often take a white male minister to repeat or vouch for what I had just said, particularly on Indigenous rights and social justice issues, before I felt folks would listen. Of course, there were also the expressions of surprise at how I was not what certain people imagined an Indigenous person would be like. I remember vividly the first conversation I had with one of my Cabinet colleagues, who exclaimed to me that I was the first Indigenous person she had ever met. It remains a reality that I, like so many women, had to tolerate a certain level of ignorance in order to get to the outcomes I wanted to achieve.

But, of course, in life the real lessons come from unexpected places. While I certainly had some successes, there were an increasing number of red flags around what was not happening. Vitally important issues—my priorities—would be interfered with and delayed more and more. On issues in which I had first-hand and lifelong experience, the PMO seemed to insist they knew better. In addressing racism and the legacy of colonization, and in tackling overrepresentation of Black, Indigenous, and other marginalized people in the justice system, I was told time and again to slow down. The PMO knew what was right. From my perspective, the message I was getting was: approve a pipeline first.

Undoubtedly these delays and lack of will, on the part of the PMO, to take action on these critical issues was the root of some real tensions that were building. I frustrated them and they frustrated me. I do think these tensions could have been managed and good results still been reached. But that can only happen when everyone is pursuing a shared goal of advancing decisions. It took me some time to realize this was not really the case. While I have no doubt that Cabinet understood that Indigenous reconciliation and criminal justice reform are serious and challenging issues, over time I learned that they were not taken seriously from a political perspective. They do not drive people to the polls, are not often sources of partisan advantage, and frankly are rarely politically expedient. They are also hard to sell, hard to explain, and hard to understand. So why do them?

I was starting to see more clearly our government's answer to this question. Which is that we wouldn't do them. Like governments past, we would tinker around the margins, but mostly the plan was to stay with a mix of lofty rhetoric and little action. I did not accept this. My Indigenous schooling in relentlessness would not let me accept this. I wanted to keep making decisions, like we had on MAID and cannabis. I wanted this government to keep doing the hard things that made people's lives better. So I pushed. And I pushed more. And for some I obviously pushed too much.

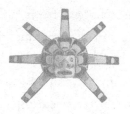

SIX

Justice

We live in an amazing country. But it is a country that is still riddled with implicit bias, discrimination and even outright racism—in the rooms and halls of Parliament and from coast-to-coast-to-coast. There are young kids across that country today who are growing up with a far greater likelihood they will be a Colten and Tina, rather than a Jody or Kory (and even this is a difficult distinction). This is wrong.

Some of these words were recounted in an opinion piece I wrote for the *Globe and Mail* on systemic racism and bold criminal justice reform following the tragic death of George Floyd. They also reflect sentiments I had shared internally throughout my time as MOJAG and especially in 2018, when these issues were in the headlines.

My sentiments, while heavy on policy prescriptions, were also heartfelt; they reflected my own emotions and hope that the government would finally act to undertake comprehensive criminal justice reform and specifically to get rid of mandatory minimum penalties. These feelings were particularly intense after the verdict in the death of Colten Boushie, who was from Red Pheasant Cree Nation in Saskatchewan, that saw an all-white jury acquit Gerald Stanley of second-degree murder. The verdict had set off a firestorm across the country. Both the prime minister and I had sent tweets that expressed compassion and concern, which caused some controversy. These events were also in the shadow of the murder of Tina Fontaine, a fifteen-year-old girl from the Sagkeeng First Nation in Manitoba. She went missing in July 2014; her body was found wrapped in plastic and a duvet cover in Winnipeg's Red River. In 2018, a jury acquitted Raymond Cormier of second-degree murder, and the Crown did not appeal. Tina's tragic death renewed calls from activists for an inquiry into missing and murdered Indigenous women and girls.

The controversy over our tweets was that some felt it inappropriate for the prime minister and me to offer an opinion on a criminal matter. But our tweets were not about that. They were about the systemic challenges of racism and disproportionate representation in our justice system. Of course, since 2018 there has been a significant awakening about these issues in Canada, the United States, and around the globe, exemplified by the Black Lives Matter movement. In 2021, for example, an independent commission found that the RCMP racially discriminated against Colton's mother, Debbie Baptiste, upon notifying her of her son's death. I expect that if the prime minister and I had sent those tweets today there might not have been a controversy. But 2018 was a different time, and I reflected on and spoke out on this issue in many ways publicly and within government. I voiced how, despite the criticism, responding to the verdict was the right thing to do—something that previous generations of leaders had not had the courage to do. As leaders we have to engage and encourage the national conversation and, perhaps, strengthen options for reform.

Critics tried to push the narrative that we were wrong to speak out, that somehow our institutions were being undermined through our demonstration of leadership. Within this narrative was the not-so-subtle assertion that the status quo of our justice system was the uncontested norm and must remain unchanged.

I believe it became clear that we had the high ground. Our actions were different than what people were used to from past prime ministers and attorneys general, but different does not mean there was anything wrong with them. Different is not the same thing as wrong.

I wanted to be seen as playing the role of AG differently than in the past. When thousands of Canadians march in the streets concerned about events in the justice system, as they did in 2018, one would hope the AG would take notice and look at it carefully. I believed then and believe now that our justice system and the rule of law are not fixed. They exist in the context of peoples' lives and experiences. The health of our democracy partially rests on the ability of our institutions to adapt and be responsive to the changing realities in Canada.

I had previously been warned by the PMO, strenuously, to never raise the issue of mandatory minimum penalties with the prime minister again. I had heard the term "out of runway" used many times in relation to this issue while in government. I understood this to mean that the only things that were cleared to "take off" at this time were issues linked to the next election and partisan advantage. Some of my staff, as much as I loved them, were strongly advising against ever raising the issue of MMPs—passing on a warning they, too, had received from the PMO. But I could not be silent.

There has always been a direct connection between silence and injustice. Silence in the face of injustice is a self-interested form of cowardice. Silence sustains and ultimately feeds harm, while speaking out can drive progressive change. Indigenous peoples know this all too well. It is a simple fact that as we have made our voices heard, and more and more Canadians raise their voices as allies, change in the direction of justice emerges. This is equally true in our daily interactions where racism and discrimination rear their ugly heads, as well as in broad societal change.

Well, here I was, the "Indian" in the Cabinet, being effectively told to shut up about a fundamental matter of justice because it was not timely or politically expedient. My God.

•

Along with bold criminal justice reform, two of my core priorities were the recognition and implementation of Indigenous rights, and judicial appointments. Indigenous issues, of course, were deeply significant and personal, and central to my decision to enter into mainstream Canadian politics in the first place. As a lawyer and former prosecutor, I was also deeply concerned about the need for greater inclusiveness, transparency, and diversity of experience in the judiciary. This required taking the politics out of how judges are appointed.

Of course, all of these justice issues—Indigenous rights, criminal justice reform, and judicial appointments—are interrelated and share common themes. They are all about ensuring that our government and institutions are acting justly, respecting basic human rights, confronting the legacy of colonialism, including systemic racism, and ensuring the rule of law is upheld to its fullest for all peoples in this country, regardless of who you are.

I was determined to set an aggressive pace of change on Indigenous reconciliation from the very beginning of my time as MOJAG. The Liberal Party had committed itself to this in its own platform, and it had been confirmed to me time and again by the prime minister that I was to help play a lead on these matters for the government. I knew we did not need to spend years reinventing or developing the overall policy approach. I was bringing with me the solutions and approaches that Indigenous peoples had shaped and advanced over decades. As with the related topic of environmental policy, these approaches have been supported by more reports, studies and commissions than is the case in almost any other area of public policy in Canada.

For generations, Indigenous leaders and others have recognized that they have to work on multiple fronts at once. On one hand, there is the need for nation and government rebuilding; on the other is the transformation of relations between Indigenous nations and the federal and provincial governments, including through changes in Crown laws and policies. Collectively, this work is about confronting the legacy of colonialism and creating cultural, social, and economic well-being that addresses the day-to-day realities that Indigenous peoples face. The formation of nation-to-nation and government-to-government relationships should have been reflected in our Constitution at the time of Confederation. It was not, and we still have to address that reality today.

Invariably—at different times and in different ways—Indigenous leaders will focus on particular aspects of these challenges. My grandmother primarily focused on the rebuilding of our Nation's internal structures, sustaining our culture and language, and the well-being of our communities. In our Potlatch, the highest-ranking male leaders are called *Hamatsa*. In our system, I am a *Hiligaxste'* (a role always held by women). One of my jobs is to lead my Hamatsa, the Chief, into the Big House. This role can be translated as one who "corrects the Chief's path." We show them the way—a metaphor for life. In the Potlatch, this is symbolized in our rituals when the power of the Hamatsa is "tamed" and he is ready to be Chief.

My dad shared much of his mother's focus, but he also spent years helping to lead provincial and federal Indigenous organizations including the Union of BC Indian Chiefs, the Native Council of Canada, the Congress of Aboriginal Peoples, and the negotiations to establish the treaty process in BC. He became more focused on the external relationships with non-Indigenous peoples and creating the collective space for rebuilt nations to take their proper place in Confederation.

I have tried to follow the example set by both my grandmother and father and in doing so recognize that all of this work is ultimately integrated. As was the case with my father, much of my work and more of my time has been spent on transforming relations with the federal and provincial governments through leadership in Indigenous organizations and now as an MP. This helps to establish the external mechanisms to support reconciliation. But I view the heart of this work as creating the space and support for Indigenous peoples to rebuild their governments and nations so they can take care of their own citizens, steward their lands and resources, and make the best decisions to meet their needs and secure their futures.

As MOJAG, I was focused from the outset on creating that space and support for Indigenous peoples to undertake the necessary work of rebuilding. This meant changing federal laws, policies, and the practices within government that are obstacles to Indigenous peoples controlling their own lives, communities, and governments. Yes, of course, that means the Indian Act. It is an amazing thing—a shocking thing—to imagine that in Canada the central piece of legislation about Indigenous peoples is still the Indian Act—a segregationist, colonial, and racist law passed in 1876. The Indian Act is the principal statute that our Parliament enacted concerning Indigenous peoples, their governance, and their relationship to the Crown. And it remains the case. There is no excuse for this. It is because of ignorance, fear, greed, and lack of will that it is still on the books; in other words, it is still in place due to all the hallmarks of racism. As long as there is an Indian Act there will always be institutionalized, systemic racism in Canada with respect to Indigenous peoples. Ultimately, we must be rid of it.

But the way you get rid of it is by creating pathways that support nations to determine their own governance models based on their Indigenous legal orders and traditions and to move out of the Indian Act on their own terms—at their own pace and without the federal government as a gatekeeper. This includes making sure that

Indigenous governments—as they take greater control over land and resource decision-making and designing and delivering the services their citizens need—have the necessary access to revenue streams, like any government does.

Why hasn't this happened yet? For many reasons, but primarily because federal and provincial governments have lacked the political will, and the understanding and capacity, to make this change. To deconstruct and rebuild, it all must start from a place of principle and the recognition of rights. Getting rid of colonial laws such as the Indian Act, and changing laws, policies, and practices that run counter to nations rebuilding and that ignore Indigenous governments and peoples, means that Indigenous rights—the basic human rights in the United Nations Declaration on the Rights of Indigenous Peoples (UNDRIP) and section 35 of our Constitution—have to be taken seriously. But governments have not taken these rights seriously. Indeed, the pattern followed by governments over the years, including today, is to invest vast resources in continuing to fight Indigenous peoples in court to try to prove that these rights do not exist, or mean little or nothing, rather than to get on with recognizing and implementing them. Believe me: I know this first-hand, and I also know how hard but important it is to change this reality.

In running for federal office, I was determined to be a part of changing this. Recognizing Indigenous rights is urgent and overdue. And to be clear, this is not only what is right and needed; it is also essential for Indigenous peoples and for all Canadians. When Canada was founded, Indigenous peoples were left out. They were not there when the so-called Fathers of Confederation got together. Through tremendous effort and leadership by Indigenous peoples, we are increasingly aware of how wrong that was. The costs and challenges of that exclusion are massive. There has been an enormously dark legacy in the lives of Indigenous peoples, who suffer under vastly higher rates of poverty, homelessness, suicide, and addictions than the rest of the population.

The challenges are in our social systems, including the roles that have to be played by education, health, and family protection services. They are in our economy and environment, where the disregard of Indigenous rights has led to massive uncertainty about investment and land and resource use. They are present in our culture and languages, where knowledge, insights, creativity, and innovation have been marginalized, ignored, or lost. And they are there in our cohesion as a country, where deep, unresolved wrongs and tensions fester and cause confusion, unrest, and conflict.

The prime minister and everyone in government knew this was a central priority for me. I also believed it was for them, as they had said so time and again. The prime minister affirmed this when he set out in all of his mandate letters to ministers that, "No relationship is more important to me and to Canada than the one with Indigenous Peoples. It is time for a renewed, nation-to-nation relationship with Indigenous Peoples, based on recognition of rights, respect, co-operation, and partnership." It was fantastic he did this, and I was excited.

Of course, some people will view my optimism as naive, and indeed many have called me naive at various times. If part of being naive means having hope and expectation that people will hold high ideals and live up to them, then I have no problem with the label. I don't subscribe to the view that cynicism and low expectations regarding the conduct and aspirations of our elected leaders is healthy or helpful. We should always be striving to make the changes to the status quo that are needed, and always doing and being better. The way things have always been done are not and cannot be the way things are. Indeed, such a view is ahistorical. We have always changed. Everything is always changing. Our responsibility is to push that change in directions that create more justice, freedom, and opportunity for all people, and to support each individual to meet their potential and aspirations in life. Saying "this is the way things are" is often given as a justification for doing little or nothing. It justifies nothing. It is the excuse given by those who have abandoned their responsibility to advance real change.

The vision to get this work done, which had been set out broadly in the 2015 Liberal Party election platform and to which I expected the government was committed, requires moving away from the long-standing pattern of slow, incremental, minor shifts and towards laying the transformative foundations that are needed for proper relationships. This means government needs to establish a new framework in law and policy that recognizes and implements Indigenous rights and that adheres to standards and principles in policy and decision-making.

No more of this hypocritical double standard about how the individual rights in the Charter are implemented but the collective rights of Indigenous peoples in section 35 of the Constitution are not. This also means ensuring legislation is consistent with Indigenous rights—including the UNDRIP. In addition, a transformative approach means creating clear mechanisms for First Nations to move out of the Indian Act, bolstered by new institutions and supports that help them rebuild their governments and nations. Finally, to make all of this work, government needs to be accountable—which has not been the case in the past. Our history as a country includes treaties being broken, rights being ignored, and court decisions not being implemented. No more. Oversight mechanisms are needed, along with new modes of dispute resolution that can monitor and make sure progress continues.

In the early months of government, focused as I had to be on MAID and cannabis, there was not much visible to the public on the process for building the framework for these mechanisms. We did not "virtue signal" in DOJ as much as maybe other ministries did—including, of course, the PMO, who were the masters. We focused more on getting work done rather than signalling we were going to do it. That said, the effort to get our own house in order within government to do this work in partnership with Indigenous peoples was taking place, and this did lead to some initial public steps. There was considerable behind-the-scenes work going on in tandem with the more public face.

This was why, for example, we developed the Principles Respecting the Government of Canada's Relationship with Indigenous Peoples, which the government released in July 2017. The ten principles, which I understand are still hung on the walls, in both French and English, in every CIRNA and ISC office across the country, were intended to start preparing the public service for the larger shifts to come in how we work with Indigenous peoples. The goal was to set initial guidance on the recognition of rights—"to support efforts to end the denial of Indigenous rights that led to disempowerment and assimilationist policies and practices."

A number of months before the release of the ten principles, the Working Group of Ministers was formed. This new and unique structure of Cabinet ministers was created to help provide political guidance and coherence to the effort of turning the vision of a transformed relationship with Indigenous peoples into reality. The mandate of the Working Group was to review laws and policies to ensure that the federal government was meeting its constitutional and international human rights obligations as they related to Indigenous peoples. This was part of an effort at a historic renewal of relations with Indigenous peoples. I was appointed chair of the Working Group, which included Carolyn (INAC), Jane (Health), and three other ministers.

The development and release of the ten principles and the formation of the Working Group were advanced as part of the effort to address a whole suite of challenges within government. However, it was clear, and wholly unsurprising, that the government system—which included most of my Cabinet colleagues—simply did not understand what the recognition and implementation of Indigenous rights meant, or how to effect it. While I know they wanted a different relationship, they did not know what that relationship should look like or how to build it. This was particularly true of INAC—which was partitioned in August 2017 into Crown-Indigenous Relations and Northern Affairs Canada and Indigenous Services Canada—and frankly remains so to this day. Indeed, government abandoned the vision of a broad and comprehensive framework for recognition and implementation of rights. It is not talked about much anymore, and they do not frame their work that way because they are not doing it and do not really know how.

From a policy perspective, I felt isolated on Indigenous issues in this early period. I spent a lot of time explaining and sharing a vision of how to move forward, but the PMO and many of my colleagues did not really get it. My department tried, and produced lots of materials, but there were struggles. By 2017, I had brought in some additional internal expertise to help with that work, and was continuing ongoing contact with external experts. This helped in getting the principles out the door and the Working Group up and running, but it also became an issue with the PMO and part of the building tensions I was experiencing with Carolyn. From my perspective, CIRNA, including Carolyn, appeared to feel they knew better what needed to be done. The increasing efforts by the PMO to interfere with and dictate my work and to determine my staff seemed in part to be a tactic intended to bring my office more in line with CIRNA's vision of Indigenous relations. Hmm. Doesn't this sound typical of Indigenous experience in Canada? The government saying to an Indigenous person "trust us," "do as we say," "we know best," and taking steps to keep pushing that view? Am I describing how the legacy of colonialism continues within our federal government? I am.

But even with these challenging patterns emerging I was still excited. I certainly knew that governments had talked big on Indigenous issues in the past, with little getting done. But this felt different. The government had adopted the Indigenous language and frame of reference for this work. I felt that Indigenous peoples were being listened to and that my voice at the Cabinet table could be one channel for this. As noted, there was a core group of Indigenous leaders providing external advice based on years of experience. The renewed relationship with Indigenous peoples was going to be rights-based and principled. Small steps were beginning to be taken—steps that broke the period of long darkness epitomized by the Harper era and reflected in the rise of Idle No More. Real change, I believed, was coming.

On June 14, 2016, some seven months into the mandate and a year before the ten principles were published, I had my first sit-down with the prime minister on Indigenous issues—a "stocktake," as these meetings were called. Carolyn was also there, as were our staffs and deputy ministers. The meeting was a good one. I expected that the prime minister would weigh in on these issues directly. There is an important truth that proper relations with Indigenous peoples require direct engagement by the prime minister and senior ministers with Indigenous leaders. The prime minister would repeat this sentiment within government to Cabinet colleagues and publicly soon after. This truth is how the nation-to-nation relationship is viewed by Indigenous peoples. Indigenous peoples have long said that the unfinished business of establishing proper relations must be done with the highest leaders directly involved, because this is how proper Crown-Indigenous relations should and could have been established before and after Canada was founded. This is also how many First Nations across the country understand their treaties. The prime minister was poised to demonstrate this publicly. In the past, prime ministers seemed to have been reluctant to be this bold, to get as deeply involved in this work, or to make it a personal priority. And when they had gotten involved the results had not followed. Only former prime minister Paul Martin had really embraced this "file," but he was only in office for a short time. I was happy Prime Minister Trudeau understood that he had to get his hands dirty and dig in personally if this was going to succeed. This was progress.

From day one, publicly and within government, I was clear and also blunt about what needed to be done. I delivered the same message I had been delivering over the past many years to Indigenous leaders as well as within government—basically, to anyone who would listen. This included the idea that we need to challenge Indigenous peoples. Yes, while we as the government had tough work to do to get our house in order, Indigenous peoples also had much to do. We had to put the proverbial "ball in their court" and give them what they have been asking for and what we all know is needed: a confirmation of the political, governing, and legislative space for self-determination, including self-government, and community and nation rebuilding. The prime minister had shared with me in various ways over the years the sentiment that First Nations have no idea how to respond to a government that gives them what they want. I did not feel this was a disparaging thought. It was a reflection on the reality we had before us—the hard reality of deconstructing the colonial legacy and rebuilding. I believe that government has a responsibility to give Indigenous peoples what they have been asking for and wanting, and that Indigenous peoples would then have to lead to self-determine how they wished to govern into the future and rebuild their nations. As I said to the Annual General Assembly of the AFN on July 12, 2016, just one month later:

> I want to talk about the nation-to-nation relationship and share some thoughts on how we can focus our efforts to collectively set in place a course of action over the coming months that ensures we can turn all the good words, the good will, and the golden opportunity we have into meaningful progress with practical and discernable benefits on the ground within Indigenous communities. To undertake transformative change.
>
> And I challenge the critics that say it cannot be done—those who, on the one hand, say the government is not serious or sincere, and on the other, say that Indigenous peoples do not have what it will take or the resolve, or that the task is too great.

And I make this challenge confident in the knowledge that there is no one in this room who would suggest that decolonization is easy—and that we all appreciate that trust, especially where trust did not exist before, must be earned, and that it can just as easily be lost—and that we all understand that the stakes are high—incredibly high. We are talking about the lives of future generations of Indigenous children within Canada—about the very survival of our distinct cultures and ancient languages—about a way of life . . .

Now is the time. The political and legal ducks are aligned. There is a friendly government. But we need your solutions. As a government we are not going to impose solutions. With your leadership we can and will make enormous progress. There is no need to refight battles that have already been won. Limited resources, time and energy have to be expended on building— not fighting. On creating—not destroying. On empowering— not protest. Pressing social issues must be addressed now. But nations need to be ready to assume jurisdiction and the responsibilities that come with it. And while the federal government has a crucial supporting role to play, the hard work is going to be in the community. As I have said in the Commons, only the colonized can actually decolonize. No one else can do it for you.

So are we ready to implement the UNDRIP? Are we ready to finish the unfinished business of Confederation? I say we are. I know we are. So let us get on with it. We have much work to do and I look forward to doing this work together.

While I was happy about how well the June 14 stocktake went, I did not have any illusions that many in government understood what this all meant in practice. That to do what I described, government would have to be far bolder and more courageous on Indigenous issues than it ever had before. It would take a cross-government or horizontal approach to allow for dramatic changes in the role of government, including ending the colonial role the government had played through the Department of Indian Affairs. An exceptional amount of policy work would have to be done.

*

In addition to progress on Indigenous issues, I also was excited and optimistic about what I was seeing early on in criminal justice reform and judicial appointments; the launch of the MMIWG Inquiry, announced in December 2015, was progress as well. My mandate letter gave me an expansive direction to review and effect change in the criminal justice system, including: sentencing reforms that had been made over the previous decade; reducing Indigenous overrepresentation; increasing the use of restorative justice; and addressing gaps for Indigenous peoples and the treatment of those with mental illness.

When I became MOJAG we immediately began working with the department on what criminal justice reforms were needed. We started a series of engagement sessions with experts and stakeholders and did tons of work with the provinces and territories. The first big engagement session was in Toronto on May 20, 2016, and included former prime minister Kim Campbell, who had been the first female minister of justice and attorney general. From that first session, and in all subsequent ones, the issue raised most consistently was mandatory minimum penalties. It was a prime topic of conversation, with calls for widespread reform.

MMPs take away a judge's discretion when imposing a sentence, and for many offences require a certain prison term. When I was MOJAG, there were seventy-two offences that had MMPs attached. The vast majority of these were introduced in the Harper era. There were six offences with MMPs in 1892, twenty-four in 2004, and seventy-two in 2015. Their use has long been controversial. Many MMPs have been found to be unconstitutional by our courts, as a form of cruel and unusual punishment violating section 12 of the

Charter. There is also extensive evidence that MMPs disproportionately impact Indigenous people and other vulnerable and racialized populations, contributing to their overrepresentation in the prison system. Discretion is vitally important so that a judge can consider the distinct circumstances, background, and context of a particular offender and impose an appropriate sentence that can both act as a deterrent and help effect rehabilitation. Removing this discretion does not help in meeting the core goals of sentencing, including the maintenance of a just, peaceful, and safe society.

I began to echo what I heard during the engagement sessions on MMPs in every venue I could. I spoke about getting rid of MMPs (among other justice reforms) all the time—in speeches, during question period, and with my Cabinet colleagues. I was taking time with the engagement sessions because I wanted to ensure that we had all of our bases covered, including directly seeking feedback from Canadians. I wanted the strong case for bold change to be watertight and to reflect the best ideas we had heard in the engagement.

The department was amazing on this work. You could sense it was something they really believed in and were eager to see done. I got the distinct feeling that people had been waiting for this and now realized we might actually make it happen. So we started work on a huge justice reform package with MMPs as a centrepiece.

I also was jumping in headfirst on judicial appointments. As MOJAG, you are responsible to appoint all federal judges and all superior court judges in the provinces and territories. There was a big gap to address, with a large number of judicial vacancies across the country. Ironically, the opposition parties were quick to point out I was not doing this work fast enough. The truth is we did not want to continue to rely on the existing process in making appointments, as other ministers had. The power to appoint judges is an incredible responsibility that comes with significant long-term implications; it should not be exercised lightly and certainly not with any partisan or self-interest. I knew instinctively that the system I was now in charge of had to be more open and transparent if the bench was to, over time, reflect the diversity of Canada—to look more like Canada. This will take time. We needed a system that would become well known to the public and that would serve the needs of Canada beyond the life of one government. A system that would build on our foundation of judicial independence. I think many Canadians are appalled at the way partisanship affects how judges are appointed or elected to the south of us, and while the system I inherited was nowhere near as problematic as in the United States, it still was not, in my opinion, rigorous enough. I could see how previous ministers, while not outside of the law, had made judicial appointments that did not always pass the smell test.

I was slower out of the gate on changing the superior courts' appointments process than I had planned; it was a priority but did take a bit of a back seat to MAID initially. The task was to bring more openness and transparency into the process, make it more merit-based, increase inclusiveness, and insulate the process from political interference. In essence, to make it more accountable to Canadians. With respect to both improving the process and the eventual appointment of judges under a new process, I had to hire a judicial affairs advisor. I found an amazing one in Katie Black, a brilliant lawyer and passionate justice advocate who was a former clerk to Chief Justice Beverley McLachlin. We set out to review and improve the process.

I am very proud of this work, although more work remains. During my time as MOJAG, I appointed 250 judges. Diversity was improving and will continue to do so over time if the process remains, is strengthened even more, and is not compromised.

As we were overhauling the judicial appointment process, Justice Thomas Cromwell notified the government of his intention to retire early, meaning a seat on the Supreme Court of Canada would be coming vacant earlier than planned. As MOJAG, I would advise on the process to select the replacement and then prepare a recommendation for the prime minister. I felt humbled to do so. It was a significant responsibility and one I did not take lightly. Not only did it come with the possibility of shaping the court, and by extension the law, for years to come, but it was also about the process of determining what was important and who had the qualities required to oversee the issues the court considers.

I wrote a memo to the prime minister with contributions from my political staff and based on advice from the independent and non-partisan advisory board that we had established in July 2016 for just this purpose. It was long, but I wanted to be thorough and detailed given the momentous importance of the decision that needed to be made. As always in life, I erred on the side of providing more information, not less, on the big things. Because of the memo's length, Katie and I wrote an overview summary with my recommendation at the top.

By this point, we had been in office almost a year. While there were challenges, I could see progress taking shape on Indigenous issues, criminal justice reform, and judicial appointments. If we did what we set out to do on these things the country would be changed, for the better, in ways that were important and transformative. Yes, it was hard, and there had been struggles and warning signs. But as the summer moved into the fall of 2016, I viewed those struggles as the growing pains of a government and group of ministers, including me, who were green and still learning the ropes. The political staffs were also green, at least on the federal stage. It was always going to be hard, but good intentions and serious commitments were still evident.

I guess I was still sleeping at night. Not for long, but soundly. This general sense of optimism that I was feeling turned out to be short-lived.

•

I remember a minister saying to me late one night, "If you had to choose between Indigenous issues and MMPs what would you choose?" He went on, "Would you be okay with getting 70 percent of what you wanted on MMPs?" I was confounded by these questions, and even more so by the thinking they represented. Why would one try to do things halfway? Why would we choose to do less when we are able to do more? Why is it a trade-off, one or the other? How can one think about basic social justice issues and matters of rights in such crass transactional terms? I suspected this question did not come from him alone but from somewhere else.

That same minister introduced me to the term *red-meat issue*. If I had lived in this world of partisan politics before coming to Ottawa, I imagine I would have known the term sooner. It was repeated again and again around many tables, and I came to realize it was usually used by ministers who had been given an indication by the PMO, prior to the meeting, of what needed to be said or emphasized. A red-meat issue is one that is not politically expedient to tackle. It may cause us grief in discussions that take place around the dinner tables of Canadians, and may result in a loss of votes. As the days tick by and you move closer to the next election, red-meat issues become more and more part of the political calculus.

I hated the term then, and still do. The whole idea of it. Not acting on critical issues, urgent issues, because of a fear of losing votes. It remains so wrong. How will things change if this is the culture of our politics? Honestly, if you have no intention of moving on a red-meat issue, even if you know it needs to be dealt with, then do not run on it or give people the impression you will do something about it.

My limited exposure to federal politics at this level admittedly contributed to some of my challenges. Not knowing the "playbook" and ways of "doing business" as well as some others was a challenge. But at the same time, ignorance is bliss (and maybe a virtue). My ignorance of the way things are "supposed to work" allowed me to continue to act based on the standards, principles, and values I was raised to lead with. I was less worried about compromises for political purposes and more focused on debating substance.

With respect to MMPs, perhaps I should have found ways to push them faster, tie them in with other issues that were viewed as more politically expedient, and tactically identify the ways and means to do so. To help make them more politically expedient for the party bosses. This is not to say that I was not pouring my heart and soul, and my blood, sweat, and tears into these issues. My office and the department were working flat-out on all of these priorities. As was I. But the reality, as I came to realize over time, was that the government did not have strong intentions to move on these matters. The end result was that on much of the key work we could have done and were prepared to move on, Indigenous issues and MMPs specifically, the government did not act. And on judicial appointments, while our main important reforms went through and hundreds of fantastic merit-based judges were appointed—something I am so proud of— the possibility of political interference in the appointment process has not been eradicated as fully as it could have been.

In addition to my conversations on red-meat issues, another early sign of how the challenges were going to build came from a series of meetings, calls, and discussions between August and October 2016 with the prime minister, senior officials, and others within and out- side government. For a short time, I began to doubt whether I was doing my job well enough and wonder what I might change. Looking back, rereading my notes, and talking with people who were with me then, I now see why it was such an awful and challenging time. I still feel there was an element of gaslighting and signs of prejudice.

In August, the prime minister had used one of his favourite bor- rowed lines—that "hard things are hard"—when speaking of the work of reconciliation. There were high-level discussions around the need for clarity in our interpretation of a proper nation-to-nation relationship and the need for consistency. The messaging from the prime minister had been good. He confirmed, as he had conveyed already, that he would be directly involved. That this work would require hard decisions and repairing relationships. He emphasized it was incumbent upon government to demonstrate our genuine commitment, and that Indigenous peoples would have to lead their own rebuilding work, including their governance capacity. "We will have to take the hits on this one," the prime minister had said at one time. I thought this meant that maybe this would not become one of those red-meat issues.

But I soon began to realize that these words were not translating into clear action and moving the agenda forward. In October, my growing sense of foreboding started to become a reality. We seemed to be continually revisiting *why* we would take big steps on the Indigenous agenda, as distinct from actually taking them. Questions were being raised like "what is reconciliation" and "what is a nation-to-nation relationship." And yet, these were matters around which an agenda had been laid out since well before the election. Mandates were already in place to do this work. As well, as was not atypical for the PMO, they liked to seek advice from outside "experts." On Indigenous matters they brought in author Joseph Boyden. I think Boyden had been invited because Gerry had just read *The Orenda* and was a fan. At that point, people still thought Boyden was Indigenous.

From my perspective, the process around the Indigenous agenda was seriously flawed. We were falling back to a more conventional approach for the federal government, such as establishing new ad hoc negotiation processes that would take place over years and years, while at the same time starting long consultation processes about what more fundamental changes should be made. I did not agree with this. In my view, the basic solutions and fundamental changes government had to make were long established, and we had already said, including in our platform, that we were going to make them. I feared government was slipping back into old colonial patterns.

And then there were some upsetting dynamics in my relationship with the prime minister and the PMO. The prime minister and Gerry both felt I was being "defensive" in meetings when pushing back on the need to maintain the course on the agenda to which we had all committed. For God's sake, we had only been in office for one year, and yet here they were, moving away from how they had defined the "most important relationship." I was not defensive. I was not pleased and, frankly, I was upset that our government was starting to look like other governments on Indigenous issues. At the same time, they launched the broadside attacks on my staff and officials that I noted earlier. This came out most strongly at a meeting on October 12. I cannot share the substantive content of the meeting; however, the prime minister was purportedly concerned about the quality of support I was getting from my deputy, my chief of staff, and my Minister's Office on issues of importance—from Indigenous issues to the appointment of judges. For me, these concerns were unfounded. I had complete confidence in my team—both my political staff and in the public service. I also always wanted to do everything I could to give the prime minister my best advice, and not to be a burden to him or cause him concern. But if I am being honest, I have sometimes wondered if there was some gaslighting going on with some of these dynamics. The reality from my vantage point was that the prime minister had a lot more emerging issues with his staff than I ever had with mine. More than once I have thought to myself that if he did not see it, he was blind. And if he did see it, he was part of it, if not leading it.

I was taken aback, to say the least, and the meeting was a gut punch. We were all working so hard and were doing a good job by any measure. And I thought we were doing what the prime minister wanted—serving him well. Was the mandate letter an illusion? I knew I would stay up nights thinking about this conversation.

I left the meeting feeling very distressed. Regarding the substantive matters I cared so much about, yes, but also due to an unease over the fact that it seemed the PM thought I was not doing my job right or serving him in the way he wanted. I was also incensed that my staff, my deputy, and my department were seemingly being thrown under the bus.

As relationships become complex and interpersonal dynamics become more challenging, I believe that all individuals bear some responsibility. Of course, it is easier to look at how others are acting than to take a hard look in the mirror. That is no different for me. For any of us. As things got harder in my relationship with the PM and the PMO, I certainly felt insecurities, and confusion set in. Was the lack of progress on the Indigenous front because of me? What were my actions slowing down? How come I seemed increasingly to be in tension with some around the table, including, at times, the prime minister? Was it my fault? I had not experienced this in my life previously.

Again, I remember working very hard during this period, but I was energized by the work and our team was a well-oiled machine. Perhaps it is a reflection of my personality and my way of doing things before coming to government that my primary response to these challenges was to encourage everyone to keep working, keep pushing, and keep pushing through. Perhaps there were other options that might have yielded different results. But this is what I knew how to do, and how I had been raised to understand what leadership means.

One way I pushed forward was to ensure my views were directly communicated to the prime minister. Of course, I did not have the prime minister's phone number. It was not the practice, as far as I knew, for Cabinet members to be given his number. We were told to go through Gerry or make a request through the PMO switchboard. I still find it puzzling that a person in such a high leadership position would not make himself directly accessible to the small group of people who were meant to be his closest advisors. So, one thing I did was write memos on critical topics and give them directly to the prime minister. These memos were of varying lengths and on myriad topics. I am not sure if the prime minister read all of them, but I know he read some. I would typically turn to writing one of these memos when

I was at the "end of my rope," so to speak, and when all other avenues to advance an approach or issue seemed to be stalled or even closed.

I know that the Privy Council Office and the PMO did not like this memo-writing practice. The clerk warned me that I had to follow the process, that there was a process for a reason. I also was told of a similar displeasure from the senior folks in the PMO, who complained about the memos. I have to be honest: a minister of justice communicating directly with the prime minister, their boss, seems necessary to me, especially on important and essential matters. Again, one would hope that a prime minister would want to hear directly what ministers think, and not have those thoughts packaged or mediated through political officials or the public service. This does not mean that process is not important or that those means of communication do not have a vital and essential place. They do. But in my view there is room, and a need, for both.

As far as the PMO was concerned, I had become a problem. Yes, I admit I was relentless in pushing. But that was not the problem. The problem was that they were unable to control me in the ways they wished. The PMO wanted the control, and I certainly was not content to let PMO staffers have control over substantive matters. Amazingly, there were times when the PM actually told me that this or that person on his staff was his proxy.

On June 5, 2017, Lea, who was then my chief of staff, was called to the PMO to meet with Gerry and Katie. They laid into her about me. "What is wrong with your minister? She is fighting with everyone," Gerry said. They listed all my transgressions—including pushing on MMPs, pushing on Indigenous matters, and staffing. The "prime minister is not in a happy place," they told her. "She can't be in the room alone with the prime minister"; "she hears what she wants"; and "she cannot give documents to the prime minister." Further, "Jane and Jody should not hang around together."

When I heard about this encounter, I was angry, sad, incredulous, and everything in between. If that is how they felt, it is a wonder they did not shuffle me sooner. But I was performing well and doing my job. I was doing what people had elected us to do. I was carrying out the Liberal platform and ticking off the directions in my mandate letter. And so, I did not change anything. I was going to continue to get stuff done and was going to keep trying as hard as I knew how.

One day in question period I was sitting near the prime minister in my usual seat. I had given him one of my memos earlier that day, and I asked him if he had read it. He obviously had, and we got to talking. Eventually the conversation moved to how we would describe certain people and their approach to work. I asked the prime minister how he would describe me. I acknowledge this was a somewhat self-centred question, but in light of everything that was going on, I was really curious. He was silent for a period of time, looking thoughtful. Then, with a half-smile, he said, "You, Jody, are challenging and infuriatingly headstrong . . . but that is why we love you." Hmm. I remember thinking about that and resolving for myself that "challenging" and "headstrong" are within the parameters of traits for a good MOJAG. After that, I began to sign my memos in a different way: "Your challenging and infuriatingly headstrong, but devoted, MOJAG."

They say hindsight is 20/20. I am not sure it is. Maybe I should have taken the prime minister's words in the House as a warning that we were heading into troubled waters. Not on the SNC-Lavalin affair—that was not even on the horizon at that point—and not even because of clashing personalities or an inability to work together, but rather on substance. On principles. On the right decisions. Because things did get far harder. On these core justice issues, and where leadership was required and decisions would need to be made on more substantive issues, getting to the finish line was going to become significantly harder. Ultimately, it turned out to be impossible. And not without coincidence, that honeymoon period of being left alone to get the big things done—as had been the case with MAID—was ending.

The PMO staff's efforts to control slowly became the norm and not the exception, and extended to attempts to establish greater control over my political staff as well as my department.

As I mentioned, by the summer of 2017 the Working Group on Indigenous issues was underway. At first, it seemed as if it could be an effective vehicle for change. Ministers were engaged and organized. I remember sitting in some of our early meetings just marvelling at the reality that the conversation was happening. A clear schedule was set, with three core items moving forward: getting the ten principles out; having initial meetings with Indigenous leaders and experts that summer; and reviewing a plan for a process and approach to working with Indigenous peoples on a recognition and implementation of rights framework. All of this work started out just fine. The principles came out and were generally well received. The British Columbia government effectively copied them for their own use and publicly released them. The principles did continue to cause some concern throughout the government; they meant change, and people sometimes struggle with that. But they were intended as a starting point for education, innovation, and pushing within government, and they were playing that role. Over the summer the Working Group had meetings that included Indigenous and non-Indigenous experts and leaders on issues of Indigenous rights. And by the end of the summer the Working Group had approved a high-level approach to working with Indigenous peoples on the framework. Although not a formal Cabinet committee, this was progress.

At the same time, though, negative things were still happening—almost counterintuitive to the work and progress being made through the Working Group. A sudden and especially odd one came that August, when Jane, Carolyn, and I were suddenly called into the Prime Minister's Office regarding a Cabinet shuffle. All three of us were down at the Slater building having our second major engagement session of the Working Group of Ministers. Many Indigenous leaders and experts were there. We were called out, one by one, and asked to go see the prime minister. It was awkward, as everyone attending the Working Group meeting knew something was going on. Jane was called up before me, and when she came back I could tell she was upset. I think others could tell as well. I started getting anxious.

I was called in next, right when the Ontario Chiefs were about to present, which was not a good look. As Lea and I walked up to the prime minister's office, I started to wonder if I was being shuffled, though I did not think it likely.

I was not being shuffled. But what became public soon after was that the prime minister was splitting Indigenous and Northern Affairs Canada into two ministries. Jane would move from Health and become the minister of the new Indigenous Services Canada, and Carolyn would head up Crown-Indigenous Relations and Northern Affairs Canada.

The idea of splitting up INAC had been around for a long time, at least since 1996, when it was recommended by the Royal Commission on Aboriginal Peoples (RCAP). In the RCAP recommendations, the split was part of a staged and coherent plan to effectively get rid of INAC in a principled way. It was an acknowledgement that a minister responsible for implementing the colonial Indian Act could not also be responsible for establishing and having proper nation-to-nation intergovernmental relationships. It was also premised on the insight that INAC cannot be the entity that supports Indigenous nations to rebuild their governments consistent with the inherent right of self-government when INAC is legally responsible for governing over them. INAC is a colonial institution. Self-government is the inverse of that. Ultimately, INAC needs to disappear, and to be replaced by Indigenous institutions that support Indigenous government building and exercise of jurisdiction.

At the Working Group, our recently formed plans included some dialogue with Indigenous peoples on such a breakup of the department. But this decision came out of the blue. It didn't appear to be framed or supported by a clear vision of why it should be done or where we were heading. I knew the necessary detailed policy work and planning had not been done, which is why this decision left me feeling a little panicked and with many questions. A more comprehensive approach and strategy was needed. It also felt unexpected and premature. We needed the framework first, along with a legislative package that would have included amending or repealing the act that had established and continued to mandate the Department of Indian and Northern Affairs Canada, as it was known then.

I was asked to attend the Cabinet shuffle ceremony, even though I was not being shuffled. I was happy to be there for Jane. We'd planned to drive over to Rideau Hall together, but I received a call from Gerry early that morning basically forbidding me from hitching a ride with Jane. He said it would be an insult to Carolyn, given the "media are already going to crucify her for not being able to do her job." I took my own car.

While Carolyn and I had been friends for some years, as the days and months passed, I felt we were increasingly not seeing eye to eye on how the core Indigenous work should unfold. The intricacies of the policy debates are multi-layered, but in essence I think it came down to this: I saw as fundamental to any path forward comprehensive legislative and policy shifts in how the federal government approached all relations with Indigenous peoples; basically, that government had to get its house in order in a big way to break the patterns of Indigenous-Crown relations. Carolyn was more focused on having negotiation tables, and seeing progress and establishing mandates through individual agreements. She had set out to establish dozens of new ad hoc "recognition of Indigenous rights and self-determination tables" across the country. We actually need both. But putting your faith in negotiations when the government's mandates are not clear and the policies and mechanisms for foundational change are sketchy or non-existent is not a recipe for success.

It puts too much pressure on individual negotiation tables to mould the national policy. This has been the long-standing pattern: to focus primarily on negotiations and long, drawn-out consultations in the absence of a principled framework that recognizes and implements Indigenous rights. The most typical result—and this remains the case today—is endless years of negotiations, at huge expense and with limited outcomes. An inconsistent and incoherent set of agreements and arrangements.

We need a proper foundation of national legislation and policy. This includes establishing mechanisms to support self-government. We need laws and policies that affirm and uphold core self-government powers, just as our Constitution upholds distinct and clear powers for different orders of government. Those are not negotiated province by province—though how they are implemented and exercised is distinct. Of course, there will still be much to negotiate, but to negotiate distinct arrangements about the basic and core powers that Indigenous governments must exercise on a case-by-case basis will not work. It will lead to a patchwork system around how jurisdiction and power is structured and shared—one that is incoherent and will effectively continue to shift (likely for the worse) as future governments go through cycles of pulling back and slowing down the work while others try to push ahead. In other words, Indigenous self-government will remain at the whim of the political focus of the government at any particular time. Of course, this is not just a federal government challenge. It has also been an approach favoured by some Indigenous groups that think everything needs to be negotiated, and who resist government actually doing what they have long asked and recognizing core aspects of those rights so they can focus on implementation. There has long been talk of the "Indian industry," a term that speaks to the ways in which lawyers and consultants can dominate aspects of the work of reconciliation. Many lawyers and consultants are fantastic—champions that we need. But there is also an industry, and some in that industry probably think there is less money in recognition and quick results. At least in the short term. Conflict and endless negotiations can be good for business.

In any case, I did not believe—and still do not—that changes in approaches to negotiations can be effective without fundamental shifts by government to recognize and implement Indigenous rights as the framework for relations. The shift has to occur first if we want to speed up and succeed in negotiations and have some consistency in relations between and among recognized Indigenous groups. Finally, while negotiations always have a place, we are wrong to think that "negotiating rights" should be the focus of all of our work. Take self-government, for example. My view—which is supported by both section 35 and the Articles of the United Nations Declaration on the Rights of Indigenous Peoples—is that the fact of Indigenous self-government and the core powers that Indigenous governments have are not matters of negotiation. Consider the following articles from the UNDRIP:

> **Article 3:** *Indigenous peoples have the right to self-determination. By virtue of that right they freely determine their political status and freely pursue their economic, social and cultural development.*

> **Article 4:** *Indigenous peoples, in exercising their right to self-determination, have the right to autonomy or self-government in matters relating to their internal and local affairs, as well as ways and means for financing their autonomous functions.*

What is needed, in the case of First Nations, is for the federal government to recognize the rights to self-determination, including self-government, and legislatively establish the mechanisms through which they will back off controlling First Nations through the Indian Act in cases where a First Nation says that this is what it wants. This approach was different from what Carolyn wanted, which was to maintain a focus on negotiating self-government, including its recognition and what powers a First Nation may have.

As the months passed, Carolyn and I would find ourselves increasingly at an impasse and would even have a few blow-ups about issues like this. I felt there was a paternalism emerging in the exchanges, and it made me push back even harder. There was a sense that somehow she and CIRNA knew best. This is an attitude that is all too familiar to Indigenous peoples and, as history shows, is just not true.

At one Working Group meeting in the fall of 2017, the tensions that had thus far been private broke out into the open. Carolyn said I was being "prescriptive," but followed that up by saying that I was "amazing and we need to protect you." She said we needed "the smart people" to weigh in. I was not pleased—substantively because it is the opposite of prescriptive to have Canada properly and legally recognize self-determination and self-government and create mechanisms to support their implementation. I also certainly did not need to be protected.

Even with these tensions we did collaborate on moving things forward. Carolyn and I sent a joint letter to the prime minister recommending that the government endorse NDP MP Romeo Saganash's legislation (Private Member's Bill C-262) to implement the UNDRIP, which was coming to the floor of the House, with the caveat that we be clear in our view that the bill was just a starting point. More was needed, including a recognition and implementation of a framework to operationalize rights on the ground in communities. The prime minister agreed, and I announced our government's support, with Carolyn in attendance, at a conference in Gatineau, Quebec, on November 20, 2017. As events unfolded, that endorsement reflects what I knew to be true then. For me, that bill was not nearly enough: it did not bind government to meaningful concrete action; it did not establish mechanisms, institutions, and supports; and it had a limited possibility of effecting real change. For government, however, that bill was ultimately the upper limit of what they were willing to do at the time in terms of recognition and implementation of rights. This is evidenced in how—more than two years later and with great fanfare—the government brought forward its own bill (C-15) that was basically a carbon copy of the C-262 bill from 2017, and frankly, in some respects could be considered weaker. (Bill C-15 received royal assent on June 21, 2021.)

The inside story of the rise and fall of the recognition and implementation of a rights framework encapsulates all of these tensions. After the Working Group endorsed the approach in the summer of 2017, I was intent on getting it moving as soon as possible. With staff and the Justice Department, I prepared a lengthy discussion paper that could be used publicly for engagement about the framework. The discussion paper gave the history and context of the struggle for recognition of Indigenous rights, detailed the kinds of solutions that had been brought forward over generations through the work of Indigenous peoples, and laid out preliminary ideas about the types of legislative and policy work that could be co-developed through the process and form part of the framework. The draft of the discussion paper got caught in an endless game of tag between my office, the PMO, and CIRNA. Ultimately, even though the PMO committed to its release, they simply blocked it. To this day it has not been released.

I could also see the government lining up to do what it so often does—focus on the "moment" rather than the "substance." The moment would be a speech, ultimately given by the prime minister, announcing a recognition and implementation of an Indigenous rights framework in the House of Commons. This ended up being planned for February 14, 2018. In the lead-up to the speech, there were what seemed like endless efforts between the PMO, my office, and Carolyn's office to develop comprehensive materials addressing hard issues and questions that would be asked about the framework and what it meant. For weeks on end these went back and forth in cycles. All they ultimately revealed was that the government did not have a clear understanding of what the recognition and implementation of Indigenous rights meant, and had no intention of following through. All of these materials were abandoned as there was no agreement on what could or would be said. There was just a speech.

February 14, 2018, and what happened in the aftermath offers a perfect reflection of so many things that were wrong with this government and how I was caught up in it all: how the government functions and where it puts its priorities; where control in the government really lies; the fraying of relationships I had with some of my colleagues; and my growing realization that it was becoming unlikely that my time in this government would or could last as long as I had once thought it would.

In the months ahead of the speech there had been also a fair amount of discussion about what engagement on a framework would occur, who would lead it, and how it would unfold, but it all remained murky. There was a general idea that Carolyn would lead the engagement with Indigenous peoples, and that I would meet with experts and certain groups. I would also give a number of speeches across the country that would provide details of the framework. The use of the discussion paper was also murky, but I was still being told it would be released around the time initial engagement got under way in early March. I was also hearing, however, that CIRNA was preparing other materials that would be used.

A final version of the prime minister's speech was shown to me on the morning of the 14th. Some of it was good, but some of the language was off-key from an Indigenous peoples' perspective. I was frustrated to be seeing it at the last minute, but I went ahead and suggested a number of edits and forwarded them to the PMO. They accepted a few. Midday, Carolyn popped into my office with a member of her staff. A number of my staff were also milling about. We got into a conversation about the speech, the framework, and what we should be doing. It became very heated, no doubt a release of tensions that had been building up. The staff were clearly feeling uncomfortable, and Carolyn and I ended up speaking alone. It was not good.

My sense of inner conflict was immense and intensifying. Based on all that had transpired up to this point, I knew there was not a clear understanding, focus, or plan for this work to unfold. At the same time, there was a part of me that always wanted to give the benefit of the doubt. My frustration and disappointment was complete. This government—the government I was a part of—would go down the same path as previous ones when it came to delivering on what was needed to address the legacy of colonialism. But I also so much wanted to believe that the right thing could still be done, and I had to be relentless in trying to push my colleagues to that place.

This inner conflict played itself out as I told some of my staff that I was thinking of not going down to the House for the prime minister's speech. Some of them started to panic; their sense was that if I did not attend the wrath of the PMO would be over-the-top. I ended up with some downtime before the speech, which was to be given after question period that afternoon. I called Tim and sat in my office with a few trusted advisors coming in and out, including Roshan Danesh.

I often teased Roshan that he was too much the skeptic and too cynical about government and its willingness to effect change on Indigenous issues. While that was not totally fair, this day was different; it featured something of a role reversal. As we had a meandering chat about how we had arrived at this place and what the journey had been (which included some emotions), he gently started encouraging me to go down for the speech. He knew all of my concerns and frustrations, and how upset I was. But as we talked, I remembered all the work and leadership—from so many people—that it had taken to even reach this moment, a moment where governments would start to talk properly about Indigenous rights. We had the ten principles. At the very least, a speech about rights recognition, delivered by the prime minister, would go on the public record and offer a retelling of some of our history in useful ways. As that discourse shifts, opportunities for change will increase. And there was still my hope against hope that this government would act. We went downstairs for the speech together.

I was moved by the prime minister's remarks. The speech was historic. The prime minister delivered it well and the words were important ones.

> *This Framework gives us the opportunity to build new mechanisms to recognize Indigenous governments, and ensure rigorous, full and meaningful implementation of treaties and other agreements. With this Framework, we have a chance to develop new tools to support the rebuilding of Indigenous communities, nations, and governments; and advance self-determination, including the inherent right of self-government. This Framework could establish new ways to resolve disputes, so that collaboration becomes the new standard, and conflict the exception rather than the rule.*
>
> *By including tools that oblige the federal government to be more transparent and accountable, we can build greater trust between Indigenous Peoples and government. And through this new Framework, we can better align Canada's laws and policies with the United Nations Declaration on the Rights of Indigenous Peoples, a declaration our government supports without qualification.*
>
> *. . . [B]y fully embracing and giving life to the existing Section 35 of the Constitution, we will replace policies like the Comprehensive Land Claims Policy and the Inherent Right to Self-Government Policy with new and better approaches that respect the distinctions between First Nations, Inuit, and Métis peoples. This will give greater confidence and certainty to everyone involved. The federal government's absence over generations in recognizing and implementing Indigenous*

rights has resulted in social and economic exclusion, uncer-
tainty, and litigation—when our shared focus should have
always been on creating prosperity and opportunity for every-
one. Better opportunities for Indigenous Peoples, and certainly
for Indigenous youth, are precisely what we hope to achieve
through this Framework.

After the speech, the PM gave me his marked-up copy of the speech with a handwritten note on the front page that read, "Thank you Jody, for leading us all on this journey!" Signed and dated.

That was to be the last of such moments.

After the speech, Carolyn began rolling out her engagement efforts across the country. CIRNA produced materials without our input that frankly were insulting. I heard from many Indigenous leaders about how insulted they were. One of them memorably asked me why they were being engaged by Canada through a "colouring book." The AFN was fuming about the whole approach, and also felt it was not working. CIRNA refused to allow some of our staff and officials to attend Carolyn's engagement meetings. Despite the PMO's promise, they blocked the use of the discussion paper. I did give one of the speeches I was slated to, at the Business Council of British Columbia in April 2018. I specifically addressed issues of Indigenous consent and economic certainty, but also laid out my vision of the framework, the same one I had been supporting for some years. After that, though, there really was nothing to be done. Predictably, Indigenous peoples were not impressed by CIRNA's poorly conceived plan and approach. Nothing was clear about what was intended, and it was obvious the plan for any real reform was dying. The federal government never even speaks of the framework anymore, nor about bold legislative change or their core platform commitments. The change that is truly needed—that we have known is needed for decades—is not being pursued. The reality today? More endless negotiations on the same subject matters bereft of a rights recognition framework and without clear mandates. The "Indian industry" continues to be fed. The real work of nation rebuilding is still delayed, pending the signing of agreements. The progress that has been made—such as through legislation regarding Indigenous languages as well as Indigenous children—does have important elements and touches on critical issues, but it is piecemeal and not comprehensive. The calls to action of the Truth and Reconciliation Commission and the calls to justice of the MMIWG Inquiry continue to languish.

As all of this was playing out, I had also been advancing and wanting to release, as the attorney general, a directive on how my department approached civil litigation involving the rights of Indigenous peoples. The directive was an application of the ten principles and designed to help the process—gently—of moving reconciliation out of the adversarial courts. As I said in the directive:

> *Litigation is by its nature an adversarial process, and it cannot be the primary forum for achieving reconciliation and the renewal of the Crown-Indigenous relationship. This is why a core theme of this Directive is to advance an approach to litigation that promotes resolution and settlement, and seeks opportunities to narrow or avoid potential litigation. Our Government is committed to pursuing dialogue, co-operation, partnership and negotiation based on the recognition of rights.*
>
> *. . . I hope that, in time, this litigation Directive will be recognized to have brought about a significant shift in the Government of Canada's positions and strategies. I hope, too, that litigation will be recognized as a dispute settlement forum of last resort, as trust and good faith allow collaborative processes, including facilitation, mediation and negotiations, to be the primary means of resolution.*

There had been struggles in having the system finalize and release the directive for months. I spoke about these struggles in a speech

I gave to the BC Cabinet and First Nations Leaders' Gathering in November 2018. Ultimately, I released it on my last day as MOJAG. Almost a year earlier, in February 2018, I had what would become a typical run-in with the PMO about the directive. One official basically forbade me from releasing it. I guess he was the attorney general now? This triggered all sorts of internal speculation for me, again, about how long I could stay in this role. My acting chief of staff took a lot of the brunt of my frustration, and that of the PMO, at this time. At one point another PMO official said to him: "I mean, we are dealing with the India trip [a reference to the public relations disaster around the PM's trip to India, where his penchant for dressing up in costume became a national embarrassment]—we can't deal with justice issues now." That pretty much summed things up.

By the late summer of 2018, I was feeling that greater honesty and transparency inside of government was needed to talk about these challenges. If all of this focus and effort on Indigenous reconciliation was not going to result in any actual legislative or significant policy change, then it was necessary to be truthful about what the challenges still were.

I also decided that I would include some of my thoughts in upcoming public speeches. The idea was to include hard talk about these challenges, to basically lay out for others what I had been thinking and saying internally. I always gave my speeches to the PMO in advance.

On September 13, 2018, I gave the first of these speeches at the University of Saskatchewan in Saskatoon, immediately after a two-day Liberal caucus meeting. I said:

> *Words have meaning. We live in a time where language is often appropriated and misused, co-opted and twisted—made to stand for something it is not.*
>
> *"Recognition" for Indigenous peoples across this country, and as a basis for true reconciliation, has meaning. It means*

that Indigenous peoples governed and owned the lands that now make up Canada prior to the arrival of Europeans. It means that Indigenous laws and legal orders that stewarded the lands for millennia, remain and must continue to operate in the contemporary world. It means that the title and rights of Indigenous peoples are inherent, and not dependent or contingent on court orders, agreements, or government action for their existence, substance, and effect. It means that treaties entered into historically, must be fully implemented based on their spirit and intent, oral histories as well as texts, and consistent with the true meaning of a proper nation-to-nation and government-to-government relationship. It means that the distinct and diverse governments, laws, cultures, societies, and ways of life of First Nations, Métis, and Inuit are fully respected and reflected.

For Canada, recognition means resetting our foundation to properly reconcile—to finish the unfinished business of confederation. What is more, for many Indigenous peoples, recognition is the lifeline that will ensure the survival and rebuilding of their cultures, languages and governing systems within an even stronger Canada.

But words are also easy/cheap. And too often we see the tendency—especially in politics—to use important words that have real meaning and importance, carelessly. We see them being applied to ideas and actions that in truth do not reflect their actual meaning—even, sometimes, their opposite. We see "recognition" applied to ideas that actually maintain "denial." We see "self-government" used to refer to ideas or processes that actually maintain control over others. We see "self-determination" applied to actions that actually interfere with the work of Nations rebuilding their governments and communities. We see "inherent" in the same breath as the contradictory idea that rights are contingent on the courts or agreements.

When we see this being done it does not advance reconciliation. It actually undermines it. It causes confusion, chaos, and division. It treats a challenge—a challenge that is vital for the survival and well-being of children, women, families, and communities across this country—as a "game of rhetoric." It trivializes—often out of ignorance or political expediency—a moral, social, and economic imperative for our country.

Words, in the work of reconciliation, are also cheap without real action—action that goes to the core of undoing the colonial laws, policies, and practices, and that is based on the real meaning of reconciliation. We all need to understand this.

The path of justice and equality is not advanced or achieved through half-measures, good intentions, or lofty rhetoric. And it is certainly not achieved through obfuscation or confusion about what we mean when we speak. Hard choices, innovative actions, transformations in laws and policies, new understandings and attitudes, new patterns of behaviour—this is what is needed.

A parliamentary secretary was in attendance at the lecture. At dinner afterwards he was enthusiastic about the speech, and recognized it was different than what CIRNA was currently advancing. I am not sure he fully understood how directly I was criticizing the government, but I appreciated his sentiment nonetheless. I gave three more speeches like this before the end of the year. And at the same time the idea of this government recognizing and implementing Indigenous rights died its death. The government moved on as if the prime minister had never given a speech on February 14, 2018.

On September 17, 2018, I was to meet with the prime minister. I had requested the meeting to deal with the collapse of the rights recognition agenda. The meeting would become infamous later due to the SNC-Lavalin affair. But as I walked up to Centre Block and waited outside in the horseshoe, my focus was on trying to convince the prime minister to do the right thing on Indigenous issues.

Maybe this was my last chance to convince him to carry out what the February 14 speech had promised. Ever the optimist, I felt it was a good sign that he had accepted the meeting. I was surprised when I walked in and saw Michael Wernick. Immediately, the PM asked about SNC-Lavalin. In hindsight, I think he had accepted the meeting because they really wanted to pressure me about SNC-Lavalin, and this was the best way to do it. He could not very well schedule a meeting to do so. Apparently, more important than Indigenous issues or justice reform was figuring out how to get this company out of hot water. And it was the most challenging issue for them, because on it I was acting as the attorney general. On Indigenous issues and MMPs and so many other things, I was minister of justice. In that role, I was working to dialogue, debate, and find policy solutions as part of government decision-making. Not as attorney general, where by law I had to play an independent role, and they could not influence or shape my decisions.

Well, that September 17 meeting has now been well documented; this is when I flat-out challenged the prime minister on whether or not he was trying to pressure me—an incident that is now public knowledge. We did eventually get to talking about the rights recognition framework and Indigenous issues at the end of the meeting, but the PM's mind was still focused on SNC-Lavalin. As for Indigenous issues, he had made up his mind and that was not going to change. Towards the end of the conversation, as I was leaving his office, I exclaimed to him that my granny was rolling over in her grave.

From my perspective, MMPs had similarly derailed about a year earlier. The message I heard was that we were out of runway on MMPs, and my staff was being blamed. This was increasingly a common theme: blame the staff or the department. I even formed an understanding that trade-offs might be possible—get rid of some staff that the PMO did not like, Lea in particular—and perhaps there may be progress on some issues. I just could not back down. We were on the wrong side of history on this—progressive states do not throw away the key on marginalized peoples. I would hear things like *we don't have the support* and *we don't want you to lose a vote on the floor of the House of Commons*. I got it. As that minister said: red-meat issue. Which meant two years into a mandate, core promises and issues were DOA. Ugh.

I could not reconcile this in my mind. I did not know how I would be able to look myself in the mirror if we did not do this. For all my efforts, I felt that I was just making the prime minister angry. I knew he was facing challenges on multiple fronts, and the pressures were mounting. The prime minister, as is undoubtably always the case, was under immense pressure those days. But I felt it was always the right time to do the right thing.

So I kept pushing—sometimes to the point of utter frustration and tears. Especially after the events regarding Colten Boushie and Tina Fontaine. But I knew it was to no avail. The political case was clear in his mind: this would lead us to lose the election. For some, this could have been the straw that broke the camel's back. The prevailing wisdom that I could discern at the time was MMPs were a political loser, and a winner for the Conservatives. It felt like the issue went round and round. And just kept going in circles.

.

Undoubtedly there were some choices I could have made better or differently on these core justice matters of Indigenous rights and MMPs. I could have been more strategic, at times more co-operative, and in some ways more flexible. But I am not sure much would have changed substantively. I think little would have been done on these issues regardless, just in ways that might have been less intense for many of us.

The course judicial appointments took—and have continued to take—reflected this. I loved making the calls to new judges to tell them of their appointment to the bench. They would always know a call was coming, as they were well planned. Many of these calls stick in my mind. I remember one person responding to my call by recounting how she had applied before, during the Harper years, and telling me: "I'm a lesbian." Another time I caught someone in their car and asked them to "please pull over your car—I don't want you to break the law." Another person responded by asking, "Can I have time to check with my wife?", which was a little strange. There were tears, and screams, and plain and simple happiness.

Despite all of the work and the commitment to removing political interference from the judicial appointments process, and the quality of the judges who were being appointed, as time passed there were unfortunately attempts at interference. Some of this became public, when stories were published in the media. Beyond what has been reported, many other tactics were used to try to influence appointments, such as the PMO insisting on receiving my detailed and confidential lists with the raw data of feedback from validators and other processes about appointees. Sometimes there would be a full-court press from the PMO, ministers, other MPs, and influential Liberals who would contact me trying to advance a particular appointment. This even occurred when a particular individual had not been recommended through our comprehensive vetting process. Of course, another way to influence appointments was simply to delay them. None of these attempts to influence worked or impacted my appointments.

In one of my little black notebooks, I have a quote that Katie Black from my office shared with me: "Beware of moderate liberals who tell you the timetable for seeking justice!" I guess that sums up well my time as MOJAG on these issues. As had always been my way, as taught by my granny and others, I pushed for big change. On Indigenous reconciliation headway was made, but truly tangible and long overdue changes—which are urgent—remain outstanding.

On MMPs, the government simply would not move. On judicial appointments, we have a more diverse bench, but the process is still not insulated enough from politics.

In 2020, in the midst of the COVID-19 pandemic, we saw how government is capable of making big, bold change quickly when there is a crisis before them. Simply stated, government does not see the dire reality that many Indigenous peoples live in as a crisis. It can wait. Until government says the time is right. It has been that way for more than 150 years. We continue to wait.

Granny and my great-uncle Billy,
circa 1925–26.

Auntie Donna, Granny, and Dad,
circa 1948.

Me as a baby with Dad, 1971.

My sister, Kory (*left*), and me, in 1974, in Grandma's crocheted dresses.

Me, at about four years old, sporting my favourite barrettes, Vancouver.

Granny and me dancing at the Potlatch where I received my name, at Gilford Island, BC, circa 1976.

Dad and me watching a soccer game in Kingcome, BC, circa 1979.

My granny, Pugladee, circa 1980.

Hemas Kla-Lee-Lee-Kla, K'ómoks
Big House, Comox, BC, circa 1985.

Pugladee, painted by Leonard Peltier,
oil on canvas, circa 1990.

Me, at age twenty-two, with Granny,
at her kitchen table.

Granny and Dad,
sharing a moment.

Kory (*left*) and me, graduation day, UBC Law, 1999.

With Tim, on our wedding day, Cape Mudge, BC, November 29, 2008.

Cape Mudge, on the southern tip of Quadra Island, BC.

My nieces Kaija, Kaylene, and Kadence, in the summer of 2008.

Kadence, Kaylene, Kory, me, and Kaija, in Vancouver, June 2018.

One of many speeches as Regional Chief at a BC Assembly of First Nations gathering.

Kwakwaka'wakw Potlatch, 'Namgis Big House, Alert Bay, BC, April 2014.

Tim and me, election night, October 19, 2015.

Lea Nicholas-MacKenzie (*left*), Kory, and me, on Parliament Hill, November 3, 2015.

That photograph, Rideau Hall, November 4, 2015.

The Cabinet room sign.

Kory and me, Honouring ceremony (soon after becoming MOJAG), at the Chief Joe Mathias Centre, North Vancouver, December 12, 2015.

Jane Philpott, then minister of health, and me, standing in the lobby outside the House of Commons upon the introduction of Bills C-45 (cannabis) and C-46 (impaired driving), April 13, 2017.

Mumma and me, Cape Mudge, BC, May 2017.

Me in the Cabinet room in Centre Block, a couple of weeks before leaving for Bali, December 12, 2018.

Speaking at a Rideau Hall press conference, after being sworn in as minister of veterans affairs, January 14, 2019.

Front page of the *Globe and Mail*, Ontario edition, February 7, 2019.

Jane Philpott and me, with parliamentary security, leaving the Confederation Building through the tunnels, on February 12, 2019.

At the House of Commons Justice Committee hearing, February 27, 2019.

Musgamagw Tsawataineuk Chiefs and me, at an honouring and cleansing ceremony, Kwanwatsi Big House, Campbell River, BC, March 30, 2019.

Jane Philpott and me being honoured at a BC First Nations Justice Council meeting, April 24, 2019.

WILSON-RAYBOULD, THE HON. JODY

My seat as a new Independent, back corner of the House of Commons, April 2019.

My Independent campaign launch, Marpole Neighbourhood House, VanGran, BC, May 27, 2019.

Federal election campaign 2019, corner of Granville and Broadway, VanGran, BC, September 12, 2019.

Election night celebration, Hellenic Community Centre,
VanGran, BC, October 21, 2019.

Signing the Test Roll and being sworn in as a member of Parliament,
with friends and supporters, December 3, 2019.

Totem at Cape Mudge, BC, March 2020.

Looking north from our beach up Discovery Passage,
from the red hammock at sunset, Cape Mudge, BC, June 2020.

Granny.

SEVEN

The Shuffle

My January 2019 notebook has the following on the inside cover: "Jan 2019 In Nusa Dua—Year of Work starts with a call from the PM—oh my—who knows what about." The "oh my" is a tell. I write that—to myself and in texts—when I feel emotions building up, whether beautiful feelings of love or negative feelings of trepidation and uncertainty. This "oh my" was of the latter kind. I could feel something big was coming.

That morning, I was preoccupied with thoughts about that scheduled phone call. It could be about SNC-Lavalin. It could be a shuffle. It could be both. I doubted it was the struggles on major policy issues. The government was already abandoning the ones I cared about. While these were not happy days within government, I imagine it was probably typical for any government that is starting to see the end of its mandate creep up. Exhaustion, distraction, frustration. People getting tired of one another. Given all of that, I was not sure what exactly the prime minister wanted to discuss.

Tim and I were on holiday in the southern part of Bali, Indonesia, trying to get some much needed downtime after the difficult events in the months leading up to Christmas. But given the message that had reached me from Ottawa, I knew Bali would not make for much of a vacation—even with our incredible surroundings. To be honest, ministers do not really get vacations, at least in my experience. Every trip I took for personal reasons while MOJAG ended up interrupted by some crisis or urgent work that had to be dealt with. Bali was a prime example of a crisis vacation: as it turned out, that's where I learned I was going to be fired as MOJAG. Ultimately, I would end up having to confront one question: Was I going to stay in government at all?

I know there is no suspense for any of you reading this. I stayed and served as the minister of veterans affairs for twenty-nine days (from January 14 to February 12). I resigned pretty much four weeks after being shuffled. From that moment, my life, Tim's, and the lives of some who were close to us were irrevocably altered.

As for the one question? I made the right choice.

·

I struggle writing about these events. To me, it all feels kind of boring—a blow-by-blow of phone calls, texts, dialogue, and decisions. I have detailed notes about everything (rest assured that I will deal with the details in the next chapter). There is too much, and a lot of it is really "inside" stuff: who said what to whom about this or that and when. And I know my telling of this part of the story here is a little out of order. By this point, all of the government's efforts to pressure me on SNC-Lavalin had already happened. The public, of course, would only learn about those events about a month after I was shuffled. But I guess recounting the ins and outs of these events is important to reveal my state of mind at the time, and that of others. It also reveals some of the misogyny and racism that remains in our public life. So here it goes—some of the important bits, anyway.

When I was told by Jessica on the morning of January 7, 2019 (well, it was the night of January 6 in Ottawa—which is thirteen hours behind Bali), that the prime minister wanted to speak to me "on an emergency basis," I wrote in my notebook: "3 letters, SNC." The government's attempts to pressure me on the prosecution of SNC-Lavalin had reached a peak in December in the now infamous, and thankfully recorded for posterity (more on this later), phone call with Michael Wernick before the holidays. In that call on December 19, I had been warned that the prime minister would get what he wanted on the matter, and I figured this new call would be about doing just that. I knew shuffling me was an option. Install a more compliant attorney general. Was I supposed to act like Trudeau's very own Bill Barr and do his bidding?

I did not have to wonder for long. Jane called. She was being shuffled to be the president of the Treasury Board. She said the line being used was that the shuffle was happening "because Scott Brison [who was the current president] resigned." She did not know all of the dynamics of the shuffle, but she did know I was going to be shuffled to Indigenous Services. The prime minister had told Jane that he needed her help to convince me.

Let there be no doubt: from the first second I realized I was being shuffled I felt it was because of SNC-Lavalin. Indeed, Jane later told me that the second the prime minister told her that I was being shuffled she immediately thought it was because of SNC-Lavalin, too. I still have no doubt, even after listening to every explanation, rationale, and prevarication provided to me. And there is ample evidence apart from my own beliefs, and the beliefs of many others, that illustrates this to be the case. Of course, everyone is welcome to their own conclusions.

I waited for the call. It was around 10 p.m. in Bali (9 a.m. in Ottawa). Tim was in an adjacent room, already stewing angrily. His views of the prime minister had only deepened over these years. We'd had a lot of time to talk and speculate about what was to come. Tim knew that I had had some very unpleasant, inappropriate, and significant run-ins with PMO and the Privy Council clerk. I think part of the reason we'd decided on a holiday so far away was to try to have a break and a real escape before whatever was to come. But Tim did not know all the gory details or the potential seriousness for the government and the country if the madness were to continue.

The prime minister's call came through from the PMO switchboard to my phone. He came on the line and shared that a situation had occurred over Christmas and that Scott was stepping away from politics. I was surprised by this, as I had not gotten the impression from Scott that he was checked out or wanted to leave politics. I would later learn that Scott had informed the PMO on December 12 that he was resigning.

Let us stop there for a second. So, Scott Brison was resigning. What did that have to do with me? Put Jane in Treasury Board if that was really what you needed; she is fantastic and has clear knowledge and experience, having already served as the vice-chair of the Treasury Board. There were lots of great candidates to replace her at Indigenous Services. I even recommended one directly in the coming days—Marc Miller. I was told he was not ready. Of course, he became the Indigenous Services minister some ten months later. Or do not move Jane—she was a star in Indigenous Services. And there were other great options for Treasury Board. Carla Qualtrough, whom I also directly recommended. Or Jean-Yves Duclos. He actually ended up in the job, also ten months later. Joyce Murray? I was told she was not ready either; Joyce would become Treasury Board president seventy days later, after Jane resigned.

"We need our best players to move," Trudeau said. He then started talking about Indigenous Services: "We need our best communicator there—someone with real influence in the lives of Indigenous peoples in the country. Your voice, your leadership is needed—to show how seriously we take Indigenous peoples and their issues." He shared that I had already introduced all of my legislation—basically stating that there was not much left to do at Justice—and that I had skills as a communicator. He used sports analogies. I admit I always respond poorly to sports analogies, as I do not watch many sports. I also find it a little offensive to the seriousness of governing when we talk of it in terms of sports. Especially when politics is called a blood sport. It orients our politics in completely the wrong way.

"I want you, Jody, to be the Indigenous Services minister." I have in my notes: "OMG!!" I was floored. I was angry, but at the same time I also felt an overwhelming sense of anxiety and calm. My calm came from the realization that my time in this government, one way or another, was changing, and likely would be coming to an end. Mostly I wanted to get off the phone. I did not want to say something that I would regret, that would be disrespectful.

Let's take another pause. Why was I so stunned? I was stunned because, as you now know, I had made it abundantly clear I could never serve as the minister of INAC, now ISC. I could not and would not be the Indian agent. They knew this, and had been told on multiple occasions—including the first time I met the prime minister and was vetted for Cabinet. It was not a matter of being a team player. One does not choose to go against basic principles and values—in this case agreeing to be in charge of implementing (not changing) oppressive laws and structures that apply to one's own people—in order to fit on a "team" and be a "team player." Or if one does, that is pretty sad. And, frankly, I would not be on a team with such a person.

I can't help but think of the words my grandmother spoke about the Indian agents who imposed and administered the Indian Act. How the Indian agents would take kids to residential school. How my grandmother never stopped her practice of speaking of the "white man" and the things they had done. When she was speaking angrily of the "white man," I know she had the Indian agents in mind. I also thought of my great-grandfather, Hemas Johnson, who had been arrested, taken to New Westminster, and thrown in jail (Oakalla prison in the lower mainland) for potlatching in the early 1920s, a time when the Potlatch was outlawed in Canadian law.

I did not say anything to the PM for what seemed like minutes. When I did speak, I said that I was quite shocked and that I did not know what to say, at least not at that moment. I said I would have to think about it. What I also managed to get out was that it did not make sense to me; this merely led the prime minister to repeat that this was the only option . . . Scott Brison . . . our need to be compelling to Canadians . . . to show transformative change on Indigenous issues.

I finally said what I was really thinking. "I cannot help but think this is because of another issue—one where I would not do that which I was being asked." I was, of course, referring to SNC-Lavalin, but I was being careful, given that I did not know if there was anyone else on the call. "No," the prime minister replied. I reiterated something I had said to him, Gerry, and others many times before—that ISC was not where transformative change happened. "I will think about it," I said. "Okay," the prime minister replied.

So, yes, I was adamant in my belief that I was being shuffled because of SNC-Lavalin from the first moment, while the prime minister and Gerry Butts were adamant that this was not the case. These positions have never changed. I presume they never will. But I challenge them to demonstrate that SNC-Lavalin was not a factor or on their minds at the time. It is for them to explain, for example, why Michael Wernick informed the deputy minister of justice on January 11, 2019, that one of the first conversations the new attorney general would be expected to have with the PM would be on SNC-Lavalin.

After I hung up, I sat in my chair trying to wrap my head around the call and what had been said. I called for Tim, who was still in the other room. He came in and said the conversation had been loud, that my voice had sounded elevated on the call, and that he had paced back and forth throughout it. So began a lot of debating, planning, and preparing regarding the next steps I would take.

I had to confront questions about the right and best thing to do— for the country, the government, and, yes, for me. I had to decide whether to stay in government. I believed I was being shuffled for a bad reason—frankly, an improper and unethical reason. And it was a reason nobody would know about when the shuffle was made public. I knew, too, that I could not be the minister of Indigenous services, which they well knew. And there was another reason—a third reason—that I was not sure I could stay: the vision and commitments that had attracted me to Justin Trudeau and his Liberal Party in the first place were now distant glimpses in the rear-view mirror. There was little that could be done, at this stage, on the pivotal priorities that had brought me to Ottawa originally. At what point was I just staying for the wrong reasons: for power, prestige, a role? Acting like a "politician" in the worst sense of the term? My litmus test of being able to look in the mirror each night was haunting me. Could I do that if I stayed in this government, which was so focused on power and partisanship and so little interested in principle? That was more about image than substance? Was there a difference I could still make? Was there a purpose, a reason, to stay?

No decisions were coming easily. Gerry and I agreed to talk. We ended up talking several times over the next number of days. I repeated to him what he already knew—that I could not be the minister of ISC. I also told him on the phone that I knew this shuffle was because of SNC-Lavalin. We did not get far and did not say too much. He hypothetically floated whether I would consider being minister of CIRNA. I said I didn't talk in hypotheticals and was getting uncomfortable with Cabinet positions being talked about so loosely. We knew we would be in touch again very soon.

I also was back and forth with Jane and Jessica. Neither of them was going to push hard one way or another, of course. I really appreciated their thoughtful counsel. This was especially true when it came to Jessica, who would be so directly impacted by whatever I decided. I was quite concerned about how any decision I made would affect

Jessica and all of my staff. But Jessica was supportive while giving me the space to weigh all options—a true friend and professional. I could tell what they both thought: fight on. Even if it was to try to keep the government's feet close to the fire on Indigenous issues and criminal justice reform. And also on SNC-Lavalin—which they both, of course, knew all about. Even if I was being shuffled because of that issue, it would be harder for the PMO to do what they wanted if I was still in Cabinet and staring them in the face every day.

But I still had a problem. Even if I were to stay, I could not go to Indigenous Services. I called Gerry to tell him definitively that I would not be minister of ISC. He seemed very surprised and told me that I was making a "huge mistake," that it "would cost me personally and cost the government," that politics is a "team sport," and that we all have to work together to push for change. Gerry said, "You are out of Justice, those wheels are already in motion" and "We cannot have someone with no experience at Indigenous Services [a reference to Marc Miller]. We need our biggest players, Jody." Gerry was getting mad. Fair enough. I realized I was basically telling the prime minister I was not accepting his will. In an exasperated manner, Gerry said that he had "never experienced something like this before in all my years . . . unprecedented." To which I replied, "I am not trying to make history here, Gerry."

I acknowledge this was serious, and somewhat insubordinate given our parliamentary system. But it just was not possible. And honestly, I think Gerry was more concerned about another issue in all of this: the optics. I knew, and they certainly knew, that the "this whole shuffle was because Scott Brison resigned" line was not going to fly publicly. It did not make sense, and it was an insult to people's intelligence. They were moving multiple pieces on a checkerboard all at once, but the explanation they were offering really only required one or two moves to address. It didn't wash.

And then there were the specific optics around me. As I said earlier, I always knew there was an element of symbolic tokenism in my appointment, certainly for the politically minded folks. Moving me made that symbolism hard to uphold. Why were they moving Canada's first Indigenous MOJAG? What was the reason? There was another complication, too. The Wet'suwet'en protests were heating up in British Columbia; the issue was getting national attention. People were responding and starting to take action. Firing your Indigenous MOJAG in the midst of all of that could be a big blow. Putting me in Indigenous Services might help with their optics a bit. But that was not going to happen. What to do?

"So, what now? What are your plans?" Gerry asked.

"I have no plans—it is not up to me what now," I replied. At the end of the call, Gerry said he was going to have to go tell the prime minister. The way he said it felt like a question, like he was asking if I was sure I wanted him to tell the PM. I thought that was so strange. It was as if he believed I would be scared or upset that he was telling the prime minister about a decision I had made with clarity and without regret—a decision they had been told would be the case ever since they'd met me.

The next day I was put on the line with the prime minister. It was testy from the outset. I could tell immediately from his voice that he was not happy. Angry even. He said he understood the "Indian agent" thing. He said that he was acting against advice he had been given, which I understood to mean he was saying he had been advised to shuffle me out of Cabinet altogether. "Are you open to being veterans affairs minister?" he asked. I was confused, as this option had never come up before. Veterans Affairs? In that moment I did not know what to say and told him I would think about it. This irritated him immensely. He started shouting. I said, "I am open to it," but I also again mentioned how inexplicable this whole shuffle was. He shouted, "It's the situation Scott put us in," and pretty much hung up.

Lordy, Scott was causing so many people so much trouble! I am not sure Scott had ever been so powerful.

Are you tired of this yet? The back and forth does get tiresome, and it made me feel so uneasy. It was basically rounds of the same. I got sick of it; I am sure they did too. The bottom line is they were intent on moving me. I certainly did not want to move. I loved being MOJAG. But more than that I did not want them to get their way on SNC-Lavalin; I felt a profound duty to protect the integrity and independence of the prosecution. I decided not to resign from Cabinet and to accept the position at Veterans Affairs.

Serving our veterans and their families is a great honour for anyone. I felt this and knew it was an important portfolio, one that needed some close attention and assistance. There were important issues, including around court cases involving veterans' services, built around the underlying principle of how much we truly owe those who sacrificed so much for our safety and protection. There also was a need for government to reorganize how the ministry operates to better respect and serve our veterans. This is vitally important and needed work, and I would be proud to try to help with it.

At this point, though, some panic also set in. I wanted to ensure that my years as MOJAG meant all they could for change. Specifically for Indigenous peoples, I wanted to know that it was not all for nothing. I knew we had done so much, but the panic came from knowing how government works on the inside. There was still so much left to do, and I would no longer be pushing things forward as MOJAG. But I did have one last piece of work that was ready to go—the litigation directive regarding Indigenous rights. This work had been a long time coming; we'd been tweaking it for well over a year. I asked my department to get it out the door by making it public on the DOJ website. The deputy did this. I was thankful. She knew it was important for the work of reconciliation in Canada. It came out on my last weekday as minister—a Friday. It did not get much, if any, media attention at the time, and it still really has not to this day. But it is important. And I was very proud of this directive. I still am. I just hope that it is strongly implemented by government and used wisely by Indigenous peoples.

There were other flurries of activity in these last days as MOJAG. I released a year-in-review report. I wanted to make sure that there was a record of what had been accomplished. I also had to consider staffing matters—I knew this shuffle would affect many people. Specifically, I needed to confirm if Jessica was going to come with me to Veterans Affairs. And then there was the looming issue of optics. How would the shuffle be spun by the PM and his team, and what did it mean for me?

I knew what was going to happen. Explaining my shuffle would be a mess, and in the warped, dysfunctional political culture we have, the best move for some in the government would be to create a smear campaign against me. They would try to spin it to make it look like the shuffle had to do with me—my abilities and personality—even if they had to do so subtly and through innuendo. They had done this to other ministers. I had come to know these people and their tactics. I was already hearing the rumblings that were to come from those "unnamed sources" in the days ahead: I was difficult (bitchy, they meant). I was not up to the task (I was not a regular politician, they meant, or I was incompetent). I was not a team player (I was an independent Indian, they meant, not part of the old boys' club). Knowing all this, I needed to be prepared.

Of course, the government would never admit any of this. They shared with me their "lines" for the public and their plan. In response to my continued cautioning about what was happening, Gerry texted to reiterate what they were going to communicate: Because Scott had left, Jane was needed to step up at Treasury Board. It was going to be presented as everyone doing what was needed for the team, and since there were currently less-pressing matters at Justice than in other major ministries I was the one, among the senior ministers, to be moved. Sure. Whatever.

Given all of these factors—SNC-Lavalin, the incoherence of the shuffle, the growing blockades and Indigenous unrest, and the expected coming smears—I admit I made an unorthodox decision, one that fits my character but certainly not that of the traditions of a Cabinet minister. I decided that if the public smears started to come as I expected they would, I would explain my shuffle myself. I would release a statement reflecting on my three years as Canada's first Indigenous MOJAG. I began working on it right away.

My emotions on that long journey back to Vancouver from Indonesia were of sadness. Being MOJAG was such an incredible opportunity and responsibility. The loss of the opportunity to finish the work that had been started—including work that I, like other Indigenous leaders, was raised to do—was devastating. I was also saddened by the reality that politics is treated and played like a game by so many. A game with the ultimate goal of achieving victory— keeping power—and not addressing an important wrong or an injustice unless that is expedient. Could Cabinet really be shuffled to do a dirty deed, or cover one up, or shape a "team" for the next electoral cycle, but not to get important stuff done? It was clear that I did not really know the rules of this "game," and I had broken too many of them. Many of the players are simply trying to stay on the field. I did not know that scoring—doing the things that really mattered and had an impact on Canadians—ultimately did not count. What I did know is that it did not have to be this way.

As I flew back to Ottawa the next day, I continued to work on the statement that I would eventually release, though at the time I was not sure I would do so. Tim stayed in Vancouver, not wanting to be in Ottawa. I did not blame him. I did not want him to have to endure this reality by coming to Rideau Hall.

I arrived in Ottawa on the night of January 13—all tanned and, yes, jet-lagged—but prepared for the shuffle the next day and the swearing in at Rideau Hall. The only person, other than Jessica, I asked to be there for my swearing-in as minister of veterans affairs was Lea, who already knew what it was like to be unfairly ostracized and exiled by these people. When I arrived at the airport Jessica and another dear staff member were there to pick me up. Such sadness. They were trying to be positive, but I saw the tears in their eyes. I was trying to keep my shit together as we moved through the airport and waited for my bags. There was no way I was going to cry . . . not yet. But as we hugged they started to tear up, and I did too. Gawd, I would have liked my bags to have come more quickly that night.

The three of us drove to my Minister's Office at the DOJ on Wellington for what would be the last time. On the way we talked about SNC-Lavalin and how it was behind all of this. They were as certain of that as I was. My office had already been packed up by my staff. Another senior staff member came in, and there were some more tears. Nathalie, my deputy, also came by my office briefly one last time and handed me a one-page summary of all our biggest achievements. "I've thought a lot about what I want to say to you. It is this: great women are only appreciated the second time around," she kindly shared.

By this point, I was fine-tuning my draft statement with Jessica and the two other members of my staff and making plans for its posting the next day, if and when I requested. We also were making plans to tell the rest of the staff, who were still not aware of what was happening. Then we simply started sharing memories and appreciation of what we had done, and of each other. I shared how much I valued each of them—so much—and that all things would be okay. We hugged and said goodnight. I walked out of the DOJ and saw my coloured ministerial photo hanging on the wall, knowing that the next day it would be gone—replaced by a black-and-white version that would hang, instead, in the long row of former ministers of justice and attorneys general, as was the custom when a new minister came in.

Lea arrived at our condo shortly after I did and we talked much of the night away, while still tweaking the statement. We spoke to

Jane and Tim a few times as well. When I finally went to bed I sat there, lost in thought about so much and nothing all at once. The last memory I have is of thinking to myself, *Tomorrow will really suck. Big time*. I fell into a deep sleep.

•

The next morning I put on an outfit that reflected my pride in being Indigenous—a wrap given to me by Hereditary Chief Robert Joseph and his family. It was red and black, which are the Kwakwa̱ka̱'wakw colours. It has two wolves on the front and a moon on the back—wolves symbolizing strength, intelligence, and devotion (particularly to family) and the moon a protector or a guardian spirit that is associated with transformation. Kathy, my driver, dropped us off in front of Rideau Hall shortly before the Cabinet swearing-in was set to start. I got out and walked past the throngs of media, with Jessica and Lea, my amazing current and past chiefs of staff, following behind. I did not say anything to the media at that time. As we waited in the dining room at Rideau Hall to go into the ceremony, I saw the soon-to-be new minister of justice and attorney general, David Lametti. He appeared somewhat apprehensive to approach me, so I went up and congratulated him and then proceeded to offer my assistance in anything he needed. He was gracious and said that he would take me up on it. Then, purposefully, with Michael Wernick standing within earshot, I offered Lametti a warning: "Be careful, all is not what it seems." I looked directly at the clerk when I said it. Lametti replied, "Noted."

The ceremony took place and I was sworn in. When it came time to acknowledge the prime minister, I extended my hand. He reached out to kiss my cheeks as he had done some three years before. I was cold. I could not smile. Not for him. I knew I was supposed to, but I **could not**.

I met my new deputy—General Walter John "Walt" Natynczyk. I liked him immediately. He gave me the VAC pin, which I put on. I told him, genuinely, that I looked forward to working with him and for our veterans and their families, and that I would put everything I had into our success. I told him I had a few things I still had to do that day, a reference to the statement I was probably going to have to put out. I did ask him for any key messages that he would like me to relay to the media, which he gave me. I reassured him of my commitment, and told him that regardless of any media and spin that might come I would serve proudly, and that this file was incredibly important. I was sincere in this. I really did not want the attention that would inevitably swirl around me and the shuffle to affect the work at VAC, or the perceptions people had of my commitment to our country's veterans.

Soon it was my time to go outside to face the press. As expected, the smearing had kicked into high gear while I was being sworn in. I remember the exact words of the first question I was asked and the reporter who asked it. It was about whether I was disappointed about being "demoted." I replied, "No, and I would say that I can think of no world in which I would consider working for our veterans in Canada as a demotion."

The reporter then started digging into my competency: "We heard rumblings in the past few months that you might be shuffled because of a performance issue. If you had to do it again, is there anything that you would do differently?"

I responded sarcastically, and then laid out all that had been accomplished:

> *Well, I can't imagine where you have been hearing that. But in terms of the three-plus years that I spent as minister of justice and attorney general of Canada, I am incredibly proud of the work that I did, supported by an amazing minister's staff and by dedicated and hard-working public servants.*
>
> *We accomplished essentially my mandate letter, plus. I was very proud to introduce thirteen pieces of legislation ranging from issues, complex issues, of Medical Assistance in Dying*

to cannabis, to impaired driving to incredibly broad and bold reforms to the criminal justice system and family law, the latter two currently in the Senate. And I am very much looking forward to seeing the new minister shepherd these through to become law.

In addition to the legislative agenda, which was entirely robust, as I said, we have accomplished amazing things in renovating and renewing an open and transparent judicial appointments process.

I had the pleasure to appoint 250 judges to the superior courts, extraordinarily meritorious and diverse judges, and I had the pleasure to appoint more judges than any justice minister in the past two decades and create seventy-five new judicial positions.

The work that we've done beyond the legislative work has been very rewarding. I am confident in terms of releasing a directive on Indigenous litigation, as the previous minister, releasing principles about how as the attorney general I engaged in Charter litigation—has opened up the role of the attorney general and provided a window into how attorneys general make decisions, in particular around Charter and in particular Indigenous litigation.

So to close, I am incredibly proud of the work I have been able to do. We've been very successful in advancing justice in this country. I look forward to bringing the hard work, the only kind of work I know how to do, and my strong commitment to serving the veterans of this country.

And that was only the start. As the hours and days passed, the smears that had been fed to the media by the government came fast and furious. That same day, one reporter said this in a question posed to the prime minister: "[We have been] hearing for months now from people in your government saying that she has been underperforming, many Liberals in your government who were disappointed . . . " As CBC reported, "Several cabinet colleagues, political staffers and some public servants have told CBC News they found her difficult to deal with." And: "Some who spoke on background said she could be dismissive and quick to leap to confrontation when a more constructive approach to policy differences might have been employed." Indeed, "Her supporters said she wasn't hesitant to push back when she was confronted with policy she thought was wrong-headed. It is a personality trait she did not try to hide in her public statement."

The PMO, as was their style, played dumb when it came to the media and leaks, thinking they were playing smart. On January 19, I had a mid-afternoon text exchange with Gerry. He indicated that word was out with the media that I had been offered the job at ISC and had turned it down, and that he would be telling journalists that government would never go into details about a Cabinet conversation (though some of it would end up being revealed in testimony at the House of Commons Justice Committee during the SNC-Lavalin hearings). He indicated that what he said to media was that the PM had asked me to move to take on a vital role and that I had agreed to move for the good of the team. I told Gerry that no one around me would ever say a word about my being offered the job at ISC and that the leak was coming from somewhere else. Gerry said that he had let many reporters know that it was expected that someone may prefer MOJAG over Veterans Affairs, just as Jane would have preferred Health over ISC, but he added that we were both team players who would do what was needed when the unexpected happened. And he said that I would still be MOJAG if it weren't for Scott's decision to resign.

The confusion my shuffle caused, especially among Indigenous leaders and people, also started building at this time. Six prominent Indigenous experts wrote in the *Globe and Mail* of the "bizarre and incoherent removal of Jody Wilson-Raybould." "Her demotion from the vital portfolio has been accompanied by insider whispers, based on poisonous stereotypes that Indigenous peoples, and women in particular, face every day: that she was angry, difficult and uncompromising." They went on to say that "one finds reflections of many ugly notions that we're still confronting today: that Indigenous peoples are not as capable, or not as responsible for the achievements and success that they have. That somehow the marginalization of Indigenous peoples, and in particular, women, can be justified. And that Indigenous peoples somehow are not ready to lead and govern in today's world." Reflecting on what this says about the government's commitment to its most important relationship with Indigenous peoples, the experts stated: "By moving her from the high-profile role, the government is reinforcing that the comfortable status quo trumps the real work of reconciliation—that half-measures and rhetoric can suffice over real change. The racial and gender stereotypes being used to diminish her only prove that the status quo has already won, yet again. Mr. Trudeau's professed most important relationship remains one grounded in oppression, colonialism, and paternalism—and the events of the past few days demonstrate that."

The rolling out of these narratives made it all the more important to release the statement I had written. It reflected everything I believed, and still believe, about the unique role of the minister of justice and attorney general, the accomplishments we made as a government, and my hopes going forward as minister of veterans affairs. It also, more critically, included a veiled warning to the government, and to Canadians, that the rule of law was potentially in peril in Canada and abroad, and this was not a good thing. This was part of my continuing effort to keep warning the government on SNC-Lavalin.

There is a slippery slope. I firmly believed that once the basic norms of a democratic system and respect for the rule of law are violated from within a government it can contribute to our democratic norms and institutions starting to fail, like we see in other countries. I still believe that. When AGs are "yes men"—acting more as the leader's lawyer than the lawyer for Canadians—we are all in trouble. And in typical Canadian style, because of the structure of our parliamentary system and the centralization and conglomeration of power in our media, these episodes tend to play out here more in the dark than in the light. Which makes it even harder to fight against their corrosive impact. At least in part, I saw my statement as a way to shine a light on these concerns.

Statement from the Honourable Jody Wilson-Raybould, Minister of Veterans Affairs and Associate Minister of National Defence, and Member of Parliament for Vancouver Granville (January 14, 2019)

I have received many questions and inquiries about the Cabinet shuffle announced today and why I am no longer the Minister of Justice and Attorney General of Canada. Thank you for all the kind words. While I can understand the interest of Canadians in this matter, I will not be commenting. In our system, decisions regarding the appointment of Cabinet Ministers are the prerogative of the Prime Minister.

Moving forward, I am very proud to be the Minister of Veterans Affairs and Associate Minister of National Defence. Any opportunity to serve and support Canada's Veterans is a great honour, and I look forward to meeting with Veterans across the country, engaging with the crucial matters that must be addressed, and continuing our Government's progress to support and honour Canada's Veterans.

I do, however, on leaving the office of Minister of Justice and Attorney General of Canada (MOJAG), wish to share with Canadians some reflections about my time in that office.

Serving Canadians as MOJAG for the past three plus years has been one of the greatest privileges of my life. I was directed in my mandate letter to pursue and achieve a broad, progressive, and ambitious agenda and I am tremendously proud of our accomplishments. There is very little, if anything, in my mandate letter we have not done or is not well under way to completing, and we have also achieved much beyond it. I have attached an overview of these accomplishments to this statement. I thank my amazing Minister's office staff and the hardworking and dedicated public servants within the Department of Justice for their tireless work and for so ably supporting the advancement of our agenda. I also thank the residents of Vancouver Granville, and all Canadians who have been overwhelmingly kind, generous, and supportive as we worked together to help build an ever stronger and more just Canada. This work goes on, and I remain dedicated to it, whatever public or private roles I may play.

I firmly believe that as a result of our achievements, the state of the justice system in Canada is stronger and better positioned today than when our Government took office. Most importantly, the ongoing work of protecting the fundamental rights and freedoms of Canadians has advanced. As I have said before, the Minister of Justice and Attorney General of Canada is in many ways an ambassador for the Charter.

The Minister of Justice and Attorney General of Canada is somewhat distinct from other Cabinet Ministers because the role is a dual one. The Minister of Justice is the legal advisor to Cabinet. In this capacity, the Minister is concerned with the administration of justice, including policy in the areas of criminal law, family law, human rights law, and Indigenous justice. The role of the Attorney General of Canada carries with it unique responsibilities to uphold the rule of law and the administration of justice, and as such demands a measure of principled independence. It is a pillar of our democracy that our system of justice be free from even the perception of political interference and uphold the highest levels of public confidence. As such, it has always been my view that the Attorney General of Canada must be non-partisan, more transparent *in the principles that are the basis of decisions, and, in this respect, always willing to speak truth to power. This is how I served throughout my tenure in that role.*

At a time when the functioning of democracies around the globe is increasingly under strain, and democratic norms are in peril, the unique and independent aspects of the dual role of the Minister of Justice and Attorney General of Canada are even more important. I know Canadians across the country expect such high standards to continue to be met—especially in the uncertain times in which we now live—and I expect this to continue.

With respect to Indigenous issues, as MOJAG, I have publicly expressed my opinions in various venues about the ongoing challenges in transforming what the Prime Minister has stated is the "most important" relationship, that between Canada and Indigenous peoples. One of my main motivations for seeking public office was to see the work of reconciliation accelerate and advance in real and tangible ways.

The work that must be done is well known. We have the solutions. Indigenous peoples have advocated and brought forward what must be done for decades. Countless Commissions, studies, reports, and analyses have reiterated the work we must do together to reconcile.

The foundation for moving forward is understanding that the dire social and economic realities that Indigenous peoples continue to face—including lack of clean drinking water, over representation in the criminal justice system, inadequate housing, high rates of poverty, and violence against Indigenous women and girls—are directly linked to legislative and policy regimes that have disempowered and divided Indigenous peoples, eroded their systems of governance, laws, and responsibilities, harmed their economies, and denied their basic rights and systems. Long overdue legislative and policy changes based

*on the recognition of title and rights, including historic treaties,
are urgently needed, so that Indigenous peoples can accelerate
and lead the work of re-building their Nations and governments, and a new climate of co-operative relations can emerge.*

*While our government has taken some very important steps,
and hard work is being done, the necessary shifts have not yet
been fully achieved. Rather, a number of the proposals that our
government has been pursuing so far require substantial work in
co-operation and collaboration with Indigenous peoples to reset
the new foundations for this most important relationship.*

*As a Member of Cabinet, I will continue to be directly
engaged in advocating for and advancing the fundamental
shifts in relations with Indigenous peoples that are required
and will continue to work with my colleagues and to ensure
my voice is heard.*

*Again, I express my deepest gratitude to the residents of
Vancouver Granville, and all Canadians, who have shown me
such kindness, patience, and support over the past three plus
years, and I am excited to continue to build a better Canada
alongside you in the days and months ahead as the Minister of
Veterans Affairs and Associate Minister of National Defence.*

Gilakas'la,
Jody Wilson-Raybould, P.C., Q.C., M.P.
Minister of Veterans Affairs and
Associate Minister of National Defence
Member of Parliament for Vancouver Granville

◆

There are four people who have most shaped who I am today. Three
of them are women: my grandmother, my mother, and my sister.
Like me, I do not think any of these remarkable women would ever

label themselves a feminist or a fighter for women's rights. It was not part of our way of talking or processing reality. Yes, we have had profoundly important and distinct experiences that are a result of being women. These include forms of inequality and discrimination.

But our way of talking and thinking, instilled by my grandmother, was always steeped in the recognition of the roles and responsibilities that women must play in our culture and for humanity as a whole. Balance is central to how I am taught to understand reality. Balance within ourselves. Balance between nature and human beings. Balance between the spiritual and the physical. Balance between young and old. Balance between all people, including between men and women.

Balance means that there are inextricable connections between things. To maintain balance we each have to do certain things and be supported to do those things. Our value resides in playing our roles and contributing to that balance. In life, our work and purpose is to restore that balance where things have become lopsided, and to nurture it and strengthen it where it does exist.

The necessary balance between men and women needs restoration if humanity is going to flourish. When this balance is not there, humanity is like a bird with a broken wing.

Generations upon generations of people—women and men—have worked and are working on this restoration. Ultimately, this work requires significant shifts in mindsets, understandings, behaviours, ways of relating, and laws and structures.

I think this is why I responded as I often did to the sexism around me in government, including in the aftermath of the shuffle. I perceived my own experience of being marginalized within government, and being smeared in ways that only women are, as part of the evidence supporting the existence of this lack of balance. I felt that pushing back on these realities was part of restoring that balance. I would show them. I would prove them wrong. I would walk on through. And when I called it out, it would be part of a broader effort to educate and build understanding. That was part of our method of restoring balance.

My experience of being a woman in government was in some ways different from my experience of being Indigenous and the racism and paternalism that was one part of it. Central to my teachings is the idea that we are all human and all part of an interconnected human reality. It is a fact of history that humanity has divided itself, often violently and oppressively, on racial lines. Addressing racism is a necessary part of building conditions of justice that will allow humanity to once again recognize the ways in which it is fundamentally interconnected and interdependent. This is, I think, why I have dedicated much of my life to Indigenous rights, to overcoming this injustice, to calling out the violation of those rights.

It is also why I responded as I did to the racism I experienced throughout my time in government. It infuriated me, though I think the smears that came after I was shuffled were more typical of being a woman than being Indigenous. It also hurt me. How blind they were to their own paternalism, to how much they embodied a colonial mindset. The constant attitude within government was that Indigenous peoples—not only me, but Indigenous peoples generally—did not know what they need or what needed to be done. There was a constant insistence and insinuation that they knew best, and knew better, what Indigenous peoples need. I found this to be the attitude of some of my colleagues in government. I also found it to be the case for some parts of the public service. Of course, it had always been this way. This is at the heart of colonialism: We know better. Trust us. We do.

In the aftermath of the shuffle, it was the fact that racist tropes would be trotted out, without a recognition of the racism, that really upset me. For example, there were cartoons of me bound and gagged with the prime minister being egged on to beat me, which is completely inappropriate given the reality of MMIWG; another had me knocked out by the prime minister in a boxing ring; there was also one of me dressed like an Indigenous person wearing stereotypical "buckskin" clothes and feathers in my hair. Together, they showed me how far we still had to go as a country. That I truly was the "Indian" in the Cabinet. Separate. Apart. Different. And expendable, when not playing their game in their way. As Indigenous peoples have always been treated by governments in this country.

But here is one thing about the sexist, racist tropes that were trotted out against me: they didn't accomplish much. In fact, I think they backfired. Far more people called out these pernicious acts than engaged in them. Those who knew me spoke out—Indigenous leaders and those who had worked with me; staff; and others. But there were also so many I had never met who were just not having it. This included a lot of the media, who didn't buy the incompetence narrative that started the second I was shuffled. In fact, some in the media even apologized for their early reporting, and they deserve credit for this.

So as I was grappling with real concerns about why the shuffle had happened, and with the terrible things that were being said, I was also reminded of how much progress we have made as a country. While the smears upset and hurt me, the overwhelmingly positive responses to them buoyed me. I am proud to be Canadian, and I was again shown why Canada continues to get stronger. I was also reminded of the importance of the sacrifices that so many have made, and continue to make, to build greater equality, inclusion, and justice. As had been the case so many times over my years as minister, it was Canadians who picked me up and made me feel able to keep going on.

EIGHT

SNC

I am writing this on January 6, 2021. On the television in the background are images of a mob storming the United States Capitol. It is violent, and deeply frightening and upsetting.

Am I surprised? Not completely. In the United States, partisanship and division are heightened in the extreme, fuelled by a political culture of blind loyalty, rampant self-interest by those who lead, and a comfort with lying. It has been a politics filled increasingly with actual and deliberate disinformation, rather than a case of being economical with the truth or ignoring the facts.

It is late at night, and as the effort to certify the election of President-elect Biden reconvenes, members of Congress are making statements condemning the events of the day: "We gather due to a selfish man's injured pride and the outrage of supporters who he had deliberately misinformed for the past two months and stirred to action this very morning," states Senator Mitt Romney. Gulp. "Selfish." "Injured pride.""Outrage of supporters.""Misinformed." These words hit close to home. They are words that resonate and speak to me when I reflect on the dynamics of the SNC-Lavalin affair and how it all played out and is still playing out. They describe aspects of Canada's political reality and culture as well.

Now, please do not get me wrong. Our democracy, along with the institutions that support it, is very different than for our southern neighbours, and the decline is nowhere near so precipitous. As we Canadians love to tell ourselves, "We are not the United States." But this does not mean we do not have some of the same unhealthy dynamics in our politics or issues with our institutions when it comes to supporting and ensuring good governance. We do. They are often more subtle here than in the United States, and are often countered by different, sometimes healthier aspects of our particular society. Also, the dynamics tend to play themselves out beyond the public eye, usually at the very centre of power. SNC-Lavalin is a prime example and a warning to us all.

The story of the SNC-Lavalin affair, like many of the south-of-the-border stories we decry, is one of partisanship and power-seeking over principle. It is a story that highlights a lack of concern with the basic democratic norms that are the bedrock of our system of government; selfishness and injured pride; and the perils of not being straight and simply speaking the truth to Canadians.

For me, it is a depressing story. Certainly, it is a story I do not like, wish I never had to tell, and wish had never happened. But I know I have to tell it.

In continuing to tell this story, I will not take you through events moment by moment or even day by day. A great deal has been seen on television and written in the media—much of it excellent and for the most part very accurate. Goodness, my public testimony before the House of Commons Justice Committee went into great factual detail and lasted for approximately three and a half hours, providing a blow-by-blow account. This was followed by additional written testimony that included an audiotape of a phone call between me and the clerk of the Privy Council.

There is also the "Trudeau II Report," which includes the findings of Conflict of Interest and Ethics Commissioner Mario Dion. This report provided additional substantiating evidence, as it concluded the prime minister contravened the Conflict of Interest Act by using his position of authority over me to seek to influence, both directly and indirectly, my decision on whether to overrule the director of public prosecutions' decision not to invite SNC-Lavalin to enter into negotiations towards a deferred prosecution agreement. Dion tells us, though, that his office was unable to fully discharge all of its duties because of decisions to deny his office further access to Cabinet confidences. He was critical of not being able to access all the information and fully examine witnesses. I agree. At the time of writing this book, the RCMP were continuing to examine this matter carefully with all available information.

We may never know the entire backstory to the SNC-Lavalin affair, what people's full motivations or roles or relationships were. But that is not my focus here. At the time my office was dealing with the "pressure" to defer the prosecution of the company, my staff and I were not privy to all that the power brokers in Ottawa were doing around us. We still do not know. I will leave that to others to figure out, if they can or have any desire to do so. At the end of the day, the gory details about and nefarious goings-on of the power elites are immaterial to how I discharged my responsibilities as Canada's attorney general. There were broader principles at stake with respect to the independence of the attorney general, irrespective of the motivation or attempted justification for people's actions, and regardless of how bad those actions may have been.

What I will do, though, is walk you through the time between September 2018 and April 2, 2019, the date when I was kicked out of the Liberal caucus, along with Jane Philpott, by the prime minister. I will reflect on some of the key moments, share what I was feeling and experiencing, and explain why I did what I did and when. And why I have no regrets.

I will also share why, today, nothing motivates me more to keep speaking out and pushing for change to our politics than what happened over those months—what I learned and what, collectively, we can do about it. The events and lessons of those months motivate me because they reveal the worst and most dangerous aspects of how we are governed. They show that if we do not keep vigilant and constantly work at our democracy, making changes to our laws and institutions when necessary, our ability to proclaim how different we are from our southern neighbours will keep shrinking. And, even then—even when we have the institutionalized checks and balances in place—personal integrity matters. Integrity based on some deeper value system beyond representative and partisan "politics." Call it cultural, spiritual, or religious. For me, it is the teachings of our Big House. My experience with SNC-Lavalin brought those teachings into greater focus for me as an Indigenous Canadian.

◆

Here is the Coles Notes version of what happened.

SNC-Lavalin, based in Montreal, is a large Canadian company that provides extensive engineering, procurement, and construction services around the world. In February 2015, the company was charged with fraud and bribery based on work it had done in Libya. Their prosecution was one of the largest corruption cases in Canadian history.

In 2017, the government began working on an amendment to the Criminal Code that would allow for a "deferred prosecution agreement" (also known as a "remediation agreement" regime), which provides prosecutors an additional tool with which to hold corporate offenders to account. A DPA is a voluntary agreement negotiated between an accused and the prosecution under which criminal prosecution is suspended for a period of time. During this period, the accused must comply with the terms of the agreement. If the accused complies, the charges are withdrawn when the DPA expires and no criminal prosecution is pursued. If there is non-compliance, charges may be revived at any point during the DPA and a prosecution may be pursued and a conviction sought.

The DPA law was passed in June 2018 and came into force on September 19, 2018. In early September, I received a "Section 13" notice under the Director of Public Prosecutions Act from the director of public prosecutions. It stated that she would not be offering an invitation to SNC-Lavalin to negotiate a DPA. After undertaking my own due diligence inquiry and considering all of the circumstances, including the explanation given by the director, I determined that my intervention was neither necessary nor appropriate. Section 13 provides that the director has a duty "to inform the Attorney General in a timely manner of any prosecution, or intervention that the Director intends to make, that raises important questions of general interest." This duty arises from the relationship between the attorney general and the DPP, since the attorney general may rely upon information provided and take such course of action as they deem appropriate. Such action can extend to issuing a directive to the director with respect to the initiation or conduct of any specific prosecution, or to assuming conduct of a prosecution, both after having consulted with the DPP and publishing intent in the *Canada Gazette*.

Between September and December 2018, efforts aimed at "pressuring" me to give SNC-Lavalin a DPA began. This started in earnest during a meeting with the prime minister on September 17, 2018, described earlier in this book. As noted, I had asked to meet the prime minister to discuss Indigenous matters, but he immediately focused the meeting on SNC-Lavalin. These efforts to pressure me— either directly or through Jessica—continued. Eventually, eleven officials from the PMO, the Privy Council Office, and the Office of the Minister of Finance made attempts. Over that four-month period there were approximately ten phone calls and ten meetings about SNC-Lavalin, culminating in a phone call I had with the clerk of the Privy Council on December 19, 2018. That was the call that I audio-taped. During that call, Michael Wernick said, among other things: " . . . it is not a good idea for the Prime Minister and his Attorney General to be at loggerheads . . ." and "I am worried about a collision then because he [the Prime Minister] is pretty firm about this . . . I just saw him a few hours ago and this is really important to him." Within a few weeks I was shuffled out as MOJAG.

Why did I refuse these attempts to ensure that SNC-Lavalin would be offered a DPA? Simple. Because it was wrong and an affront to the rule of law and prosecutorial independence. And while they tried to pressure me, I did not feel pressured. I was simply doing my job of ensuring the law was followed, and trying to ensure the government did not engage in wrongdoing.

In the end, after much public drama, testimony, and the failure of a political system to get the whole truth before Canadians, things came to a head. Along with Jane, I was kicked out of the Liberal caucus by the prime minister on April 2, 2019. He also told each of us that we were no longer the confirmed Liberal candidates in our ridings for the upcoming federal election. Our expulsion was shown on television, accompanied by a cowardly display of cheering Liberal MPs. Perhaps even more cowardly was that the powers that be did not allow MPs to vote on our expulsion, which they were required to do by the Reform Act.

Ultimately, in December 2019, many months after the public became aware of the SNC-Lavalin affair, the company pled guilty to a single count of fraud, which required it to pay a fine of $280 million.

And that is it. The rule of law in Canada was frayed. The Liberal Party damaged itself. The prime minister revealed some of his lesser qualities and character. Doing politics differently was a sham, an empty slogan. Our system of government was brought into disrepute.

Some folks lost their jobs or quit. And my five-year journey as a Trudeau Liberal was, thankfully, finally over.

◆

Throughout those months when the prime minister and those around him were attempting to pressure me, there was never any question of what I was going to do. I knew what my job was as attorney general, and I knew what was right. I always felt grounded, and I know where that came from. It has to do with aspects of my upbringing.

What did build up in me over those months was an exasperation at their continued efforts, and their whole approach in trying to pressure me. No meant no. I may never have accepted "no" from the PM and his staff on Indigenous issues or MMPs, and in that context have been labelled "difficult" (and not because I was a woman), but this was different. This was not a matter of policy disagreement or advocacy but rather a matter of law; it was about acting in my capacity as the chief law officer of the Crown, responsible for conducting all litigation for the federal government and for upholding the Constitution, the rule of law, and respect for the independence of the courts.

What really irked me was the casual persistence of their actions and how that followed the dynamics of much of my time in government. They would be passive-aggressive at times, until they snapped and you saw their real colours. Of course, the prime minister directly indicated what he wanted to happen during our meeting on September 17. But after that he left it to others. Months later, the ethics commissioner would see right through this story to what I and others already knew. This all followed the Trudeau government's pattern: access to the prime minister controlled by Gerry Butts and Katie Telford, and a structure of power where the prime minister—whether as part of a clear plan of his or designed by others (I still am not entirely sure)— appeared to maintain distance from and deniability on certain issues.

On SNC-Lavalin, as with so many other things, it was the PMO trying to be the government by controlling ministers and what they do. They did this directly by trying to tell me what to do, and indirectly by instructing Jessica to control me. For example, Jessica was summoned to meet with Gerry and Katie on December 18, 2018. They wanted to know where I was at on "finding a solution." Gerry said, "There is no solution here that doesn't involve some interference." Katie said, "We don't want to debate legalities anymore. If Jody is nervous, we would of course line up all kinds of people to write op-eds saying what she is doing is proper." The meeting was tense, upsetting, and intimidating.

As I said earlier, the only difference between the events around SNC-Lavalin and the efforts to control me and other ministers that I recounted in previous chapters of this book is that the former was about messing with a criminal prosecution. This is a fundamental difference. The very act crossed a line, even raising questions in some minds about potential criminality. This is not just about a policy choice that may or may not be made. This is about the rule of law and the norms and core principles of our democratic system. So my approach to it was, of course, different. I was the attorney general, for fuck's sake. I knew from the outset that even the conversations that were happening were dangerous and wrong, and that we should not be discussing the matter casually or loosely. I took measures accordingly.

What did I do? Having decided that I was not going to interfere with the prosecutor's decision, I then used every conversation that came up about this matter to issue a warning to those raising it that this was not appropriate. And I continued my usual practice of making contemporaneous notes. The content of these notes was revealed in great detail during my testimony before the Justice Committee. I also instructed Jessica to keep a comprehensive record and notes— on every conversation, email, and text that related to SNC-Lavalin. And she did.

And then, of course, there was the December 19, 2018, telephone meeting with Michael Wernick that I recorded. This is a decision I would never go back and change. I would do it again one hundred times out of one hundred. A few days before sitting down to write the first draft of this chapter I was watching reports about the audio-recorded call between Georgia secretary of state Brad Raffensperger and President Donald Trump as Trump was pressuring him to "find" 11,780 votes for him in the 2020 presidential election. As one reporter commented about the call, "If you think someone is trying to involve you in a crime and may lie about it later, it may be a good idea to record that person to avoid any dispute about precisely what was said. Assuming the law in your state permits it . . ." Hmm. Interesting analogy to my own thought process, in which I felt there may have been attempts to draw me into ethical violations, and that some people might not be truthful or straightforward in the future about what happened.

Let me add a bit more, if that was not blunt enough. I needed the "receipts," the "insurance" of a recording. I was the attorney general, and the political actions and reality unfolding around this issue and others—and around me—at this time were a nightmare. I did not trust these people. Their actions were extraordinary, and not in a good way. They were trying to do something that crossed the line, and they'd been trying it for months. It had been building up. I was fed up, and also worried. They did not stop and would not stop. It was also undoubtedly clear, by this point, that I would not bend. And yet they kept coming. And coming. I was increasingly afraid they were going to do something drastic to get their way. Getting rid of me as MOJAG was one obvious option. I wanted clear evidence of what they had been doing. If they did get their way and issue a DPA, at least there would be some incontrovertible evidence that Canadians could see as to what had transpired. I had no way of knowing the phone call with Wernick would be the last one before the shuffle calls, but it was clear the breaking point on this issue was being reached.

There was another dimension to consider as well. A pattern had developed within government of the PMO looking to deflect blame from itself when issues came up that hurt the government. The "blame game." This was the source of their continued insistence that I was not being staffed well and that our people did not know what they were doing. Thank God they *did* know what they were doing; if they hadn't, we never would have accomplished all we actually did on the policy front, and I may not have weathered the storm as well on SNC-Lavalin. As a leader, you are only as strong as those around you.

I made the decision to record the call that same day it was scheduled, not long before it took place. I had contemplated recording calls before, and had mentioned this to Jessica, but had never done so. I had no idea what Michael would say and had no real way to prepare in advance. I just had a premonition that it was going to be unpleasant and bad.

I was sitting in our condo in Vancouver when the clerk and I spoke. And yes, it was unpleasant and bad.

MICHAEL: *Hello.*

JWR: *Hello, Michael, it is Jody.*

M: *Hi, sorry about the phone tag.*

JWR: *That's okay.*

M: *Um . . . I am not calling you about the litigation directive. I am calling about the other unpleasant one—the deferred prosecution agreement thing and SNC and so on—I wanted to pass on where the PM is at . . . so our intelligence from various sources is that the company is getting to a very serious point now . . . the board has asked consulting firms for options* *for the board for their next meeting which could be selling out to somebody else, moving . . . you know, various things.*

JWR: *Yep.*

M: *So, and it seems to be real and not a bluff. Um, so there is another rising anxiety as you can imagine about a signature firm and job loss and all that coming after the Oshawa thing and what's going on in Calgary and what not. So, the PM wants to be able to say that he has tried everything he can within a legitimate toolbox to try to head that off. So, he is quite determined, quite firm, but he wants to know why the DPA route which Parliament provided for isn't being used. And I think he is gonna find a way to get it done one way or another. So, he is in that kinda mood and I wanted you to be aware of that.*

JWR: *Okay.*

M: *So, um, I don't know if he is going to call you directly—he might—um and he is willing—I think he is thinking about getting somebody else to give him some advice . . . you know he does not want to do anything outside the box of what is legal or proper—um . . . but his understanding is—you know—the DPA tool is there and you have options that we talked about before to ask for reasoning from the DPP or even take over the prosecution. He just wants to understand more at this point why the DPA route isn't being taken up in this route. So, he is thinking about bringing in somebody like Bev McLachlin to give him advice on this or to give you advice if you want to feel more comfortable that you are not doing anything that's inappropriate or outside the frame of . . .*

JWR: *I am 100 percent confident that I am doing nothing inappropriate.*

M: *Yeah, no, but would not be if you decided to use some of these tools under the law . . . um cause I think he feels that the government has to have done everything it can before we lose nine thousand jobs . . . and a signature Canadian firm.*

JWR: *Right so—um—I again am confident in where I am at and my views on SNC and the DPA haven't changed—this is a constitutional principle of prosecutorial independence that, Michael—I have to say including this conversation, previous conversations that I have had with prime minister and many other people around it—it is entirely inappropriate and it is political interference. And I . . . the prime minister obviously can talk to whomever he wants—but what I am trying to do is to protect him. I can have a conversation with Beverley McLachlin . . . I can call her right now . . . um . . . I am just—um—issuing the strongest warning I can possibly issue that decisions that are made by the independent prosecutor are their decisions. We gave her, and them, the tools—the additional tools—I made it very clear at the Cabinet table and other places that these tools are the discretion of the prosecutor—and everybody agreed to that and there was no guarantee that there would be a DPA in this or any other case. So, we are treading on dangerous ground here—and I am going to issue my stern warning—um—because I can't act in a manner and the prosecution can't act in a manner that is not objective, that isn't independent, I can't act in a partisan way and I can't be politically motivated. All of this screams of that. So, I am actually uncomfortable having this conversation, but I am happy to talk to you. I'll call Beverley McLachlin . . .*

I cannot even imagine her feeling in any way, shape, or form comfortable interfering with the independent prosecutor.

M: *Okay, but I think that is where people are talking past each other. I mean I think the view that he's formed—which I think I share—I am not the lawyer in any of these conversations— and Elder [Marques, senior advisor, PMO] and others is— um—it's not interference—the statute specifically has these other provisions in it that allow you to ask questions of the DPP and that is provided for and that is not interference . . .*

JWR: *But I would have to issue a directive, I would have to gazette this . . .*

M: *Yes.*

JWR: *The prosecutor—the director—whom I know and understand after having several conversations with her about another directive on HIV that I issued—she is a by-the-book person. If this is gazetted—this will be—and I hear you on the jobs and wanting to save jobs—I mean, we all want to do that—this goes far beyond saving jobs—this is about the integrity of the prime minister and interference—there is no way that anybody would interpret this other than interference—if I was to step in. It does not matter how I would look in doing that—I would be a mockery—and that is not the problem— the bigger problem is what it would look like down the road for the government. It is not about jobs—and I know that jobs are important, so I do not want anybody to misinterpret that I don't care about those jobs—this is about the integrity of the government and recognizing that there is the ability to issue a directive under the act . . . um . . . it is still irrespective of the ability that I have to do that—One, it has never been done* *before, but two, this is going to look like nothing but political interference by the prime minister, by you, by everybody else that has been involved in this politically pressuring me to do this.*

M: *Well . . . um . . .*

JWR: *I actually really feel uncomfortable having this conversation because it is wrong, and I hear the prime minister obviously can call me . . . like I said to you I will have a conversation . . . I am going to call Beverley McLachlin and have a conversation with her about this.*

M: *Well . . . of course it has not been done before because Parliament only created the instrument barely a year ago . . .*

JWR: *No no no . . . this instrument was . . . you mean the directive—the directive on a specific prosecution has never occurred . . . And this happened . . . cause Harper brought this law in, as you probably know, ten years ago. The directive—or the DPA has never been used because it just entered the Criminal Code back in September, so I understand that this is the first case. The prosecutor sent me what is called a section 13—you told me that you hadn't seen it before—but I read it and I have reread it—and the Prime Minister's Office has a copy of it. She explains in it why she is not doing it in this case—we have to, I have to be—unless it is something outrageous—comfortable with the decision—recognizing it is the first one likely and obviously I am confident wasn't entered into lightly—made the decision not to enter into a DPA with respect to this case. And she explained why.*

M: *So, when did she convey that to you?*

JWR: *She issued the section 13 back in September when I was down in Australia for that. . . . Five Eyes—and then all this transpired . . . I mean, I have a timeline of every single conversation and everything that everybody has said to me on this so . . . um . . . So, like . . . anyway . . . again—I am surprised that you and I are having this conversation, but I am just saying that I really feel uncomfortable about the appropriateness of this conversation.*

M: *Okay, I understand that—but I mean, I think his view is that he is not asking you to do anything inappropriate or to interfere. He is asking you to use all the tools that you lawfully have at your disposal . . . um.*

JWR: *I know I have a tool under the Prosecution Act that I can use. I do not believe it is appropriate to use it in this case.*

M: *Okay, alright . . . that is clear—um—well he's in a very firm mood about this so um . . .*

JWR: *Does he understand the gravity of what this potentially could mean—this is not about saving jobs—this is about interfering with one of our fundamental institutions—this is like breaching a constitutional principle of prosecutorial independence.*

M: *Well, I don't think he sees it as that . . .*

JWR: *No one is explaining that to him, Michael. Like this is . . . we can stand up in the House of Commons on [Vice-Admiral] Norman on—totally appropriately on Norman—on extradition and we can talk about the rule of law—um . . . . The cases aren't dissimilar—the principle or the integrity of how* *we act and respond to the tools we have available and what we should and shouldn't do—again . . . I just . . . I don't know . . .*

M: *Okay, then I am—I respect where you are coming from . . . I just think . . .*

JWR: *You know what—I hope that you do because I do not think anybody respects this . . . The conversation that Gerry and Katie had with my chief of staff, and I have it—like she wrote down what they said—saying that they don't want to hear any more about the legalities—but want to talk about jobs . . . entirely inappropriate.*

M: *Okay, well, I was not . . .*

JWR: *Okay, I have it . . . I have it all.*

M: *Okay, but you are not just the attorney general, you are the minister of justice in a Cabinet and . . . you have context within which you exercise your roles and responsibilities . . . I am not seeing anything inappropriate here but . . . um . . . I mean . . . you are right . . . and the PM . . . people are talking past each other . . . I think the way he sees it and the advice he is getting is that you still have things you can do that are not interference and are still very much lawful so . . .*

JWR: *It is not that they are not lawful . . . the perception and what will happen is that it will be deemed political interference from day one when people were talking about why we are entering into a or putting in a DPA regime in place . . . Everybody knows that it was because of SNC. Whether that is true or not that is what people will think.*

M: *It is a tool used in lots of other countries though . . .*

JWR: *Fair.*

M: *. . . for these kinds of purposes and especially if there has been a change of ownership or management of the company that is being prosecuted . . . it is a public policy tool.*

JWR: *Fair, but in our MCs [memorandums to Cabinet] all the way up and in the law that we changed we gave the director of public prosecutions the discretion to enter into the DPAs and a judge to oversee the regime. There is no guarantee in any particular case—this one or the ones that will come—that they'll enter into the DPAs or think it is appropriate to do so. And that's what we consciously made the decision on when we decided as a Cabinet to enter into this process and I amending the law.*

M: *Is there anybody that can talk to Kathleen [Roussel, director of public prosecutions] then about the context around this or to get her to explain why she is not . . . or I guess the company has talked to her directly . . .*

JWR: *The company has . . . but Michael, there was a preliminary inquiry—I am still trying to get an update on what happened at the preliminary inquiry. Like the suggestion that I made ages ago, which Gerry talked to you about in Montreal was . . . nobody from the company ever contacted me or sent me a letter expressing concern—had that happened I would have done what I believed to have been appropriate, would have been to forward that letter on to the director of public prosecutions.*

M: *I think they have made direct representations to the prosecutor though . . . and they tried to make the public interest argument and so on and so on. But they gave the impression that they are not being listened to so . . .*

JWR: *Yeah . . .*

M: *Alright . . . um . . . well, I am going to have to report back before he leaves . . . he is in a pretty firm frame of mind about this though so . . . I am a bit worried . . .*

JWR: *Bit worried about what?*

M: *Well . . . it is not a good idea for the prime minister and his attorney general to be at loggerheads.*

JWR: *Well, I feel that I am giving him my best advice, and if he doesn't accept that advice then it is his prerogative to do what he wants . . . But I am trying to protect the prime minister from political interference or . . . perceived or otherwise.*

M: *Alright, I understand that . . . but he does not have the power to do what he wants . . . all the tools are in your hands so . . .*

JWR: *. . . Okay, so then . . . I am having thoughts of the Saturday Night Massacre here, Michael, to be honest with you, and this is not a great place for me to be in—I do not relish this place—but what I am confident of is that I have given the prime minister my best advice to protect him and to protect the constitutional principle of prosecutorial independence.*

M: *Okay . . . alright but . . . I am worried about a collision then because he is pretty firm about this . . . I just saw him a* *few hours ago and this is really important to him ... Okay ... um ... there is not much more we can cover for now then ... um ... I understand where you are coming from ... Um ... sorry ... The section 13 argument or response from Kathleen ... you're saying Elder has that or had a version of that?*

JWR: *The Prime Minister's Office has had it since September, since I have had it.*

M: *Since September ... okay, that is important. That is new to me so ... okay. Alright ... um ...*

JWR: *They'll tell you that they have not received a copy of it ... Elder and Mathieu [Bouchard, senior advisor, PMO] said it to me when they came to my office ... um ... but we have documented evidence in terms of emails et cetera where that has been provided ... so they do have it ... maybe they have misplaced it. I can send it back over to them, but I know that Jessica asked the other day when she was over at the PMO's office ...*

M: *And what did they tell her ... that they didn't have it or that they never seen it ... ?*

JWR: *I have to ask and I will tell you exactly what they said. I will have to ask her.*

M: *I think ... well ... My advice is that Jessica should send it to Elder then just to make it "triply" sure they have it.*

JWR: *Okay, I will get her to do that right now.*

M: *Alright, thanks for calling me.*

JWR: *Thanks.*

M: *Thanks for calling back so quickly.*

JWR: *No problem.*

M: *Okay, he is still around tomorrow so . . . (inaudible)*

JWR: *I am waiting for the big . . . the other shoe to drop . . . so I am not under any illusion how the prime minister has and gets things that he wants . . . I am just stuck doing the best job that I can . . .*

M: *Okay, alright. Will talk again.*

JWR: *Thanks. Bye.*

Between that December 18, 2018, phone call and February 11, 2019, when I flew back to Ottawa after telling the prime minister I was going to resign from Cabinet, a great deal had happened. I had been shuffled from being MOJAG, for one. I'd also become the subject of a media firestorm after the *Globe and Mail* story about what would become known as the "SNC-Lavalin affair" broke on February 7. I had no idea how things were going to unfold next.

What I knew for sure was that I had to do two things immediately. First, I had to talk with Jessica to let her know what was happening and to ensure our staff was taken care of as best we could. As political staff, you serve "at the pleasure," which means when the minister is gone so, too, are you. Second, I had to write and release a resignation letter, something of a follow-up to the "demotion" statement I'd released on the day of the swearing-in. Beyond that, I really had no idea what would happen next. There was no "playbook" for this.

I was certain I would need to speak publicly at some point, but I knew I was constrained from doing so by solicitor-client privilege and Cabinet confidentiality. I had already hired Judge Thomas Cromwell, a former Supreme Court of Canada justice, to provide legal advice on what I could and could not say. I did not know what the prime minister and his office would do next. I was not sure if the story would keep growing or peter out. I did expect it would be chaotic. Did I ever imagine it would unfold quite as it did? Never.

The resignation letter was done on the fly. The first draft was actually tapped out by text message; a draft was then worked over and refined—discussed with Tim, Jane and Jessica—but all in the course of a few hours. Every word was specific and purposeful.

February 12, 2019

Dear Prime Minister,

With a heavy heart, I am writing to tender my resignation as the Minister of Veterans Affairs and Associate Minister of National Defence.

I want to thank all Canadians, and in particular the residents of Vancouver-Granville, who put their trust in me and supported me as the Minister of Justice and Attorney General of Canada, and as the Minister of Veterans Affairs and Associate Minister of National Defence. When I sought federal elected office, it was with the goal of implementing a positive and progressive vision of change on behalf of all Canadians and a different way of doing politics. My resignation as a Minister of the Crown in no way changes my commitment to seeing that fundamental change achieved. This work must and will carry on.

To Canada's Veterans and their families: I have the deepest admiration and respect for you. This decision is in no way a reflection of my desire to see your service and sacrifice upheld and honoured. I only wish that I could have served you longer.

To my officials and ministerial staff: thank you for your hard work in the service of all Canadians. I am truly grateful for all that you have done and will continue to do.

I am aware that many Canadians wish for me to speak on matters that have been in the media over the last week. I am in the process of obtaining advice on the topics that I am legally permitted to discuss in this matter and as such, have retained the Honourable Thomas Albert Cromwell, CC as counsel.

Again, my thanks to all Canadians. Regardless of background, geography, or party affiliation, we must stand together for the values that Canada is built on, and which are the foundation for our future.

I look forward to continuing to serve as the Member of Parliament for Vancouver-Granville.

Respectfully,
Puglaas
The Honourable Jody Wilson-Raybould, PC, QC, MP
Member of Parliament for Vancouver-Granville

•

Within minutes of the letter being released, I found myself trapped in my office in the Confederation Building with Jane, Jessica, and some of my Minister's Office staff, including Melissa Doyle, who was my executive assistant. Media were camped out at the exits of the building. One reporter actually came up to our office and opened the door and looked in. They were politely sent on their way. We stayed in there for hours, but by early evening we had to get out. The security guards were awesome, in full protection mode. They led Jane and me down through the tunnels of the Confederation Building to the

Justice Building and out to our waiting car. Staff came over to our condo. My home phone rang; Jane answered. I thought it might be my mumma, but Jane quickly hung up after realizing it was a CBC reporter. Very shortly afterwards, one of Jane's staff called her to let her know that this reporter—who had recognized Jane's voice—had already reported that we were camped out together. Ugh.

I was drained. We spent the night watching the news on TV, monitoring social media, and reflecting. Melissa has told me that what really sticks out from that evening are her memories of Jane and I listening to the PM on TV, and us saying, over and over, "He's lying," in reference to the lines he was giving about SNC-Lavalin. Of course, social media was exploding. #StandwithJody was starting to trend. There were countless text messages from all over. Some have stuck in my mind, such as one from Premier John Horgan of BC, that expressed shock and support, and for which I was grateful. Some Liberal colleagues reached out as well, including Scott Brison. This was all his fault, wasn't it? Sheesh.

The next day was more of the same. And it just kept building. The papers were full of the story. *Maclean's* called the resignation letter a masterclass in speaking volumes with few words, which I quite appreciated. But as the day went on, I became infuriated—especially about the lack of honesty from the prime minister to the public. In his press conference he made statements to the effect that he was surprised and disappointed by my resignation, and that I had never raised concerns to him about efforts to pressure or influence me regarding SNC-Lavalin. I had told him about my intent to resign on Sunday, and we had had three meetings in two days where SNC-Lavalin was the central issue. And, of course, there were the four months of efforts to pressure me on SNC-Lavalin, beginning with our meeting on September 17 and ending with the call with Michael Wernick on December 19. This revealed to me just how far this man was from the man I'd originally perceived. I am still mad at myself for that—for being convinced, at one point in time, that the prime minister was an honest and good person, when, in truth, he would so casually lie to the public and then think he could get away with it.

While my anger was there, I was feeling buoyed by the continuing support. A few Liberal ministers kept reaching out. A few others in caucus also sent messages of support, but there was certainly no groundswell internally in the party. And the Indigenous world was rallying. I saw my dad on TV, almost crying, defending his girl. It broke my heart, but I loved him so much for doing something he rarely did anymore simply because he knew I needed it. We never talked about him doing this before he did it. In fact, it was the first time I had heard from or seen him since the whole matter had blown up.

I also was relying on my lawyer, Judge Cromwell—to whom I gave the nickname "Privy Seal." I was in uncharted territory; even a former MOJAG needs a lawyer. And in this case, a good one. We were in regular contact from the outset, and primarily focused on one issue—really, for me, the only issue: figuring out what I could legally say and not say. The phrase "let her speak" would become a rallying cry for opposition parties and many in the public. At one point Minister Morneau's presentation of the 2019 budget was drowned out with chants of "let her speak" and the banging of hands on desks in the House of Commons. Figuring out what I could say would be the focus. This would be the focus right until I ultimately ended up testifying, still with limitations, before the House of Commons' Justice Committee on February 27, 2019.

The days between my resignation and the testimony are somewhat of a blur. Everything was intensifying, and dividing lines were becoming clear. On the one hand, there was a mix of denial, lies, and misogyny from the powers that be in the Liberal government and their caucus sycophants. It was gross, and so inappropriate that ultimately the prime minister would have to apologize for the sexism and racism that had been hurled at me. On the other hand, there were waves of public support, recognition, and love. It was a crazy reality—being treated like a whistle-blower without having blown the whistle. Remember: at this point people did not have any real details about what had gone on.

On February 17, 2019, I returned to Ottawa after a brief trip back to Vancouver. I had resolved to try to give the prime minister and Cabinet a push to just come clean and tell the truth. I wanted to help push them in that direction, towards what I thought was best for the country and also for the Liberal Party. I knew that, one way or another, I would eventually have to speak. The demands were becoming too much not to. But I would only do this with some form of waiver of privilege. I knew it was best if the truth came from the government and not from me. I sent the prime minister a short letter:

February 18, 2019

Dear Prime Minister,

I am writing to request the opportunity to meet with and speak to Cabinet in the immediate future (as early as tomorrow) regarding the reasons for my resignation from Cabinet. I think it is vitally important, and in the public interest, that Cabinet hear directly from me regarding these matters, and that this happen very soon.

As you are aware I have sought legal advice from Thomas A. Cromwell regarding the permissible scope of public statements I may make about the matters, which have been in the headlines. However, I do understand that a meeting of myself with Cabinet would be subject to the normal rules of Cabinet Confidentiality as well as Solicitor-Client Privilege.

I look forward to your prompt reply.

Respectfully,
Jody Wilson-Raybould, PC, QC, MP
[cc'd: Clerk and Lametti]

If a meeting with Cabinet were to happen, my goal was to lay it all out. Every detail of what happened from September onward regarding SNC-Lavalin.

Inexplicably, Gerry resigned on February 18, 2019. I have never understood this. I did think that Gerry and others should be gone for their roles in the events surrounding SNC-Lavalin. It was what I told the PM needed to be done during our three meetings in Vancouver before I resigned. But Gerry's resigning at this moment only made sense to me if it were to be part of a government shift towards finally coming clean and telling the truth, before I spoke to Cabinet. But they did not do that. The PM did not do that. Instead, Gerry resigned in a way that I feel only deepened the crisis. Validated it. I cannot imagine how the public felt (well, I guess I can; it was all trending on Twitter, all over the papers, and on TV).

The next day, February 19, 2019, I was told I could go to Cabinet. That morning at 8:15, Jessica and I met with the PM, Katie Telford, and the clerk of the Privy Council before Cabinet. The meeting was exactly what the public might expect such a meeting to be. It was tense and unproductive. Nothing was resolved. And, indeed, it mirrored the lines and messages that the public already knew at the time, and would come to learn more about in the months ahead.

The prime minister was his usual self in the meeting. Katie appeared defensive and somewhat hostile. Before the meeting, I had instructed Jessica to take detailed notes. Of course, this government's standard practice was to not take written notes about anything, write nothing of substance in emails, do everything by phone—perhaps so that it can never be discovered.

I was asked for my perspective on the events around SNC-Lavalin and I did not hold back. I reflected that everything was out of control; I could not speak and felt unfair and untrue things were being said about me and what had occurred. The smears and allegations were horrible—like nothing I had ever experienced . . . I wanted Cabinet to know what had happened. Everything. They had a right to know what happened. Then they could make their own decision.

I did not expect positions to change at all in the meeting. I knew the prime minister was dug in. Looking back at all the notes of that meeting raises for me again the issue of who this prime minister is. He had deputized Gerry Butts and Katie Telford to be the main representatives for him to Cabinet. Gerry and Katie, and PMO staff, and the clerk of the Privy Council were all part of the attempts at pressure on SNC-Lavalin from September on. And he was now saying, publicly, that he was not aware or responsible. That he couldn't have known. Huh? These are your people, who say they are doing your bidding. Are you the puppet master or the puppet? Either way, take some responsibility.

There was some discussion in the meeting about the future. What was going to happen next? Here are Jessica's notes on one of the exchanges, which mirrors things I said in my testimony and which the prime minister and others have said publicly:

> PM—*I am trying to figure out next steps here. You have a role to play.*
>
> JWR—*what do you want me to do?*
>
> PM—*what have I said that is not true . . .*
>
> JWR—*I can answer but answer my question. What do you want me to do?*
>
> PM—*I don't know how this unfolds. I want to know what you think. What was untrue?*
>
> JWR—*your first answer. That there was no direction. How you characterized me. No direction / pressure. The comments then snowballed. The AG's lines. No knowledge, etc.*

I brought up pressure to you. Face-to-face. I have no direct line to you. No phone number. No email. In early September, it took me two weeks to get a meeting with you. I talked to every senior person—Elder, Mathieu, the Clerk, Katie, Gerry. Pressure was put on me and my CoS.

I wanted to speak to Cabinet and reveal the facts to the public. I wanted to speak my truth to the public—either with the prime minister, responsibly, as leaders, or on my own through a confidentiality waiver. I wanted him to take responsibility. He, as he continues to maintain publicly, felt there was no undue pressure and that he was uncertain whether I should be allowed to say anything to Cabinet or otherwise. He was suggesting that perhaps this was just competing notes and memories of different meetings, such as the one between Gerry, Katie, and Jessica on December 18, 2018. Perhaps there were just misunderstandings when we spoke in public. I felt things were just circling around, and I believe the prime minister felt the same way.

I eventually got into Cabinet later that morning. We (Jessica was with me) waited for more than two hours before I was ushered in. The media saw when I entered into the PM/Cabinet wing on the third floor of West Block, and when I left. A narrative started being spun about whether the meeting was part of my backing down or helping the government with damage control.

It was clear my former Cabinet colleagues were not going to be persuaded. I do not need to tell you what I said and I am not allowed to. Suffice it to say that I have been consistent in what I have said, as everyone else would soon learn; most of it would become part of the public record. I wonder today if any of my former colleagues, other than Jane, wish they had taken a different approach with the "boss"? I doubt it. Most of them are still in Cabinet. I do hope at least they learned something, or perhaps paused however briefly to reflect on what happened. The quote from Solomon in the Book of Wisdom was not on the wall in the new Cabinet room in West Block.

The next day, February 20, a vote was scheduled on a motion by the Opposition about transparency and accountability aimed at the SNC-Lavalin issue. Basically, the House was going to have a vote to demand the PM waive confidences and break privileges so I could speak—to let me tell everyone what my Cabinet colleagues now already knew. I had to decide what to do. Everyone in the chamber had their eyes on me; indeed, so did much of the country. That morning there was a Liberal caucus meeting, which I attended. It was a shitshow. I will leave it at that. As for the vote, I knew I had to abstain, as it was about me (although I would have voted yea), but the issue was how to do it. Since the previous day's Cabinet meeting, the government had just repeated the same public lines and messages. They were floundering. Honestly, I was fed up. Fed up with weak people who would not stand up and speak the truth. Sick of the blind loyalty. Sick of their incompetent handling of the government's mess. Sick of the media chaos. Fed up with it all. While sitting in the House of Commons as voting began, I was debating whether to say something in the House or outside to the media. And what to say.

If you look at video of that day, you can see me on and off my phone, texting, and scribbling on a piece of paper. On the fly, I was writing the comments that I would make, still not sure where I would make them. I decided, really on the spur of the moment, that I would try to speak in the House. Still unsure of my scribbled words, I indicated to the Speaker that I wanted to speak, and then waited for my moment after the vote had been taken:

February 20, 2019—Opposition Motion—Transparency and Accountability

The Speaker:
I declare the amendment defeated.

The member for Vancouver Granville is rising on a point of order.

Hon. Jody Wilson-Raybould:

Mr. Speaker, I would ask that the record show that I abstained from voting on that matter. The reason for my abstention is that the matter, in part, has to do with me personally, and I do not think it is appropriate for me to vote on a matter that has to do with me personally.

I have said that I am seeking counsel on this matter of what I can and cannot say. I understand fully that Canadians want to know the truth and want transparency. Privilege and confidentiality are not mine to waive, and I hope that I have the opportunity to speak my truth.

At this point it would have been clear to all that I was not working with the PM and Cabinet on damage control and that the government was now going to have to react and actually let me speak. As far as I was concerned, they had manoeuvered themselves into a box of their own making.

The opposition side of the House exploded in roars and a standing ovation. Again, if you look at the video you can see a random Liberal or two clapping. The brave few. Other than that, the Liberals sat there stone-faced. I could feel their daggers piercing into me. Tim texted me, surprised but happy that I stood up and stated it as I did. "I am just tired of fucking around," I texted back.

◆

The back and forth about testifying before the Justice Committee is not particularly riveting. The substance of the issues raised, however, was important. Many fundamental principles and values were at stake.

At the core, and most important, was the transparency of government in a democracy. If you strip away all the noise and opinions, a simple question remains: When government has been accused of doing something wrong, how do we ensure that the matter is investigated and examined in a legitimate, responsible, public manner? Notice I put the emphasis on *how* we should do this. The issue is not *if* we should do this. Good governance, core democratic principles, and the trust of citizens in their government all demand it. But the simple truth is that in Canada we do not have strong, good, and effective political structures or mechanisms for publicly investigating alleged government misconduct. We do not have a full separation of powers between the executive (the PM and Cabinet) and Parliament. By comparison, Congress in the United States has independent powers related to oversight and investigation of the White House. We do have parliamentary committees, but these are microcosms of the same government-opposition relationship that exists in Parliament. In other words, they are much more controlled by the prime minister and Cabinet. We also have some independent officers, such as the ethics commissioner, but that office can only investigate a range of matters with limited consequences, and the government can hide behind confidentiality.

The lack of such independent political structures and mechanisms for oversight has two effects. First, it means that when government wrongdoing really needs to be investigated, something extraordinary is needed—a truly massive political firestorm leading to the establishment of a special process, commission, or inquiry. Short of this, little real or true investigation takes place through political mechanisms. The RCMP and criminal investigations are, of course, another matter. Second, this lack of structures and mechanisms for oversight means that many matters that do merit looking into simply are not explored. If they do not become matters of significant public attention, they simply float on by, unnoticed and unknown. With no independent arm of government with authority to look into matters, wrong acts can be simply undiscoverable. In our system, corruption and bad governance can fly below the radar.

Well, the SNC-Lavalin matter was a public storm, and growing by the minute. There was going to be some form of investigation.

As it turned out, the Justice Committee was to the main venue for this. But it is not designed or equipped for a true investigation with independence. This would become abundantly clear. Of course, the ethics commissioner was also going to get involved and carry out his own investigation.

Please understand me: Cabinet privilege and confidentiality are important principles. They are part of what allows a government to receive, process, deliberate, and utilize sensitive information—information that often needs to be kept private. Without trust that this can happen, sensitive information—often what is needed to make sound decisions—would end up being held back for fear that it might be made public and used in ways that are damaging to Canadians. Privilege and confidentiality are also needed for good governance.

But privilege and confidentiality can be abused. When not applied in a principled and consistent manner, they can be used as an excuse to shield wrongdoing or even simply keep Canadians in the dark. Without a core rationale such as national security, privilege and confidentiality can be a tool of bad governance instead of serving good governance. In Canada, we have adopted the habit of just asserting things like "it's a matter of Cabinet confidence" without really ensuring we are doing so in a principled manner. We make assumptions about what this means and the extent of it. And we have established a tradition of rarely lifting privilege and confidentiality, even as part of looking into wrongdoing. This is not good. We should have clear procedures, protocols, and mechanisms about how some information is made public, without it only happening when there is massive public pressure and political costs to not doing so.

It felt like an eternity passed while I was trying to secure a lifting of Cabinet confidentiality so I could testify before the Justice Committee. This was the main reason I had hired Thomas Cromwell—"Privy Seal"—as my counsel, and he was working diligently on it. But because of our system, there was no requirement that the government must lift any confidences of the Queen's Privy Council for

Canada, or waive privilege or any other relevant duty of confidentiality. It was strictly political. We had to ensure that the government waived confidences, and now all we could do was push for it to be the broadest waiver possible, which we did. Ultimately, the government did not go as far as we wanted. What was agreed to was a limited waiver that was confined to the period of time I was MOJAG. That is why even today—because of how our system is structured and an unwillingness by the prime minister that I should speak freely—I remain legally constrained from saying everything, although I can add little more than what I have already said and am saying here. However, others who were not deposed might have more to say. In this way our political system enables cover-ups, and on SNC-Lavalin some vital information remains covered up.

Then, of course, there is the rule of law. On SNC-Lavalin this was the heart of the matter. The attempts to pressure were a violation of the principle of the rule of law and the related principle of prosecutorial independence.

This was the backdrop to the Justice Committee proceedings. Before I was called to testify, the Liberals presented their witnesses, including David Lametti, Nathalie Drouin, and Michael Wernick. Various experts were also called to testify about the Shawcross doctrine and other principles.

I also think that agreeing to hold committee hearings with testimony might have been a political gambit, a bet. Were the PM and his staff betting that at the end of the day I might hold back in my testimony and not damage them? That I would be evasive and economical with the truth and not answer fully? In their minds, that is the way most politicians are supposed to act. I think some of the media thought this too; they suggested there would be little to see and hear in my testimony and that this would go down as nothing more than a tempest in a teapot. I mean, my God, even in the midst of them stacking the decks against me in the committee, as the public was watching in huge numbers, Katie Telford was messaging me asking what they should say to the media on some of their questions. Insanity. They were flailing. But it was too late.

The government's mantra in the media and before the committee was consistent. It did not matter to me what noise was being made; I was resolved to be deferential to the committee, including the Liberal members, no matter how infuriating the mantra and their questioning. I would answer every question as fully and as clearly as I could within the limitations of the Order-in-Council waiver. And I was determined to show how I was just doing my job, and to expose all that had occurred: what the facts were and where lines had been crossed. How was I going to do that? By simply telling the truth in excruciating (for them) detail. Liberal line #1: some types of pressure are okay, and this was an example of that. Wrong. Liberal line #2: she didn't resign. True, but for sound reasons—including trying to ensure the rule of law was upheld by the government. Liberal line #3: jobs in Quebec matter. Guess what? Jobs in Quebec do matter. But they have nothing to do with the government trying to interfere in the prosecution of SNC-Lavalin. No evidence has been provided of job losses as a result of the SNC-Lavalin affair, and the government admitted to the ethics commissioner that they had done no analysis that job losses would occur. As mountains of evidence would come to illustrate, the prosecution (and the fact that SNC-Lavalin pleaded guilty to one count of fraud over $5,000) has not resulted in job losses.

By this point I was feeling very exposed. I felt eyes staring at me anywhere and everywhere I went, and I knew the day of the committee testimony was going to increase that exposure even more. My sense of vulnerability was high.

On February 26, 2019, I pretty much pulled an all-nighter to prepare for my testimony on the following day. As was typical of me, I was still finalizing the written text of what I would say until the last minute.

The morning of my testimony, I went through a practice run of my presentation in front of Privy Seal and Jessica. We had asked the committee for thirty minutes to make my opening statement, instead of the standard ten. I had a lot to say. The committee had agreed to the extra time. I got through almost the whole practice run before I teared up and could not finish. The last words I said were so personal, so much about who I am and where I come from:

> I will conclude by saying this: I was taught to always be careful what you say because you cannot take it back. I was taught to always hold true to your core values and principles, and to act with integrity. These are the teachings of my parents, my grandparents and my community. I come from a long line of matriarchs, and I am a truth-teller in accordance with the laws and traditions of our Big House. This is who I am, and this is who I will always be.

Oh, this was tough. I was proud of the words I was going to say but hit by the magnitude of what had happened and what I was about to do. This was my telling—my truth-telling. I said to myself at the end of that practice run that I would not let them see me emotional. I would just tell it like it was. I would harness strength from my culture, which was the foundation of my ability to give the presentation. Privy Seal and Jessica were also emotional at this point. They said something like "do it just like that."

That afternoon I walked to the Justice Committee room from my offices in Confederation with some of my staff. I was early. The committee scheduled my testimony to start at 3:15 p.m., but it ended up starting about thirty-five minutes late. And there were throngs of media. Everywhere. I sat down at my spot at the table. Some members of the committee and MPs were there already, Elizabeth May and Nathan Cullen among others. They came over to speak to me and say hi. I had opened my book to my presentation but soon remembered that the media were there; I closed my book before anyone could film it. At that moment, I had a sense of calm.

I was simply going to tell the truth, the whole sordid, unvarnished kind. People filed into the committee room and assembled. Most were very friendly, except the Liberals—although I do remember the Liberal chair of the committee coming over to say hello.

Late in the preparation of my remarks, we'd talked about the testimony and how it would be so detailed—there was so much to reveal. It was suggested to me that I give the punchline right off the top, a very quick synopsis of exactly what I would be saying. We live in a Twitter world, and people needed to know what I was saying immediately, with absolute clarity and alacrity. With these words added I began my testimony:

> *For a period of approximately four months, between September and December of 2018, I experienced a consistent and sustained effort by many people within the government to seek to politically interfere in the exercise of prosecutorial discretion in my role as the Attorney General of Canada in an inappropriate effort to secure a deferred prosecution agreement with SNC-Lavalin.*
>
> *These events involved 11 people, excluding myself and my political staff, from the Prime Minister's Office, the Privy Council Office, and the office of the Minister of Finance. This included in-person conversations, telephone calls, emails, and text messages. There were approximately 10 phone calls and 10 meetings specifically about SNC, and I and/or my staff were a part of these meetings.*
>
> *Within these conversations, there were express statements regarding the necessity of interference in the SNC-Lavalin matter, the potential for consequences and veiled threats if a DPA was not made available to SNC. These conversations culminated on December 19, 2018, with a conversation I had with the Clerk of the Privy Council, a conversation that I will provide some significant detail on.*

A few weeks later, on January 7, 2019, I was informed by the Prime Minister that I was being shuffled out of the role of Minister of Justice and Attorney General of Canada.

I have to tell you, when I delivered those words it was like the room froze. There was such shock. I could feel it. I will never forget seeing one MP covering her mouth, seeming genuinely stunned as I spoke. There were audible gasps. A close friend who was watching texted me later about his experience of that moment: "I had the TV on, and you said your thing, and I was looking at social media at the same time. It was like everything froze for ten seconds. Social media was stunned. And then they realized—'OMG, she's actually going to say something real and blow the lid. Holy, that never happens from a politician'. And then the social media world exploded."

As necessary, my presentation was quite long—more than the thirty minutes I had asked for and been allotted. The chair asked if committee members would allow me to finish. There was no doubt about that. I finished my remarks. When I reached my closing words I did not tear up. Rather, I felt lots of passion and pride as I concluded. It may sound corny to some, but I felt like the ancestors were with me, especially my granny. Honestly, it makes me emotional just writing this and remembering. I do not know if I will ever be in a situation like that again or ever feel that way again, but I knew, in that moment, that I had done the right thing.

Then the three hours of questions began. I was thinking clearly and was simply telling it as it happened. Liberal members tried to trip me up, but I did not let them. You cannot trip someone up who speaks the truth. I did, however, start getting a bit irritated. I am not sure if it showed. As the hours went on, and as the Liberal questions became more hostile and repetitive, I started to push back and challenge them more directly: the lawyer, not the witness, coming out of me.

For example:

Iqra Khalid (Mississauga—Erin Mills, Lib.):
Thank you, Chair.

Thank you, Ms. Wilson-Raybould, for appearing today and sharing your viewpoints with us on this.

I've always felt that you've been a very vocal advocate on issues that you genuinely believe in, without regard to other viewpoints. You've been vocal at cabinet; you've been vocal to the Prime Minister and you've been vocal to Canadians. In fact, you've gone on the record at many public events and you've really expressed your viewpoints on issues that you genuinely believe in, such as the indigenous file.

Just going through your testimony and your chain of events, I see that there hasn't been communication between you and the Prime Minister himself from September up until the time when he called you for the shuffle.

Why is that? Why didn't you speak out to the Prime Minister when you've been so vocal on issues such as the indigenous file, and you know that you have access? Why did you not speak out to him when you had these concerns? Do you feel that you had an obligation to do so?

Hon. Jody Wilson-Raybould:
I need to say a couple of things with respect to your question. I completely reject your characterization that I do not have regard for other people's opinions. You talked about the cabinet table, and with respect, you would have no ability to know about discussions around the cabinet table.

I don't apologize for being vocal in my opinions, but that doesn't mean that I don't value other people's opinions. For the entirety of my professional career and how I was raised in terms of consensus-based decision-making, it has always been incredibly important to me to take into account the views of other people. That's how we make good public policy in this country.

You talked about indigenous issues. I'm a proud indigenous person from the west coast of British Columbia, and I will not apologize for being a strong advocate in pursuing transformative change for indigenous peoples in this country. I have worked in the indigenous world as a politician for a significant amount of time and have a very in-depth understanding of the issues that indigenous peoples face. That's not to say everybody agrees—and I appreciate hearing other people's opinions.

To your question with respect to the Prime Minister, I believe I've covered that ground. I had a direct conversation with the Prime Minister, as I had direct conversations with the people in his office and the Clerk of the Privy Council.

The chair kept asking me if I wanted a bathroom break. I was determined not to go to the bathroom or take a break but to sit there and answer their questions as long as they had them. I did, however, comment to the chair and the committee that the questions were becoming repetitive. Perhaps it was the chair who had to go to the bathroom.

At the end of the committee, I left the room. Media asked me some questions—but really, I had said all I wanted to say at that moment. Then we left and got into our car; Tim had waited outside the west door of West Block for over an hour as I finished up. He was proud and smiling, said I was amazing, and then uttered, "Now let's get the hell out of here." We drove down to the Confederation Building and walked into my office to watch all the analysis. I had received what felt like a million texts and emails. I could not keep up with all of the messages. But oh, thank goodness it was over. Jane arrived with some champagne. Thank goodness again.

◆

In Ottawa, the political culture, which includes the media, lives in a world of its own construction, quite divorced from the daily realities and lives of most Canadians. A cardinal feature of this cynical world is that it rarely, if ever, assumes that an individual might actually do something simply because it is what they believe is the right thing to do. Rather, there must always be an ulterior motive—an agenda—one that is either partisan, political, or tied to personal ambition. To get recognition, to climb up the ladder. In this Ottawa world, people are not thought of first as people who hold beliefs and try to live lives of meaning that reflect those beliefs. Nope.

Throughout the SNC-Lavalin period I felt this Ottawa world pressing on me, particularly the media. While the media talked about many aspects of the scandal, one of its main focuses was on my "endgame" and figuring out what it might be. This infuriated me. In life, is not trying our best to do the right thing—and, sure, failing lots of the time—often our "endgame"? Or even just simply trying to do our jobs? Not in Ottawa. There had to be an ulterior motive. I guess in the warped endgame reality of Ottawa it was assumed that I must have done all of this because I wanted some power or privilege I did not already have. And what? Resigning from Cabinet, telling the truth even though it was difficult for the Liberal faithful (I was still a Liberal at this point), and I knew full well that it might get me kicked out of the caucus—was all of that part of a master plan to seek attention or gain power? Lunacy. I can have no greater power and privilege than knowing where I come from, who I am, and the values that I uphold. That is power. Powerful.

I knew that once I had spoken out, my days in caucus were numbered. It was only a matter of time. As I expected, when it finally happened, on April 2, 2019, it brought with it a mix of relief, exhilaration, and sadness. The scandal had kept growing and roiling the capital. There was further testimony, including by Gerry and again by Nathalie and the clerk, but none of it was very consequential. Gerry did reveal some of the back and forth about my being shuffled out of my position as MOJAG. I think the narrative—because it was the truth—was largely settled at this point. And it is incontrovertible now. The ethics commissioner released his investigation on August 13, 2019, and it backed up my testimony before the Justice Committee.

But for me, the most important thing that occurred in the period after my testimony was the courage, integrity, and resolve shown by Jane. She did not need to also resign from Cabinet. I did not ask her to do so or to back me up. I knew she had been struggling with the question of what to do since the *Globe* story first broke. She had met with the prime minister, spoken to lawyers, sought the counsel of her husband and those close to her, and weighed every option. I know she, as she always did, gathered information and looked at all the evidence. She is a doctor, after all, and a damn good one. She finally decided to resign on March 4, 2019.

During this time I felt like a hamster in its wheel, forced to keep running faster as the world spun and spun. There was the cacophony of support and attacks, some public and some private. It kept up each day. Publicly, the prime minister and the PMO were setting things up to remove me. They started pushing their lines, talking about "erosion of trust" and how two people can "experience the same event differently."

On March 18, 2019, I was contacted in the morning by the PMO and told the prime minister wanted to meet with me.

He and I met just before noon in his office in West Block. As always, the PM hugged me. Still. This time I felt my skin crawl. He opened by talking about how much was going on in the world and how we needed to move beyond the SNC-Lavalin matter. He also said he had talked to lawyers. He made a point of telling me that both Gerry and Michael had resigned. At that point, I did not know about Michael, who actually resigned later that day. He told me that Anne McLellan was being brought in to advise on the separation of the AG role from the minister of justice role. We talked about whether that should happen, and I also raised that safeguards needed to be in place.

The conversation was stilted and not easy, but up to that point it was basically congenial. I had been in Vancouver the week before doing my usual constituency work. It was great and I loved it. While SNC-Lavalin was a huge distraction and a part of every conversation, people had their own issues that needed addressing. I also had endless lines of people asking for selfies and expressing love. The PM said he liked seeing what I was doing and emphasized our shared values. He also talked about the "erosion of trust" between Gerry and me. Honestly, give me a break.

Then the conversation got down to the real issue of why I was there—the proverbial elephant in the room. He wanted me, effectively, to signal a moving on from the SNC-Lavalin matter, to indicate that I was done wanting to speak to it. Basically, in my mind, he was saying there were two truths—mine and theirs—and it was all a big miscommunication. Please.

As for me, I was where I was always at. I wanted the full truth to just come out, responsibility to be taken, and our system improved for the future. I said the Justice Committee needed to keep working. Wrongdoing needs to be acknowledged, the full story must come out, and then we could find a way through this.

The last line was drawn.

"Absolutely no," the prime minister responded. As he continued on, I thought and then said out loud to him, "I wish that I had never met you." In that moment this is what I felt. I told him I was upset—to say the least—because I had actually believed him and what he said about doing politics differently. "I feel like a fool for that." He went on to speak about how valuable I was. I think I laughed out loud.

I knew then, more clearly than ever, that the prime minister had no intention of doing anything to make the issue right. To take responsibility. Even some responsibility. I implored him again, one last time, to do the right thing. But again he said he just wanted to turn the page. He even said he was glad I still wanted to be a member of the Liberal Party.

We went around some more. The meeting ended with both of us saying we would think about what we had discussed. There was no hug as I left. A few hours later, while I was sitting in question period, a letter was released from the Liberal members of the Justice Committee saying they wanted the committee folded. As expected, the conversation with the prime minister had just been for show. It was all fake. The decision to "turn the page" had been made much earlier.

Given all of this, I knew I had to get on the record and to do so within the confines of the Order-in-Council waiver. This meant I needed to release anything and everything else I had to say to the committee before the prime minister and his office shut it down. I wrote to the chair of the committee and told them I was going to be making another submission. It was in this submission that I decided to respond to some of the testimony made by others after I had testified. I also decided to release the audio of my conversation with the clerk. Did I debate the choice? A little. Tim and others were wavering back and forth; they thought it would really upset some people who would not understand the need to tape it in the first place. But the reality was, as you know now, I had made the decision to record the conversation long ago. It would be wrong to not say all that I could to get the truth out simply because I was worried about how people would react to the fact that I'd made the recording in the first place. After all, it was the telephone call itself, and what was said by Wernick during it, that was at the heart of the issue. Let people hear it and decide for themselves.

Near the end of my written testimony, after remarking on our institutions of democracy and the importance of the rule of law and prosecutorial independence, I offered some reflections on Canada and the Canadian public:

... a significant part of the public dialogue about this matter has touched on issues of race and gender, and, in particular, there have been undeniable elements of misogyny, much of it aimed at myself. While this is unfortunate, and unpleasant, I also see the benefits this entire episode can bring to building a stronger Canada, and strengthening our civil society. In particular, over the past seven weeks, the thing that I have heard most from Canadians is their true belief and desire to see fundamental and transformative, and not merely ephemeral, change in our modes of public discourse, the health of our institutions, civic engagement, and the standards we uphold. For each cynical commentator and commentary, I estimate I have encountered ten Canadians thinking and asking about what these events mean for the future they are helping to build. So I take the opportunity to thank those Canadians from coast-to-coast-to-coast who give me hope, and look forward to acting alongside them into the future—a future where we truly do politics differently.

When the written testimony was made public, along with the audio recording, the reaction was as expected. Some defended it, some did not.

Even in those final days before my public excommunication from the caucus, there were lawyers going back and forth to see whether some sort of statement could be issued that would close the matter. This had begun with overtures I had received from various Liberals about trying to find an approach and a statement that would work for everyone. I knew this would not work, but in good faith I still tried to have discussions. They never went anywhere. The types of statements being proposed just reiterated the divide that existed. I wanted the full truth to be said, with a recognition of the fact that change was needed. It was not going to happen. The PM and his people were just playing at their game—and this was just another ploy.

As this was going on, I was back at Cape Mudge, in my home

community of We Wai Kai with Tim. Our Chiefs had organized an honouring and cleansing ceremony at the Kwanwatsi Big House on Wei Wai Kum First Nation lands in Campbell River. I had come full circle. This was the first time I had been in the Big House since going to Ottawa as an MP. The ceremony took place over many hours. To give me strength. To hold me up. To honour and humble. To protect. To cleanse. To show love. I took it all in. Strengthened and renewed. Feeling so blessed, Tim and I then headed back to Ottawa for what I knew was coming.

I was sure by now that the PM and his closest advisors wanted me, and maybe Jane, out of the Liberal caucus. But I was not sure if he would do it himself or follow the Reform Act. Given the struggles that had occurred over the rule of law and the ongoing political fallout, I was doubtful that the legislation would be followed. The Reform Act requires that the matter of a member's removal from caucus be put to the caucus (and not decided by the leader) unless the caucus has voted to do otherwise. We had not done that.

On April 1, in anticipation of a vote I still thought might happen, I sent a letter to the Liberal caucus that included the following:

> Now I know many of you are angry, hurt, and frustrated. And frankly so am I, and I can only speak for myself. I am angry, hurt, and frustrated because I feel and believe I was upholding the values that we all committed to. In giving the advice I did, and taking the steps I did, I was trying to help protect the Prime Minister and the government from a horrible mess. I am not the one who tried to interfere in sensitive proceedings, I am not the one who made it public, and I am not the one who publicly denied what happened. But I am not going to go over all of the details here again. Enough has been said.
>
> Growing up as an Indigenous person in this country I learned long ago the lesson that people believing what they wish about you does not, and cannot ever, make it the

truth—rather than letting authority be the truth, let the truth be the authority. Indeed, if I had succumbed to interpreting the beliefs of others to be the truth, I never would have been able to push forward in the face of the racism and misogyny that far too many Indigenous women, and others, still experience every day.

Ultimately the choice that is before you is about what kind of party you want to be a part of, what values it will uphold, the vision that animates it, and indeed the type of people it will attract and make it up.

If indeed our caucus is to be a microcosm of the country it is about whether we are a caucus of inclusion or exclusion; of dialogue and searching for understanding or shutting out challenging views and perspectives; and ultimately of the old ways of doing business, or new ones that look to the future.

Unsurprisingly, the letter accomplished nothing. I did not expect it to. I did receive some very angry comments from a number of caucus members plus one comment from our BC caucus chair, who was still expecting us to chat in our scheduled caucus meeting the next day, but for the most part people were silent.

As it transpired, the decision to remove Jane and me from caucus never in fact came to a vote; we were simply removed, unlawfully. Jane actually rose in the House to ask the Speaker to inquire into whether the Liberals had properly followed the Reform Act. (The Speaker eventually ruled it was outside of his jurisdiction as not a matter of parliamentary business.)

But hey, no surprise there given that this entire scandal was about adherence (or not) to the rule of law. So why not ignore it one more time in getting rid of the two that had stood up to defend it?

It was the morning of April 2 when Jane was called in to meet with the PM. Caucus was to meet later that evening. She met him and came back to my office and told me she had been booted from caucus. The prime minister had asked her not to say anything until after the caucus was told (I guess that confirms he wasn't following the law on this point). Later that afternoon it was my turn. No real greeting. No skin-crawling hugs. He said that I was being removed from caucus and that I was no longer allowed to run as a Liberal in Vancouver Granville in the 2019 general election. After the PM said what he had to say, I looked at him squarely and without emotion and said, "Okay." I think he was expecting me to say something more. But I simply got up and left before he could say anything else.

I headed straight back to my office, where Jane, Tim, Jessica, and Celina Caesar-Chavannes—a good friend and Independent MP for Whitby, Ontario, who has since recounted her own experience of marginalization in her memoir *Can You Hear Me Now?*—and others were waiting. I had already drafted the tweets I wanted to send out. The prime minister had not told me that I should keep the news under my belt until after he had made the announcement to caucus, as he had with Jane. I hesitated over whether I should just go ahead and send them, though I am not sure why I cared at this point. Tim told me caucus was beginning to gather and said, "Get it out . . . now." And Celina, bless her, said, "Send the fucking tweet . . . what are you waiting for." And so I did:

> *I have just been informed by the Prime Minister of Canada that I am removed from the Liberal caucus and as the confirmed Vancouver Granville candidate for the Liberal Party of Canada in the 2019 federal election. More to come . . .*

> *Reflecting on what PM has done, my thoughts are w/ my constituents in #VanGran, my dedicated staff & volunteers, my family & friends & all Canadians who believed in a new way of doing politics. I will take the time to reflect & talk to my supporters about what happens next. (1/2)*

What I can say is that I hold my head high & that I can look myself in the mirror knowing I did what I was required to do and what needed to be done based on principles & values that must always transcend party. I have no regrets. I spoke the truth as I will continue to do. (2/2)
— *Jody Wilson-Raybould (@Puglaas), April 2, 2019*

Social media blew up once again. One of my favourite tweets in all the melee, which kind of hit the nail on the head, was from journalist Robyn Urback: "We are stronger not in spite of our differences, but because we extinguish them." Awful. But appropriate.

I think some of the Liberal caucus might have thought they were actually going to vote and may have been surprised it was all over as they walked in. We watched on TV in my office as the caucus cheered our ouster. The prime minister called what I did—recording an effort by the clerk to do the prime minister's improper bidding, after months of such efforts—"unconscionable." Does this not typify that Ottawa reality? Trying to pervert the law is perfectly fine. Gathering evidence and revealing that effort at perversion—unconscionable.

For some time after the April 2 caucus meeting, most Liberal MPs would not even look at me. Many of them, if they saw me in the hallways of West Block or the Confederation Building, would turn and walk in the other direction. I took it as perhaps a sign of fear, pettiness, or cowardice. Or maybe a mix of all three? Many people do not like confrontation, and perhaps some expected that would happen. It would not have; I had nothing to confront them about. I had made my choices. I think it is more likely that many of them do not like being reminded of their own choices. Of the fact that they made a choice of blind loyalty, of surrendering some of their will to the PMO, and perhaps along with it had to ignore their own values and principles simply to be members of the Liberal Party in good standing with the "boss." I made a different but not a difficult choice.

I had become a Liberal after a lifetime with no political affiliation. On the night of April 2, 2019, I was an Independent. Again. At home within myself, where perhaps I have always been.

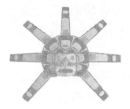

NINE

Moving Forward

My life while writing this book has been like many of yours. I am isolated, more often alone than not, and only going out for essentials. It is February 2021. Tim is in Westbank with his mother, following the recent passing of his father. I have spent much of the COVID-19 pandemic in our condo off Cambie in Vancouver, going to Ottawa to perform my House of Commons duties as needed, and, thankfully, on-reserve at Cape Mudge, in our little blue house four doors down from my mumma. Like pretty much everything at Cape Mudge, the house looks out to the ocean, and across to Campbell River on Vancouver Island, which is ten minutes away by ferry.

It was during the spring of 2020 that I began in earnest to write my notes for this book, often sitting on a red hammock down by the shore as the sun heated me up. This place is my home. I mean, how could it not be when on an almost daily basis the orcas or humpbacks swim by and bald eagles soar above. The perfect place to be inspired to write.

At that point, I had only shared with one or two people that I was even thinking of writing this book. If I am honest, I was not sure if I would go through with it. There were lots of reasons for this. With the exception of some of the SNC-Lavalin stuff, I was not sure how much of the story of my political journey and my time in Ottawa would really be that interesting. How was my story different? I was certainly not interested in writing a "vanity" piece. Also, I am not really a writer. I have never held myself out to be one. I was not sure if I was going to pull the story together in a way that made sense and was enjoyable to read. As with the anxiety I have always had about giving speeches, I am anxious writing something knowing others will read it, listen to it. As such, my approach to speech writing has always been to get extensive feedback from others. This book is no different. Many have helped me to find the right words, jog memories, and express feelings. Others who are integral to this story have shared with me what they remember, including their notes of many of the events described. And I have spent countless hours going through all of my records from my years in government.

As I started to write up my notes into prose suitable for a book, I was not sure if I was ready to dredge up everything that happened over those Ottawa years, and how I felt during all of it. If you look at the arc of the story I just told, it has the quality of confronting certain truths, both about who I am and about how we govern. Some of these truths, including the personal ones, I continue to struggle with. I wanted to see a leader and a government ready to do what I believed in and what I believed most Canadians believed in—certainly the constituents of Vancouver Granville. So I chose to believe I saw that. But it was more illusion than substance. When the image started to get blurry and out of focus, I let myself believe I could still help bring it back into focus by pushing, prodding, and challenging. But that was impossible. And as in all relationships, when one keeps trying to change who and what someone fundamentally is, to make it into what one might want, it usually ends badly—be it in government, with work colleagues, with family and friends, or within whatever community you are a part of.

The writing of this book had stops and starts that reflected some of the feelings triggered by revisiting my time in government as the "Indian" in the Cabinet. As I continued putting down my notes during the summer of 2020, the WE Charity scandal unfolded. In it I saw many of the patterns I had experienced. The attempts at cover-up and a lack of straight answers. A failure to just deal with a challenge head-on, with truth. The ridiculous partisanship of how our committee system functions. And I felt a sadness and frankly some trauma watching former minister of finance Bill Morneau resign, sensing that he faced toxic behaviours and attacks on his reputation that were similar to what I had faced.

As I watched his face on TV, I think I could see the relief in his eyes after he spoke the words, "I am resigning." There almost seemed to be a freedom in how he answered the media's questions that you really did not see when he was playing the role and giving his lines as a minister. Bill never seemed to like doing media and was always working on his presentations and answers. He did not seem to need to do so here.

I stopped writing for a while as the WE issue played out.

In writing and revisiting the events that led to the prime minister ejecting me from caucus, I have had to look at aspects of myself that I have sometimes struggled with. But one thing is clear to me now, even clearer than it was to me at the time: the end of the story had been clear from the beginning; it was never going to be any different. One way or another, my time with this government was not going to be long, for any number of reasons: Aga Khan. India. Vice-Admiral Norman. SNC-Lavalin. Blackface. WE. Payette. General Vance. There are similar patterns reflected in all of these. And all of them cut against what I originally anticipated, hoped for, and wanted from this prime minister and his government. Over time, if it hadn't been SNC-Lavalin, something was going to arise that made it clear this way of governing was not my way of governing and that I did not want to be a part of it—to be complicit. Like any breakup, it could have happened in any number of ways, and it was always going to be painful, but we make it more or less so. I will take some responsibility for this breakup being so public, dramatic, and painful, including for me. But a breakup was going to come.

Lots of people have said to me that writing this book must be a bit of a balm, healing and cathartic for the pain of those years. I am not sure if it is or isn't. Does reliving the harder moments in life make them easier to bear? Perhaps. I certainly do not regret writing it. I am grateful for it. If anything, what has come out of doing so is a greater understanding and self-awareness. That is a good thing. I also feel better having written about my time in government in my own words, and, in particular, about the political realities and policy debates that are important. Too much ink has been spilled by others who were not there. I was.

But what's next? I know I still have roles to play and work to do, though I hope never again so publicly in quite the same way. More important, where might we be going as a country? And in the struggle for true reconciliation? What can be taken from this story as the larger story, our collective story, is still being written?

On April 2, 2019, I had to start answering these questions. The answers were not easy. And they still are not.

◆

The story did not end after Jane and I became Independents. The media did not go away, and while the issues receded from the public somewhat, the SNC-Lavalin affair remains a part of what is now associated with this government. What has also remained are the challenges this government faces on Indigenous and racial issues, and on inclusion and changing the way politics is done. This was highlighted again in dramatic ways during the blockades of early 2020 and the protests and marches during that same summer—both bringing into focus a fundamental issue for the government and for the country. What does a politics of inclusion, that recognizes difference, truly look like in practice?

To be clear, I do not mean what difference looks like for the prime minister, with the PMO's line about "experiencing things differently." Many viewed that sentiment as a euphemism for saying that certain (white, male) experiences were valid and other (Indigenous, female) experiences were invalid. It was an example of politics of exclusion, not inclusion. My "experience" was so out of the norm for Ottawa that it needed to be exiled, pushed back to the margins—to which Indigenous peoples, people of colour, and women have long been relegated in this country. The prime minister's lack of recognition of this marginalization and the actions that were taken by many may be seen as reinforcing those long-standing patterns of exclusion; these were some of the most damning aspects of the whole situation. It all dredges up so much: The extent of privilege and the blind spots it creates. The depth of the focus on image over substance. The hollowness of certain principles the government professed to hold.

There was no stronger symbol of the rejection of this form of politics than the courageous act of dozens of young delegates from Daughters of the Vote. On April 3, 2019, when the PM was speaking in the House of Commons at the Daughters event, many delegates stood and turned their backs on him throughout his remarks. Afterwards, he tried to explain his rejection by these brave young people by saying that there "is never going to be an absolute one side or another. There are always going to be multiple voices." I am unsure how he could say these words with a straight face given that he had spent over a month now publicly discounting my voice, using legal means to limit what I could say publicly, kicking the only Indigenous woman who had been in his Cabinet out of his caucus, and exiling another strong woman who spoke her mind.

As I began my Independent MP reality, the media began to focus on what Jane and I were planning to do next. Would we join another political party? Would we start our own? Would we run as Independents? Were we done with federal politics? A federal general election was going to happen in the fall, so we both knew we had to make some decisions quickly.

By this point I was feeling quite low. I had been on the political hot seat and in the public spotlight for what seemed like a lifetime, even if it had only been four months. I was done with it. It was so disorienting to constantly be in a place where people act like they love or hate you. Only the extremes and no in-betweens—though I was grateful many more showed love than hate. And in the age of social media, you are always conscious that whenever you go out, there may be some picture or video clip that will end up on Twitter or Facebook; this puts you always on edge. You also know you might be spotted by a reporter and potentially hounded by questions. Yes, I realize I was a public figure—but for me this was extraordinary. I think it would have been for anyone. I could feel myself increasingly on guard, always scanning my surroundings.

I did, though, appreciate very much the countless people who approached me on the streets, or in airports, stores, and anywhere else to say hello and more often than not to say "thank you." I think this kept me going, along with Tim, my family, close friends, and community, including my amazing team in VanGran. I have never met or talked to as many people and heard as many lived experiences as I did during this time. For those of you who are reading this, I say thank you. I received so many emails and letters, and I tried to respond to all of them. People still come up to me today to talk (through masks and with social distance, in this pandemic era), and I really value each exchange. I guess it reminds me that my experience unleashed something good. I know there are lessons here.

But for all the love, I was tired. And in addition to being exhausted I was tired in a different way. You know that feeling in the course of a day where something important and serious is coming, and you experience all the anxiety and anticipation of it, and then, afterwards, there is a sense of release but mixed with tiredness? Well, I felt that now, except it had played out over years. I felt that the whole reality of Ottawa had sucked some of the life out of me, and only now, as Ottawa had receded a bit or as much as it could, was I starting to feel the full effects of all of its toxicity and intensity. I felt like lying in bed for weeks and shutting out the world.

But it was not time for that yet—for me, I am not sure there will ever be time for that. I was, of course, still an MP. I *am* still an MP and I so cherish the local "politics" of this reality and the work of fulfilling my responsibilities to my constituents. I also felt a responsibility to all of those people across the country who were so supportive, who had held me up. I felt a need to honour all the love from Indigenous peoples, which had been constant in my time as MOJAG and after. And the reality was that the immediate public spotlight was not going to recede until Jane and I said more about the future.

One of the many invitations I received at this time was to speak at an event back in British Columbia for the BC First Nations Justice Council on April 24, 2019. The conference was about criminal justice reform and the overrepresentation of Indigenous people within the justice system. It was the main forum where First Nations leaders and experts would be developing aspects of a new strategy (which has since been supported by the BC government) to transform the relationship between Indigenous peoples and the justice system. This was the kind of event that I would have always spoken at when I was Regional Chief—a gathering of Indigenous leaders, experts, and those on the front lines helping their communities deal with real-life issues. I knew a lot of family members, friends, and colleagues would be there. After talking to Tim and Jane, it was decided that both Jane and I would attend and give speeches, one after another. Our first public speeches since becoming Independent MPs.

Jane and I did not intend to say anything of substance about our political futures. We had not decided anything at that point. But we knew the cameras would be there, and it was an opportunity to give some interviews. I also knew, given how I was feeling, that the event would give me some energy and lift my spirits. I knew there would be a wave of love in the room, just as there had been at the Big House Honouring some weeks prior, and that I would be buoyed with strength. While Jane had some sense of how Indigenous peoples would embrace us, I do not think she knew quite what to expect. But I knew it would give her strength as it would me. And I was so grateful to be there and experience this with my friend.

We arrived mid-morning as the Gathering was underway. It was being held at the Westin Wall Centre near Vancouver International Airport. We had been warned the media was going to be intense. Some of the BC government ministers were speaking at the event, so their full communications contingent was involved. I had come with my constituency staff and some "VanGraners," but no comms staff. The media that day ended up being more than I could have imagined. I am pretty sure it was the biggest media presence I had ever been a part of—including when we were introducing legislation and for scrums on Parliament Hill. It was more than when I gave testimony at the Justice Committee. And I am sure it was the most media to ever attend an Indigenous gathering of this sort. Dozens of cameras and reporters. Live-streaming of the event. Endless demands for interviews.

Of course, they were not going to get the news they were looking for or what perhaps they thought they were going to get—such as the announcement of a new political party. But they were going to hear two pretty substantive speeches from Jane and me about the overrepresentation of Indigenous peoples in the justice system, among other things. I was happy for that to be seen by Canadians—these issues need attention! Also, there was going to be a ceremony and honouring of the two of us. It would be great for the media and Canadians to see how Indigenous peoples pay respect and show love to one another and, in this case, to Jane as well.

For the ceremony, we were blanketed and dressed appropriately by Elders and those responsible for cultural protocols. The process of preparing us took close to an hour. We were then drummed into the room and led into a large circle, with everyone standing around us. There were songs, witnesses called, statements made, gifts given, and tears shed. It was lovely. Most appreciated and much needed. All with cameras and reporters peering in from outside the circle.

As I passed through the ceremony, my mind was floating through the whole journey I had been on. I had gone to Ottawa as an MP to represent my riding and to create the space for our Indigenous governments to rebuild within a stronger Canada. Along the way it became clear that the government of Canada had something to learn from our Indigenous cultures and ways of being that have survived for millennia. To address the legacy of colonialism in this country, the colonizers are going to need to learn a lot from those they sought to colonize. Not just to confront their own actions, ignorance, and systemic racism, but to actually make Canadian institutions and modes of governing better by learning the different values, principles, and practices that uphold Indigenous governments and societies and which I was, at that moment through that ceremony, experiencing.

◆

When we got back to Ottawa, things were a little different. While Indigenous peoples in BC encircled Jane and me and held us up, and every day Canadians showed us love as we moved through our days, the Liberal government exiled us to the margins of the House of Commons. I made my journey from the front bench on the government side to the farthest back corner on the opposition side. If you want to see one of the true images of this Liberal government, take a look at the picture of the Black woman MP, Celina Caesar-Chavannes, and the Indigenous woman MP sitting in the back corner of the House of Commons—in one way or another sent there by the "feminist" prime minister for not doing his bidding or no longer buying what he was selling. If this is what the prime minister meant by "because it is 2015" we could do with less of it.

Jane and Green Party leader Elizabeth May were seated in front of Celina and me. There was a screenshot on social media of the four of us in the House one day. The looks on our faces could tell many stories. As Independents, Jane and I had to quickly figure out what we could and could not do. We had more than enough "friends" in the place. Many MPs from all opposition parties would come and talk to us, offer support and speaking spots, and engage with us on issues. For the Liberals, we might as well have been Hester Prynne, wearing a scarlet A. They had failed at public humiliation (and had humiliated themselves somewhat), so public shunning was what they had left. In addition to just walking away from us, there were glares and snide comments under their breath. This behaviour just reinforced what Jane and I had increasingly come to recognize: excessive partisanship is corroding truth and humanness in our politics. The Liberals were proving it.

Of course, our current system is structured to reinforce the party system of control. It can be costly to think for yourself. Such costs include marginalization, a limit on opportunity, and even removal. Some might even say that the partisan culture in Ottawa helps to create an ethic of closed-mindedness and lack of truth.

During this period of time, Jane and I talked back and forth about what we would do next. We decided that whatever we did, we would support each other. The choices: 1) Join another political party and run with them in next election; 2) Form a new political party and run in the next election; 3) Run as Independents in the next election; or 4) Say goodbye to it all. We approached the decision as we had approached tasks as ministers. We talked about it a lot. While we of course each had our own agency, somehow we knew this was a joint task, or decision. We weighed every option and all the factors as best we could. We listened to what others had to say. Both Elizabeth May and Jagmeet Singh were kind, supportive, and somewhat persistent. Andrew Scheer was kind also.

From the outset, I was always leaning in one direction: I was done with political parties. The people who were representing the Liberal Party in government were not representative of the party that Tim and I thought we had joined. They were not ethical—and they treated me and others reprehensibly. The reality of what I had become a part of went against my very nature. Was it the party or the people? Who knows. But at that point, I was not a "party" person. So I was hesitant to sign up for another so soon after that experience, or establish a new one.

Jane and I held a planning/strategy meeting on May 16, 2019, at Jane's house in Stouffville, Ontario. Several other people participated, including members of our campaign teams, to hash out the options and a plan. We eventually decided that the best choice for us— individually and together—was to run as Independents in the 2019 general election. We were happy and excited with our decisions. But we did not have any illusions. This would be different. This would be hard. As one study has shown, more than 99 percent of the MPs elected to Canada's Parliament over the last thirty years were elected as representatives of a political party. None of the Independent MPs elected were women. Jane or I, or both of us, would be the first.

We agreed that on May 27, 2019, we would hold back-to-back events in each of our electoral districts to announce our intentions. We would also simultaneously release media advisories.

At my event, I was relieved to be able to say these words:

> *After much reflection and deliberation and given all of your kind words of encouragement and support, I have decided to run again in the upcoming 2019 federal election as an Independent candidate.*
>
> *Although I was removed from the Liberal Caucus and as the confirmed Liberal Candidate for Vancouver Granville by*

the Prime Minister, I believe my time in federal politics is not yet over—there is still much work to be done. And with your support I am confident running as an Independent is the best path to advance the change we need and positively impact our evolving political system.

I have learned and experienced a lot over the past three and a half years as a Member of Parliament and as a Cabinet Minister. Much of it has been positive, including accomplishments I was proud to be a part of such as medically assisted dying legislation, the Canada Child Benefit, the legalization of cannabis, and justice reforms.

But it has also become very apparent that there can be and must be a different way of doing politics that reflects where our country is going as an evolved and fair democracy based on the rule of law.

To meet the challenges of today and tomorrow every voice must count and not just those with perceived or real power. We too often see empty partisanship trump democratic principles; sowing division prioritized over building understanding and inclusion; and the public interest being redefined to mean the interests of the few.

In 2019, we cannot afford to be complacent. Around the globe, and across the country, environmental, economic, and security challenges are deepening. And these challenges share a fundamental characteristic—they ignore boundaries between nations and peoples. They impact all of us, remind us of the ways we are interconnected, and require solutions and that see us acting with strength and recognition of how we all have a part to play.

In the face of these challenges, many places in the world have chosen to erode democracy, traffic in fear, and promote tribalism—naively thinking that the response to the interconnected challenges that affect all of us is to try to protect the few.

We have to do the opposite and build on our strengths and accomplishments that have brought us together as a nation and allowed us to prosper. When the challenges we have to meet are collective ones, we need to respond through shared and joint efforts that use the distinct ideas, talents, and expertise we all have to offer.

Rising to these challenges requires Ottawa to operate more openly and transparently in a spirit of non-partisanship and cooperation. This is what I am committed to advancing.

I look forward to continuing to earn your support so that we can continue our efforts to do politics differently and to ensure progress is made on the issues that are important to all of us.

My priorities have not changed. Both as a matter of individual and collective health and well-being, and as a matter of economic prosperity and national security, we must tackle climate change.

For myself, as an Indigenous Canadian, it is also important that reconciliation be purposeful and lead to a stronger system of cooperative federalism where Indigenous peoples are full partners in Confederation. This is simply good for all of Canada.

In our riding of Vancouver Granville, which is one of the most diverse in the country and growing quickly, we need to continue our focus on housing needs with all levels of government, which also includes ensuring that our transportation networks continue to be upgraded and improved including the timely completion of the Broadway line.

The 2019 election may be confusing to some for whom to vote. But I can assure you that a vote for JWR will ensure that you have a strong independent voice in Ottawa that will work with whichever government is in power for the betterment of Vancouver Granville and our country. When I say "independent"

I mean it in the true meanings of the word—"free from outside control; not depending on another's authority" and "not depending on another for livelihood or subsistence." The only thing I will depend upon is the vision, service, and support of the citizens of my riding and all Canadians.

Over the coming months, I will be continuing to seek your guidance on policy matters as well as uploading information to my website. One of our first tasks once re-elected will be to work across party lines to amend the rules that govern how parliament works to make it more effective. We have learned a lot in the past years to help us in this regard.

I am very much looking forward to continuing our conversations whether through email, in community meetings or on the doorstep. If you would like to join our independent movement, please feel free to contact me. Your support is most appreciated.

I was so energized by that event. There were so many people at Marpole Neighbourhood House; the place was packed. So many faces were the same ones that had worked with me in 2015, but there were many new ones as well. It was a reinforcement of the decision I had made, but also of the whole journey to this point. More people were now involved. More diverse people. More people who had never had anything to do with politics. It was a good day, and apart from being frazzled by learning that Tim had had a car accident on the way to the event (he was fine), it reminded me of what I had hoped politics would be when I first started contemplating running federally back in 2013.

•

The political path was now before me, and I was very glad for and happy about that. For my future in politics, the impact of all I had been through was evident: I was now running as an Independent. But the personal impacts, and the impact on those around me, remain hard to fully know.

For those around me, who loved me, I know there was pain. Isn't this always the case? Is it more painful to see one we love suffering, or being attacked, or struggling than to be attacked, suffer or struggle ourselves? For Tim, our parents, my sister and nieces, and close friends, there was, I think, a lot of pain. I know I was not easy to live with during and immediately after this time, and that for Tim this has all been tremendously difficult. He remains angry about how I was treated, but also about the lost opportunities for change. Many around me who are committed to seeing a transformation in the realities of Indigenous peoples, and to actually doing politics differently in this country, are as angry as Tim is. I understand why. For their part, my mum and sister and many close friends just wanted me to be away from the toxicity.

I know there are also many friends and volunteers who have worked on both of our federal campaigns who still have a deep sense of sadness. Some are still Liberals. We were all so committed. I still have many conversations with them, gaining understanding about how they feel now about politics, about where we are at, about what is needed in the country. And about what they saw in 2015 that drew them to the Liberal Party and whether they are disillusioned. What comes through is a passion to transform the way politics is done federally to ensure all voices are heard.

But passion can also become a dangerous thing, as we have seen in other democracies. If we the people do not see opportunities to be a part of moving change forward, the alternative can be very scary: hope and trust are replaced with fear and anger. This can contribute to other kinds of movements that are less constructive and even dangerous. This is why I think the image-driven emptiness of much of how the Liberal government operates is becoming dangerous. Selling lofty rhetoric but failing to act in ways that live up to it breeds cynicism and even hopelessness that change can ever take place through our regular political processes and culture.

I recall sitting on a patio with some close friends and volunteers on a sunny day in VanGran some six months or so after being elected as an Independent. One member of our team challenged me for not having laid out more effectively a plan for a movement for a changed politics. I could feel his passion for wanting to press on with driving change. It reinforced for me that it all mattered, that what I had gone through had an impact and that people cared. But I also felt a bit annoyed. Not at my friend who was passionate but at the recognition of the reality that I was still struggling with understanding it all. Understanding how I could have been so wrong about the prime minister and the Liberals. How I still was struggling to recover from what had happened, both personally and politically. How I was struggling to let hope triumph over disaffection in my own heart.

I guess writing this book is part of that struggle. And it is part of carrying the work forward and pushing on to see these needed changes happen. For me, this is not the story of an Indigenous gal from an island off the West Coast of Canada who journeyed to the capital with hopes of helping to make change and could not. It is not the story of a girl who came back home realizing that there was not the space for her and the type of change she sought to make in that place. Rather, it is a story of learning (yes, about oneself) and about revealing how much Ottawa needs to change, and the roles we all can and must play in changing it. It is not a story that ends.

⋅

Deciding to run as an Independent—and being determined to win—was in part the answer to the questions I had been asking myself. I wanted to convey an answer of hope. To show that one could stand on principles, reject partisanship, and still succeed in an election. To demonstrate that what I had gone through in Ottawa meant something, and that there was a larger message in it. To illustrate that the public respects integrity above other values in a politician.

In running, and in thinking about potentially winning, I had no illusions that returning to Ottawa as an Independent MP would give me some greater ability to effect policy change, although I would try. Like any backbench MP in our parliamentary system, one is treated a little like an empty chair by the powers that be—at least until a vote is needed. While reform of Parliament is one (albeit important) aspect of our governance challenges, it was not the main reason I ran as an Independent. Changing our system is a larger project that will require all of the recognized national parties to, counter-intuitively, relinquish some control and power. No, what Jane and I really wanted to show by running is that it is possible to stand independently in campaigns against the established traditional parties and have a chance to win; that it is possible to inject new, independent ideas and messages into political discourse. That alone could inspire more people to act independently, think independently, and vote independently. Over time, this can lead to broader structural changes to our parliamentary system.

I have been fortunate in the two election campaigns in which I have stood as a candidate. I enjoyed running in 2015 as a Liberal. It was new and exciting, a good experience. Even more, I loved running in 2019 as an Independent. It was a chance to truly do things our own way. With the experience of 2015 under our belt, we also knew more about what we were doing and how to run a campaign. There was not a steep learning curve.

Melissa Doyle—"mumma," as I call her—moved out from Ottawa to run my campaign, and would later run my constituency office. Funny, dynamic, smart, and fiercely loyal, Melissa was perfect for the campaign. She has an energy that has always helped me stay focused, and helps to keep everyone buzzing and excited. As with Lea in the first campaign, Melissa and I understood each other well; we have become close friends over our years of working together, and we could tell what the other was thinking and what was needed. We were a pretty seamless team in setting the direction for the campaign.

And what a team we had. Volunteers were everywhere. Many of them were disaffected Liberals. But there were so many others. In our first campaign in 2015, there were many non-Liberals—those from other political parties or those who decided to get involved in politics for the first time. They had seen something they liked in what we were standing for. This time there were so many more people like that. Passionate individuals who wanted to see transformative change to our ways of governing in this country. They were from every political background, age group, and demographic. They were not all from VanGran. They believed what we were doing mattered. There was Vance, for example, a kind elderly man from Abbotsford out in the Fraser Valley, who would drive in each week to make phone calls for us. And organizations like Leadnow, which were not necessarily our friends in 2015, were now very supportive.

The core backbone of any successful campaign—volunteers and money—were just not a problem. In addition to so many volunteers, the money flooded in and we raised what we were allowed to spend so quickly we actually cut off fundraising early so as not to raise more than we needed. It was amazing. In fact, some people were upset that they could not donate. And, of course, support was coming from all over the country from people who were responding to what they believed was right and wrong in the SNC-Lavalin matter: volumes of correspondence, donations (including lots of yummy baked goods), and well-wishes.

A big part of our effort was the decision Jane and I made to run parallel campaigns. While ridings are all different, and VanGran is a long way from Jane's riding of Markham–Stouffville in Ontario, we wanted to project a similar image and focus on independence. This was reflected somewhat in the images and visual style of our campaigns, and, of course, substantively in our "platforms." What a great experience it is to write messaging and blogs for a campaign when one is not running for a political party. No one person or party can tell your team what they or you, as the candidate, must say. There is no script to follow. You truly just get to say what you believe and what, in my case, I knew was important to my constituents. I could also support what really might work, and the policy solutions with the most evidence. Imagine that. This is what I tried to do in the substantive ideas I put forward in the campaign. There were certain independent themes for the platform that Jane and I had developed together through our years as ministers—around partisanship, governance reform, integrity in government. There were also certain national policy issues to be emphasized, including climate change and Indigenous issues. And then we each had specific issues that were also important to our respective ridings. This was a lot of work. In political parties, candidates are given lines that reflect a platform written by others. We were doing it all ourselves.

I could feel the difference between 2015 and 2019. In 2015, there was always that sense that, when speaking to reporters or in forums with other candidates, one had to find and parrot the party lines on certain topics. Indeed, in 2019, I remember seeing candidates from other parties flipping through their party platforms to find the lines on certain subjects. I could just say what I believed in, the way I believed it, and address what I knew my constituents thought was a priority and important. I felt liberated. It was easier and more authentic. It was personal. It was real.

Of course, it was not all perfect. The basic reality is that our system is not designed for Independent candidates. It is designed for political parties. This is the case with the Canada Elections Act, for example, in how it places more restrictions on how Independents can fundraise. It was also a struggle to find certain contractors, such as polling companies, because there are not that many of them and most were locked up by specific parties. Many did not want to venture out to support an Independent.

The media also largely struggled with how to cover and report on an Independent. It is not what they are used to, and, of course, for some of them, their work and access is dependent on the types of relationships they maintain with those in government and within the political parties. I am not ascribing motivation to any individual, but as in any profession, some reporters are better than others. Some have a high set of standards they adhere to and others do not. Some have agendas, including political agendas, which colour much of what they report.

Reflecting back on 2019, as compared to 2015, I guess I felt truly like myself in the 2019 campaign. I let myself be seen for who I was in a more fulsome way than during my first federal campaign. A few months ago, I was talking to a new friend of mine, Lesli Boldt, a communications pro in Vancouver who was campaign advisor for Mira Oreck, the VanGran NDP candidate in the 2015 federal election. We got to talking about the two election campaigns. Lesli, a constituent, said something that really had me thinking. She said that she never actually felt she knew me—as a person—until after the 2015 election. Yes, she was a competitor's campaign advisor, but her comment about me had an impact. She said she only started to understand me when I gave a speech at Simon Fraser University soon after becoming MOJAG. During the campaign, she reflected, she had not really gotten a sense of who I was as a person.

I wonder if this is the case for many candidates who are subsumed under the banner of their party and overshadowed by their leader. People do not actually see them. I guess in most circumstances we do not really elect MPs but rather parties. This is a shame. I know that pollsters tell us that the quality of a local candidate only affects the vote by a small percentage, but Lesli's comments made that real.

As I reflected on what she'd said, it brought home how I felt about political parties. Granted, I knew she and her candidate were aligned with a political party at the time, and I knew I had to shape myself around the Liberal Party in that first campaign; yet our conversation gave me great pause. I appreciated it. I was in the process of writing this book—so thank you, Lesli.

I was free to be completely myself in 2019. My conversation with my friend and the way I felt during the 2019 campaign surely says something more about our political system. How much do we hide our true selves to protect an image, to try to convince voters to believe certain things even if they are not true? How much is that the culture of how we govern? Is it especially the case with this Liberal government? And is that the cause of the disaffection and cynicism that is far too prevalent in our political system and our political class? The public knows when someone is not representing themselves authentically or being true to who they are. It is pretty obvious. With politicians, it is like we almost assume they will not be authentic. I see now how during my time in the Liberal Party, I got caught up in that reality.

I asked a few individuals who were part of both campaigns to reflect on their experiences. Ted, a passionate man who is particularly focused on seeing Indigenous reconciliation advance, shared that in 2015 he saw in me the hope for a breakthrough in federal governance with the election of the Liberal government under Justin Trudeau. That hope seemed clinched with my appointment as MOJAG. After expressing his disgust at the SNC-Lavalin matter and my treatment, Ted continued his answer to my question with the following words:

> It was a bittersweet mix of triumph and revenge to help get you re-elected as an Independent in 2019, and now to see you finding the voice muzzled by the Liberal government. It's taken all this for me to begin to comprehend what a long and painful journey you and all Indigenous people have made and still must make. I will always be an outsider looking in, but am warmed by the graciousness with which you have welcomed me and Elaine along your part of the path.
>
> Screw politics. Of course, we will vote and do our bit, but our heart went out of it the moment we heard of your getting the boot . . . but here you are still standing. We're grateful and proud

to be standing with you ... our involvement with you during the campaigns, and especially the second one, was quintessentially about the joyfulness of it all. Which was really infectious, even when it was low key, like meeting the two little girls somewhere around 13th and Manitoba, who knew who you were and had even done something about you in school. As I think about it the "in school" part is what gradually reshapes worldviews.

There were many others who shared aspects of Ted's experience on the campaign. Feeling the joyfulness and freedom of 2019, still passionate for real change, but still hurting with disgust over what had transpired with SNC-Lavalin. I felt it on the streets and at the doorsteps. Many times, my breath was taken away when people would come up to me and reflect on how what happened during the SNC-Lavalin affair impacted them, what it meant to them, and how they appreciated my speaking the truth and standing up. They conveyed that it all meant something, was important, and we needed more, not fewer, examples of that.

I heard this from a woman who stopped me in South Granville and said that what I did in Ottawa, standing up on SNC-Lavalin, helped give her the courage to leave an abusive relationship. And I heard it from a dad who told me that watching my testimony with his young daughters helped them realize they can do anything in life that they set their minds to doing.

When I said publicly at the end of my testimony before the Justice Committee that "I was taught to always be careful what you say—because you cannot take it back," essentially that our words and our voices matter, I meant it. But from these countless, wonderful, loving people sharing their stories, I felt it. And as an Indigenous woman who, like all Indigenous women, has been made to feel at one time or another that her voice and experience does not matter, I was, frankly, overcome by hearing these stories. We do matter. Each of us matters. Our experience matters. It has resonance and meaning, and when we share our realities—our ancient ways of being that have persevered through resilience—we can contribute meaning and well-being to those around us, and all people everywhere.

One would not expect an election campaign to be part of a journey back to self, a reminder of who one really is. But the 2019 campaign did that for me.

◆

Election night was bittersweet. Ultimately the Liberal Party won again, but this time only a minority. Going into it both Jane and I had some level of confidence. But we knew Jane's riding was much more difficult than mine. The possibility of me getting elected and Jane not being successful in her campaign was, we knew, a real possibility. I dreaded the thought, not just for my dear friend and for what a loss it would be to not have her voice in Ottawa, but also for the idea of having to return to Ottawa without her.

Once again, I spent election night with my mum, Tim, Kory, and our nieces, this time at Melissa's house. As it became clear Jane was not going to win (with the time change this was known well before my results were clear), we were really upset. I was tearful while texting and talking to her. As the results started coming in from the media for Vancouver Granville I was behind as well. I remember Tim sitting beside me and Melissa sitting at the foot of my chair. She started tearing up. Tim suggested losing was a possibility. I remember not feeling anything. Our nieces were upset too.

Then the results started to change—we pulled ahead. Melissa was getting pumped. My mumma was calm. The girls were happy and Tim was too. When they called me the winner, I honestly felt nothing. I am still not sure why that was. But that is what it was. Do not get me wrong: I was happy to have won, to have showed that Independents can be elected. It meant something. At the same time, Jane had lost and I would be heading back to Ottawa alone. It was a very lonely feeling.

But we had a victory party to go to. This time a huge party. The media was out in full force. It was nuts. All of our volunteers were there. I loved them so. They were so happy. The Hellenic Community Centre was packed. Walking into that room with Tim and my family to be greeted by our team—our extended family—made me fill with pride, excitement . . . yep, I was now pumped. All I really remember of my speech is saying "Holy moly." And I meant it when looking out at the sea of people. I was overwhelmed at what we had accomplished together. So, so special. I felt blessed and wrapped in a victory that was ours, a victory for really doing politics differently.

TEN

Home and Beyond

So that's it. That is my story. Is it what you expected?

It is not what I ever expected. To go from Cape Mudge to Ottawa. From Indigenous politics to Canadian politics. To drift somewhat away from who I have always been just to find myself returning—when events and relations were at their most difficult—to who I have always been and what I have always believed.

Is this uncommon? That when things get hard in life, we feel our strengths and resilience more intimately? Almost imperceptibly, I think we find ourselves rising to the challenge by drawing on what innately is within us, our capacities of human spirit, even if we forget these qualities of self from time to time. I tend to think that this calling on inner strengths is universal—a trait we all have. I think that at various times in our lives we reveal our strengths to others and ourselves, drawing on the teachings, traditions, and cultures of which we may be a part.

Globally we are facing difficult times. As I write this, millions of Canadians are still waiting to get vaccinated. We are still isolated in our national and personal bubbles. The siege on the U.S. Capitol happened a month ago, and there remain feelings of uncertainty about challenges to democratic norms and the international rules-based system. It feels like a moment of collective reckoning in the evolution of modern geopolitical relations, the fallout of which could lead us in different directions depending on the strength of global leadership. We either become more separate and apart in our political islands of misplaced nationalistic fervour, or we continue down the path of constructively recognizing our interdependence to improve the lives of all peoples of the world, and in so doing, our own. The single biggest issue that unites us all is climate change.

I do not know about you, but for me the reality of the world has prompted a considerable amount of self-reflection about the choices I make, how I live my life, what is important, and how I can contribute to what we need to do collectively to help and heal humanity and our planet. To support the progressive arc of history and the advances we have made. It has also prompted me to reflect in new ways about the role of government and what lessons I take from my time in government.

Being Indigenous means knowing all too well the harms that can be caused by bad governance, weak decision-making, and unprincipled ways of acting. This is part of why I reacted as strongly as I did to the types of behaviours I saw while in Ottawa. I so wanted the government to be better. I could not stand the thought of being a part of one that was like so many others.

I believe the pandemic has reminded all of us of the costs of bad governance—be it domestically in Canada (federally or provincially), or regionally in the Americas, or globally. Bad governance can be a matter of life and death for each of us, anywhere.

Good governance is not just an ideal that we need to strive for. It matters for our Elders and newborns and everyone in between. We need good governance, better governance, not just to thrive but to survive. This is a theme that I have often repeated in my governance work with First Nations. Governance can be done well or badly. Research tells us that the quality of governance, even more than its specific form, has a huge impact on the fortunes of any given society. And Canada, as a country, is no exception. Societies that govern well do better economically, socially, and politically than those that do not. Simply put, good governance increases a society's chances of effectively meeting the needs of its people and creating conditions where all citizens can lead meaningful, prosperous, and happy lives.

I am at times more upset, frustrated, and even angry today about what I saw while I was in government than I was when it was all happening. Why? Because it simply is not good enough. We can do better. And guess what? We had better do better or the results could be catastrophic.

I am not sure if I have taken enough from the lessons of my time in government. I am not sure I know what it all means, and why it happened the way it did. Right or wrong, and for what it is worth, here is what I have to say.

Life is a mix of the steady and the sudden. I think for many of us there are long stretches of time where life is as it is, moving along, moving forward. During those times we are focused on certain priorities, whether it be meeting core survival needs, family well-being, relationships, work, studies, or community. In focusing on these priorities, we are striving to make things better, be happier, express meaning, and make more of our life as we wish it to be. And then, unavoidably, there are moments of sudden change, transformative moments, that in a second can result in us reshaping where we focus, what we do, and even who we are. These can be joyful, like a birth, meeting someone, or a new, life-changing opportunity. Or they can be filled with pain and loss, such as a death, an illness, a sudden unexpected event. A pandemic.

My life has had this pattern, and the story told in this book reveals times when I was living day to day, focused on work, and some of the moments that were transformative and upended life in unexpected ways. My time in government ended in such a moment.

Going through the public SNC-Lavalin affair was a transformation. It changed, quite suddenly, my work, my role, what I did, how others perceived me, and how I perceived myself. And it crystallized and confirmed some of what I truly believe. Many of the effects of that transformative moment are still unknown to me. I am still learning and think I will be for a long time.

This life pattern, the steady and the sudden, exists in our collective life as well. There are times when humanity shifts in significant and major ways. Then there are long stretches when we start taking for granted that things are moving along slowly, incrementally, and while there are ups and downs, the basic way things are functioning is as it should be and does not really need to change.

In Canada—and frankly in most wealthy, Western, liberal democracies—we have been somewhat complacent, taking for granted that our way of life and the institutions and ways in which we govern are in place for the common good. We've accepted that while some things need work and will incrementally improve, the big things will not and do not need to change.

In this, I think we are wrong. Of course, it should be acknowledged that some people do know big things need to change. They push and fight for it. Indeed, many marginalized populations, including Indigenous peoples, know big change is needed. But for many, there is more of a comfort with the idea that things are fundamentally as they are and always will be.

Our government and political culture are organized around this belief. If the current Liberal Party has a vision of policy change, it is that maintaining a course of slow, progressive change, of finding compromises that (while sometimes contradictory) avoid bold action, is the way forward.

But here is the issue. Our complacency has caught up with us. We are, collectively, in a sudden, transformative moment. Of the painful kind. Humanity today is confronted, in my opinion, with three massive and urgent realities: the need for racial justice and equality (including, but not only, Indigenous reconciliation); pandemic response, including its economic and social impacts domestically and globally; and climate change. These three realities all, in their own ways, are convulsive and existential to human life, ways of living, and well-being, and will impact generations to come.

All three also share something fundamental in common. They are about the integration and interconnection of human beings. Racial justice reflects this in the most basic way: How do we live together, with equality, inclusion, and justice, when our history is mostly stories of us living apart, or with inequality and injustice? And climate change and pandemic response and recovery boil the reality of connectedness and the need for integration down to its very core. We all breathe the same air and drink the same water, and when one part of us gets sick we all do. We must figure out how to respond to these issues collectively, and take action collectively, or we all suffer the consequences. We need to do this locally, regionally, and globally.

Racial justice, climate change, and pandemic response and recovery are about our shared reality as human beings. How we respond will determine the degree of suffering felt by multiple future generations, whether at home or abroad.

I learned the hard way that our politics and system of government are not designed to respond to these existential challenges. Obviously, I stormed into government pushing transformative responses on racial justice only to realize there was not the will, understanding, or structures in place to support the response needed. Commentators and reporters, tweeters and leakers can say all they want about the struggle we faced over Indigenous policy as being a mixture of personality conflicts and tensions. It was not. It was all very simple.

I thought the bold, transformative things that the prime minister and government had said in 2015 about reconciliation were actually what the government intended to do. They were not. And now I know they do not believe that bold action is the right way to go, or even really possible. It is that simple.

Similarly, on climate change, everything almost by default has deviated to the muddy middle of taking steps—including some large ones, relatively speaking—like putting a price on carbon. But none of this approaches what is needed to actually address the challenge. Cancel a pipeline, buy and build another one.

We have to recognize that time is running out. In 2021, we might literally be in the last Parliament that will be able to take any meaningful climate action before it is too late. The United Nations established the Intergovernmental Panel on Climate Change (IPCC) in 1988, and it was in 1989 when climatologists first declared global warming a threat to human survival and ranked it "second only to nuclear war."

In 2015, when world leaders met in Paris, they came to an agreement on a target to reduce greenhouse gas emissions. It was an attempt to limit the global temperature increase in this century to 2° Celsius above preindustrial levels while simultaneously pursuing the means to limit the increase to 1.5° Celsius. We know that a rise beyond 1.5° Celsius will have catastrophic ecological, economic, and social consequences that could threaten the very foundations of civilization.

The latest reality check from the IPCC is that we need new targets to get us to 1.5° Celsius, and we only have about a decade to act. In October of 2018, the IPCC issued a special report declaring that global temperature is already more than 1° Celsius higher than pre-industrial times. In order to meet the 1.5° Celsius ceiling, the report called for reductions in fossil fuel use by 45 percent by 2030 and 100 percent by 2050. These must now be our minimum targets.

No question, these targets are incredibly challenging. But in large part this is because politicians have lacked the ability to implement the changes that were called for back in the 1990s and early 2000s, because these big issues are not easily tackled through our political systems. The harsh truth is that we are still on a path to global temperature warming in the range of 4° to 5° Celsius this century.

In another way, the pandemic response has also revealed how government is not designed for transformative action on the big issues. Yes, our government was forced to do some big things quickly and suddenly, as governments all around the world had to do. And good on them and, for that matter, all parliamentarians for rising up to face this collective challenge. But the response was also a patch on top of a patch, with more coming to patch up the earlier patches. In other words, the response is largely incoherent, because our governments and modes of functioning are not designed to address bold action, or implement bold change, to meet bold challenges.

So, what needs to change? As I have said before, there is a need for a new and principled culture of independence, inclusiveness, and co-operation. What does that mean? Let me lay out a few ideas.

Political independence is about being free from the control or influence of others in making decisions in the best interests of Canadians. Here I am thinking primarily, though not only, about the control and influence of political parties—of partisanship—on how elected representatives think and act. I will not mince words: this control and influence in our system is near total. It extends to every Liberal MP being given a piece of paper telling them how the government is going to vote on a particular issue. Sure, some representatives are brave and push back on things their party does that they do not agree with. They even sometimes vote against their own party. Often, though, they do so with the knowledge that this type of action will come with political costs—typically in terms of opportunities and positions within the party and in one's role as a member of Parliament. And good for them. But the vast majority of MPs simply follow the party line, even when they disagree with it or it fundamentally goes against their beliefs. You might wonder, then, if they are in the wrong party. But it is more complicated and involved than that. It is not only on matters of policy. Many also turn a blind eye when they see something wrong happening. The dominant factor determining what they do and say is "what does the party want?"

In their defence, the behaviour of MPs is a symptom, not the cause, of the problem of partisanship; it is the result of a system that needs to be reformed before it can address the big challenges of our time more effectively. The problem of partisanship is that it constructs division and conflict around groups of people labelled in certain ways, rather than focusing on varying approaches to policy and ideas. A different approach would allow all of us to bring our own worldviews, experiences, and perspectives to the table as part of a search for the best outcome for Canadians. The policy issues themselves become the fodder of partisanship rather than the lens through which parliamentarians can try to find and agree on solutions to the big issues we face—solutions we all need. The "loyal Opposition" becomes the disloyal critic, and the executive (Cabinet) becomes less accountable to Parliament and more the plaything of the unelected people in high office whose primary concern is that the party be re-elected. And on it goes, cycle after cycle, no matter the political stripe. That is my summary—albeit cynical—of our system, based on my lived experience.

So many times, decisions I observed while I was in government were made for no other reason but to reinforce a partisan conflict—creating division to try to elevate oneself and stigmatize another. I remember decisions being made in an effort to trigger a debate over abortion, which no one had any desire to reopen, for no other reason but to try to make other parties squirm or fuel fundraising efforts. I remember decisions on critical issues being shelved for no reason except that they may have opened an opportunity for other parties to "score points." I remember bad decisions being made simply because the better idea had already been proposed by another party. This is the ugly side of partisan politics. "Nuts," as my father would say.

Partisanship in the form in which it currently exists results in bad decisions. Plain and simple. Partisanship hinders our ability to achieve long-term solutions to complex problems that won't be solved within an election cycle. Government needs to make important but sometimes unpopular decisions.

The challenges of racial injustice, pandemic response and recovery, and climate change are of such scope and depth that their solutions can only be found by learning to work and live together in new ways. Our means and ends need to be aligned. We cannot build co-operation through divisive means. Just as we do not teach love by using force and hate, we will not meet these fundamental challenges that will require collective action through a mode of decision-making rooted in false, constructed, partisan conflict. Our parliamentary system may have been effective in the past, when society was not as compli-cated or interconnected. But it does not work as well in today's world. For example, today's social media companies use algorithms in their business models that help to perpetuate and strengthen social divi-sion, not unity. Political parties know this and use it.

I am not saying that our system is so broken that we cannot get anything done. I have seen good things get done. But we are not doing nearly as well, or as much, as we could and need to do.

I am also not saying there is no role for political parties. They play an important role in bringing disparate groups and voices together, aligning efforts, and supporting the participation of those who might otherwise struggle to get involved. Look at me. I accept that as an Indigenous woman leader crossing over into Canadian politics, I was unlikely to have had a chance of winning in Vancouver Gran-ville running as an Independent in 2015. But at the same time as I benefited from the party system, my example also illustrates the fundamental problem. Why isn't there a space, opportunity, and sup-port for an Indigenous woman leader to run and have a chance as an Independent if that is how she wishes to present herself? How many others, including people from populations long marginalized from our politics, have simply been left out because of the degree of control and influence of political parties? This is part of the challenge of inclusiveness. In order to make more room for different political voices, proportional representation—which has been debated for years—can help, as it has in the form practised by New Zealand, for example. Data has shown that countries that use proportional voting are ranked higher on the quality-of-life index.

Overt partisanship leads to decisions and choices being made to achieve the ends of political parties—to keep power or be best positioned to seize power—rather than to serve the needs of Canadians. This is but one example of how our democracy is being frayed. But it is by no means the only one, as the SNC-Lavalin affair demonstrated.

That entire episode was an attack on the rule of law for no good reason. The justifications and rationale expressed by the government for what they attempted to do in trying to pressure me—even if they were legitimate (which they were not)—were completely invalid and quite beside the point. One never has to violate core democratic or legal principles in order to have economic growth or retain jobs. Who would ever even think that way, unless one is ignorant, corrupt, anti-democratic, or anti–rule of law? One might think that way, I guess, if one is consumed by an ulterior motive that is not about democratic governance or economic growth—like, possibly, a primary focus on a self-interested goal such as getting re-elected.

I do need to say something more about the rule of law and the principles of democracy. I believe these principles are dynamic. They evolve and change over time in order to be responsive to new understandings, realities, and challenges. As I said in my testimony:

> *It has always been my view that the Attorney General of Canada must be non-partisan, more transparent in the principles that are the basis of decisions and, in this respect, always willing to speak truth to power.*

In saying this, I was reflecting what I understood to be the vital importance of the rule of law and prosecutorial independence in our democracy.

My understanding of this has been shaped by some lived experiences. I am, of course, a lawyer. I was a prosecutor in the Downtown Eastside of Vancouver so I come to this view as a trained professional and committed to certain values as key to our system of order.

But my understanding of the rule of law has also been shaped by my experiences as an Indigenous person and as an Indigenous leader.

The history of Crown-Indigenous relations in this country includes a history of the rule of law not being respected.

Indeed, one of the main reasons for the urgent need for justice and reconciliation today is that, in the history of our country, we have not always upheld foundational values such as the rule of law in relations to Indigenous Peoples.

And I have seen the negative impacts for freedom, equality and a just society this can have first-hand.

So when I pledged to serve Canadians as your minister of justice and attorney general, I came to it with a deeply ingrained commitment to the rule of law and the importance of acting independently of partisan, political and narrow interests in all matters.

When we do not do that, I firmly believe and know we do worse as a society.

We need to understand and apply the rule of law in ways that recognize that in our nation's history, the law, in fact, has been used to exclude, marginalize, and oppress certain peoples. We need to recognize that in various ways we must strive to make our society more substantively equal, and that people have diverse realities and experiences that we need to account for. We need to recognize that in upholding the rule of law we must do so in ways that promote greater justice and equality in how the law operates, and in society as a whole. This is what principles are for—to keep us on the path forward, to keep us honest, to make life more meaningful and better for more and more of us. As is said, "the arc of the moral universe is long, but it bends towards justice." This understanding of the rule of law is about continually bending towards justice.

During the SNC-Lavalin affair, there were clear attempts to bend the rule of law. But in this case, it was being bent towards injustice. Towards politically self-interested ends. Towards narrow and petty preoccupations that do none of us a service. It was gross. And it was but one example of principles being sacrificed in that way.

All of these things I am describing—partisanship, unprincipled politics, a lack of inclusion—are problems of political culture. There is nothing fixed or necessary about this political culture. It is our creation. We can change it. We can also expect more of our leaders. Integrity matters.

Arnold Schwarzenegger—I cannot quite believe I am talking about the Terminator—spoke some important words to his fellow Americans in the wake of the 2021 Capitol siege. While finishing the first draft of this chapter I saw his video message from January 10, 2021, on Twitter. I have no idea why I watched it, but it resonated. It was both compelling and emotional.

Schwarzenegger compared the events on Capitol Hill to the Kristallnacht, the Night of Broken Glass. When I watched his video, I could not help but be moved by the message of confidence in the United States, its institutions, and its ability to move forward. His message was both damning of the insurgent domestic terrorists and President Trump but incredibly hopeful at the same time. Invoking a biblical reference, it called for leaders to have a "servant's heart" when it came to what is expected of those of us who might hold office.

As powerful as his message was, I think what struck me most was that it also missed the mark in one important way. Which is this: that good governance and the protection of democratic principles primarily takes place hidden from view through the mundane and day-to-day ways in which we protect democracy, our way of life, and the rule of law in the face of those who would challenge it.

The breakdown of the rule of law and democratic governance is not always about unhinged people wielding banners and flags and storming buildings, or about going to war, including civil war, or about overt criminality by elected or appointed officials. No, it is more mundane than that. There is a need to maintain and strengthen the institutions that support the system on a day-by-day basis. This is what sustains governance over time and provides certainty and stability. Sometimes we are able to see the fragility of the system that has provided us the quality of life we enjoy only when it smacks us in the face.

It is striking when, as we saw during the U.S. Capitol riot, a guy gets dressed up like a failed *Dances with Wolves* character, wearing buffalo horns and skins, and is seen with other seditionists standing half-naked over the chair of the Speaker of the House. But that is the aberrant form of threat. Other threats are much more subtle but equally or more dangerous. These threats exist in the daily routines— some of which are seen but many of which are not—through which the system is upheld and advanced. They exist in the work that takes place every day in the halls of government power and with those who have been elected or appointed and whose actions are often opaque to the general public. Typically, this happens because of the need for confidentiality and the ability to speak freely to one's peers. In this situation, behind closed doors, the only people upholding the system and the rules are, in fact, those who are in the room—at the epicentre of power in our system. This is a place I found myself. For every SNC-Lavalin affair, there are many moments that are never seen. What happens in those moments matters. And if wrong things are happening, the danger and loss can affect every one of us.

At the extreme end of the spectrum, the system can collapse, creating chaos and disorder—even violence—if the people in that space and those closest to them are themselves the system destroyers, or the instigators of insurrection, like Trump and his enablers. Democracy is supposed to prevent that through the institutions, laws, conventions, and norms that support it.

One thing I am not is prone to hyperbole. I am not comparing Trudeau to Trump. He is not Trump. And SNC-Lavalin does not rise to the high crimes and misdemeanours we have seen committed by public officials in recent years in the U.S. and in some other democracies around the world. But at the same time, the prime minister possibly did not really understand how some of his officials were trying to exert pressure to bend the rule of law. Or perhaps he did and didn't care. Or perhaps he directed them to. Because of our system we probably will never know what motivated the full extent of these actions. The most our system can discover—given the decision not to waive full confidentiality—is that Prime Minister Justin Trudeau broke the law in contravening the Conflict of Interest Act. And this is the point. It seemed a lot of people at the top did not actually understand—or chose not to understand—the nature of how power is supposed to work in our system, what principles are important, and what is needed for good governance. And that is a problem.

Of course, we can say, looking back, that ultimately the system did work. The PM and his advisors and whomever they may have been thinking they were helping were unsuccessful, and did not get their way. That was my focus. But what an unfortunate way for the system to have to work. And it begs the obvious question: At what other times are the rules, norms, and conventions being bent? If my experience is an example of what it takes to keep our norms in place—with all the public exposure and outcry—how many times out of ten is it not? Three times? Five times or more? And is that number going up or down? For the system to work in this instance there were casualties. Jane and I were casualties. Gerry was a casualty. The PM's reputation and that of the clerk were damaged, and the clerk resigned. Because of the air SNC-Lavalin sucked out of the government, certain policy developments were casualties. The integrity of certain Liberals became casualties. And if it takes all this, then our system is weaker than we think, and we could be in a far worse situation more quickly than we might expect if the actors are more nefarious.

At one point in his message, Schwarzenegger picks up his "Conan" sword from his acting days—a prop (literally)—and he compares the system, democracy, to the steel of the sword. You heat it up, pound it, and dip it into water, and the more you do this the stronger the sword becomes. He suggests that insurrections and wars represent the pounding and the strengthening of democracy. Or, to put it another way, that democracy has been tempered. While it is a powerful metaphor, I do take issue with the idea that we need to find strength in conflict. To me, that is a very aggressive, old-school, and perhaps patriarchal view of the world.

Sure, conflict can take and forge strength. But it is much harder, and takes much more strength, to truly co-operate than to choose to fight. Co-operation takes really trying to see another person for who they are, to understand their experience, to listen. It requires checking oneself and realizing one is not the centre of the universe. It requires opening up, being transparent, and battling with one's own inner self in order to be productive. It means recognizing that everyone has value in what is at stake, and doing what one can to help others. It means being comfortable enough in oneself to know that one is not always right. It means having the strength to change.

All of the elements of co-operation take real courage. We do not have nearly enough of it in our political culture, and our system does not support it. We have so little of it that when people see it they are shocked and surprised. Instead, what we have plenty of is petty, constructed conflict—a tribalism that weakens rather than strengthens our country, democracy, and the people who are in Ottawa supposedly representing us.

So where does this leave us? We all want politicians and those who work for them to follow the rules and to act with integrity—to be ethical. Most of us expect that our structures and procedures of governance—our institutions—will support, promote, and uphold good governance. We expect that checks and balances are in place to inform decision-making and when necessary expose inappropriate action and correct it.

My experience in Ottawa has been an eye-opening learning experience. It has also been a personal reminder that while Canada, thankfully, is considered to be one of the most democratic, ethical, and least corrupt countries in the world, good governance cannot be taken for granted and requires hard work and due diligence to maintain. We cannot be complacent, and there is always room for improvement.

•

I went to Ottawa hoping to be an Indigenous woman in the Cabinet and contribute teachings and learnings from the Indigenous experience in this country to making good decisions and setting better policy. I ended up being treated as the "Indian" in the Cabinet. Became the "Indian" out of the Cabinet and finally the "Indian" out of the party. An unusual tale? Perhaps not so much.

When I set out to write this book, I was reminded by Kory that she had recorded over eight hours of our grandmother speaking about our people's ways and her life. As I said earlier, Kory recorded these tapes in 1990, when our grandmother was nearing the end of her life. Sometimes my auntie Annie and auntie Lilly and Fred are in the conversations as well. My granny and aunties move between English and Kwak'wala. All of them were recorded at my granny's kitchen table, by her window that looked out over the cherry tree to the right of the grass and, off to the left, the second green of the Comox Golf Club.

I had not listened to these cassettes before writing this book. When I played the first one on an old cassette machine and heard my grandmother's voice my eyes flooded with tears—the kind of tears that come when memories are so vivid and intimate it feels like they overtake every aspect of your being. I could feel everything of her. Her words dripped with the learning of thousands of years of oral history and the wisdom gained through a life fully lived.

On the recordings she reflects on the disruptions our system of governance has experienced and laments the contemporary reality of our people, on which outside forces have had large impacts. She asks whether we, as a people, still really know who we are. When she lovingly shares stories about my dad, she talks of how she may have named him wrong. "Your father is too voluble to be a Hamatsa," she says. As part of the Hamatsa society—as a Chief—you are not supposed to raise your voice; you are supposed to be observing, taking everything in, and maintaining balance. But in this contemporary world, because of how things have changed, Dad had to lead in the outside world, and he needed to do what he was doing because of those changes.

She also talks on the recordings about the Potlatch, about how our people maintained governing through the Potlatch even after it was outlawed by Canada through the Indian Act. She talks about how our people would disguise the Potlatch from the Indian agents that would travel to Kingcome by boat. They had lookouts along the way, on the shore. And when the signal came that the Indian agent was close by, those assembled would start singing "Onward Christian Soldiers" to trick the agent into thinking they were just being "good little Indians." When the political organization of the Native Brotherhood was in its early days, they followed a practice of singing that same hymn at the beginning of every meeting.

In the shadows, hidden from view, resilience, survival, and the work of advancing justice carried on. Our governance systems were nurtured and maintained by my recent ancestors and their generation at significant risk and cost. The struggles undertaken by them allowed our ways to survive and to come out of the shadows, and to be revitalized and rejuvenated. They knew what was needed for us, as Indigenous peoples, to once again govern ourselves in ways that respect our legal traditions and, in so doing, support the cultural, social, economic, and spiritual well-being of our peoples. This history of survival is a part of being who we are, and who we will always be.

I think of the sacrifice my grandmother and so many others had to make to keep something known and alive—to make sure it could thrive again. And I realize that throughout my journey to Ottawa I was looking at her in the mirror, and she was guiding me each step of the way. She had already shown the way, as our Elders do. She had passed on the knowledge and responsibility, and that we each have a role to play in our time. While my grandmother and the "old people" had to maintain ways of governing without being seen, I, like my father and other leaders, had to do my part with everyone seeing. While my grandmother and my ancestors used the shadows to keep something strong, I had to endure the glare of the public eye to raise an alarm about what was hidden from view.

Isn't that the way of change—the unseen becoming seen? A lot that was unseen within me I now see because of my journey to Ottawa and back. I hope some light was also shone on some of the challenges we face, and where we still must go as a country. I believe it has, and for that I am grateful.

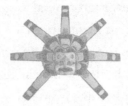

Author's Note

Throughout the writing of this book I kept in the forefront of my mind the responsibilities I hold to maintain Cabinet confidentiality and solicitor-client privilege. These responsibilities are, like the rule of law and others, some of the principles that undergird our democracy, and are critical to how our government functions. They are also important to me personally, and nothing in this Author's Note or in the book itself diminishes or undermines their importance.

But in recognizing that principles of confidentiality are among the foundations of our democracy, I believe we are also affirming how they are more than abstract and obtuse legal concepts. They exist for a purpose: to support good governance, sound decision-making, the ethical functioning of democracy, and the requirements of justice. They are living and active principles, applied by human beings exercising their judgment, in times and places that are dynamic and changing, with the purpose of supporting governments to act in an ethical manner, in the best interests of Canadians.

For me, in interpreting and applying these principles—both as minister of justice and attorney general and today—I do so through the experiences, lenses, and identities that I have. One of those is as a lawyer, which includes the obligations I hold as part of that profession. Another is as a leader, which includes upholding the ideal that true leadership is indivisible from being an example of integrity, honesty, and inclusiveness.

And yet another essential lens through which I interpret and unabashedly apply these principles is the one I use as an Indigenous woman, raised with a worldview that all things are interconnected and interdependent, and that our roles and responsibilities as individuals are to ensure that patterns of justice, equality, and truthfulness are increasingly present in both our individual and social relations. Within this worldview, and as I have stated in this book, one of the central teachings according to which I was raised—what some would call a law in my culture—is to always be careful with words because one cannot take them back. This teaching informs choices about what one says, what one does not say, and how one says it. We should use words to inform, encourage, and uplift. This teaching is also an injunction about the responsibility to speak truthfully, especially when it is a truth that is important for the well-being of the collective.

The words I swore in the oaths I took as the minister of justice and the attorney general of Canada, the minister of veterans affairs, and as a member of the Queen's Privy Council matter. Ultimately, they speak of responsibilities owed to the Queen as the head of state, to our democratic system, and to all Canadians. Upholding those oaths, and fulfilling those responsibilities, is essential, including when it comes to how they may place limits on what I can say and how they may require me to speak out. This is part of being careful with words and being truthful to what one has committed to do.

As such, throughout the process of writing I have remained mindful of the limitations—grounded in my oaths and the roles I played—that exist on my ability to speak publicly or disclose internal documents about conversations within government involving me, the prime minister and other ministers, and their senior staff and officials. These limitations are rooted primarily in conventions around Cabinet confidences. Cabinet ministers bear collective responsibility for the Cabinet's decisions and are expected to publicly support those decisions or resign. The confidentiality conventions are intended to preserve the principle of collective responsibility and allow for the full and frank substantive discussions that lead to Cabinet's policy- and decision-making. These limitations are also rooted in solicitor-client privilege relating to my role as attorney general of Canada. As attorney general, I provided advice to government on matters of law. Solicitor-client privilege extends to communications that relate to the government's seeking of or obtaining legal advice.

Although I am limited in what I can share about specific Cabinet discussions leading to decisions made (in other words, the Cabinet's substantive discussions), it was critically important that I share, as I am fully entitled to, my own perspectives on *how* decisions are made within government—or at least within this government—and the serious flaws in the processes that lead to such decisions. This is particularly true for those processes relating to the PMO's role in decision-making and the way in which decisions may be predetermined or orchestrated before a Cabinet discussion has even taken place. In my view, these permitted insights should cause all of us to re-evaluate how government performs its role. Sharing these insights is part of upholding the importance of truth-telling, and doing so in a way that uses words carefully because they matter and cannot be taken back.

Documents, particularly those prepared to assist ministers in making decisions, and agendas or minutes of Cabinet meetings, have not been reproduced or summarized in this book. These documents are at the core of the conventions and privilege that govern me. Nor have I disclosed any solicitor-client privileged communications that remain confidential. Finally, in some instances, I have chosen not to attribute specific comments to specific individuals where doing so is unimportant to the true narrative.

Of course, part of the story in this book is how conventions of confidentiality can also be abused—such as through government's selective and misleading disclosures of otherwise confidential information to create a false or incomplete narrative. Or through government's partial or incomplete waiver of Cabinet confidences so as to prevent the full, true story from coming out. Indeed, the ethics commissioner, in his report on the SNC-Lavalin affair, indicated that his request to access all Cabinet confidences relevant to his investigation was denied. This denial constrained witnesses in their ability to provide all relevant evidence. He stated that if his office is to remain truly independent and fulfill its purpose, he must have "unfettered access to all information that could be relevant" to the exercise of his mandate. That unfettered access never came.

As it turned out, the ethics commissioner was nonetheless able to collect sufficient information to determine that the prime minister, through his actions and those of his staff, sought to improperly further the interests of SNC-Lavalin. The commissioner also found that the prime minister contravened section 9 of the Conflict of Interest Act by using his position of authority over me to seek to influence, both indirectly and directly, my decision as attorney general as to whether to intervene in the SNC-Lavalin criminal proceedings to overrule the director of public prosecutions. Although I was personally vindicated—as was the rule of law—by the ethics commissioner's report, I share his expressed belief that, due to the undemocratic and non-transparent way in which he was denied access to all relevant information, he was unable to fully discharge his investigative duties under the act.

Similarly, at the time of writing, the police assigned to criminally examine the SNC-Lavalin matter remain unable to access all relevant information. Sadly, in my view, the decision not to waive all relevant confidences had little or nothing to do with the underlying importance of Cabinet confidences. Instead, it had to do with the government's desire to ensure that the full narrative never be known—whether to all in Cabinet, the ethics commissioner, the police, the media, or the public.

The time is long overdue for a critical examination of the scope of our conventions around Cabinet confidences and when they are inapplicable or should be waived, all to ensure they are not misused to immunize government from proper scrutiny of conduct that may be improper, unlawful, or corrupt. After all, when Canadians think of our system of democracy, and what makes it healthy and work properly, there are many principles and practices that are thought of as fundamental before, or at least on par with, Cabinet confidentiality: participation, transparency, honesty, co-operation, integrity, inclusion, and many more. I trust Canadians to speak to how they view the fitting together of all of these important principles and practices. Indeed—and again, as I recount in the book—when I was minister of justice and attorney general of Canada, I spoke publicly about the importance of honesty and transparency with Canadians, and how essential this is for ethical and good governance.

The government provided a partial or incomplete waiver of Cabinet confidences pertaining to SNC-Lavalin for the period during which I held the office of attorney general. Accordingly, I describe in this book some of the exchanges I or my staff had within government permitted by that waiver. In addition, the prime minister and others within government effectively waived Cabinet confidences through public statements about the basis of my decision to remain in Cabinet and about my decision to resign from Cabinet. The prime minister said, among other things, that my initial decision to remain in Cabinet "spoke for itself"—as if I had endorsed the approach he and others had taken to SNC-Lavalin. He claimed my public statements were inconsistent with conversations he'd had with me, and that it would have been my duty to speak to him directly if I were concerned that something untoward had occurred. According to him, I did not do so. He also quoted me in relation to specific conversations that would otherwise be subject to Cabinet confidences. This book provides my reflections on those statements and the events and conversations they reference, as I am entitled to do in the circumstances. Further, in my view, existing conventions permit me to explain my resignation from Cabinet since, by resigning, I was no longer bound by collective responsibility for the decisions subsequently made by Cabinet.

Similarly, the government's public statements about matters that had been discussed in Cabinet were, of course, not confined to SNC-Lavalin issues. Again, the content of this book has been informed by the extent to which the government has already chosen to publicly disseminate information that might otherwise be covered by confidentiality principles.

For me, what is unconscionable are efforts by governments to try to hide from Canadians wrongdoing or things that may look bad, or distort basic facts and understandings of events. Keeping such things hidden, while trying to mould to one's advantage what the public may know, is the opposite of upholding the teaching that words matter. Such a fear of the truth—such efforts to keep the truth hidden—is in itself the most damning evidence of guilt, and a most cynical and corrosive orientation to what good governance and democracy requires and Canadians deserve.

One expression of the integrative worldview I hold is that I am ever aware that I exist within multiple legal orders. This is true for all Indigenous peoples in Canada. For me, it is Canadian and Kwakwa̱ka'wakw law. Existing within both of these legal orders has only made me stronger and, in all my endeavours, I strive, always, as I must, to honour the responsibilities and obligations that lie within both of these legal traditions. This reality is what helped me speak the truth to power when I was within the federal government and uphold my oaths and obligations. These responsibilities and obligations have also informed the choice of each and every word in this book.

Acknowledgements

"Grateful" is the final word of *"Indian" in the Cabinet*. And grateful is how I feel when I reflect on my journey from Cape Mudge to Ottawa and back. It is a journey for which I was prepared by the wisdom, experience, and perseverance of so many who came before me, and those who have shaped, supported, and influenced me throughout my life. There are so many names that I know I cannot name each and every one of you. But I love and appreciate each and every one of you.

To all those whom I had the pleasure of working with professionally—from the courthouse on Main Street to the British Columbia Treaty Commission and the British Columbia Assembly of First Nations, from my Minister's Office at the Department of Justice and at Veterans Affairs Canada, and from the Vancouver Granville MP offices—I am profoundly thankful. To my ministerial chiefs of staff, Lea Nicholas-MacKenzie and Jessica Prince, who have back-stopped me and our work: you are both professional, principled, smart, passionate, and friends always. And to the amazing group who made the transition with me from MOJAG to MOVA: Melissa Doyle, Audrey DeMarsico, Whitney Morrison, Kathy Pinksen, Phil Jansson, and Jessica Prince—what a team. To all of the great public servants who worked alongside me, from those who were my closest aides—William F. Pentney and Geoff Bickert—to all who worked so hard on behalf of Canadians. Thank you.

To my constituency and parliamentary affairs staff (and all of our office volunteers), thanks to each of you for your hard work and dedication in keeping our busy office running smoothly. Every member of Parliament is supported by a small group of staffers, and to me you are the best.

To all of the Vancouver Granville TeamJody volunteers. You are so many, from two campaigns (2015 and 2019) and all the years in between. With every door you knocked on, every call you made, every election sign you hammered in, and every encouraging message you sent—your passion for principled politics has inspired so much. Thank you for doing your part—to people such as John Turner, who knocked on my first door with me way back in 2014, and Ted Cragg and Elaine Perry, with whom I knocked on thousands more. To Dorian Pope, who had never been involved in a campaign but became central in two. To Francis Cheng, our very diligent (and stylish) financial agent. And to Joan and Rob Conklin, who campaigned and then volunteered in our constituency office from almost the first day managing our front desks: thank you all for holding me up and for exemplifying what it means to do politics differently.

To those who assisted me in the writing of this book. First off, I am grateful to the entire team at HarperCollins Canada for your support—specifically my editor, Jennifer Lambert, and copy editor, Linda Pruessen. Thank you to my agent (never thought I would say those words!), Stephanie Sinclair, who helped guide me through the interesting world of publishing.

To my impromptu but incredibly helpful, clever, and diverse team of chapter reviewers: Jane Philpott, Melissa Doyle, Ted Cragg, Elaine Perry, Sarah Jane Barclay, Todd Barclay, Jessica Prince, Lea Nicholas-MacKenzie, Rick MacKenzie, and Geoff Bickert—thank you for your encouragement and for the many thoughtful comments, edits, and suggestions.

And to Roshan Danesh. We have worked closely together since my days as Regional Chief, through the MOJAG years, and on through the preparation of this book—from concept to completion, through all of its starts and stops. I could not have written it without you. Thank you for sharing so much with me.

In my personal journey, there are four extraordinary people who paved the way, lifted me up, and gave me guidance. To my beloved grandmother Pugladee (Ethel Pearson); my father, Hemas Kla-Lee-Lee-Kla (William Lane Wilson)—yes, I have been and will always be proud to be "Bill Wilson's daughter," though I am so grateful for your story of signing books "Jody's dad"; my mother, Sandra Raylene Wilson; and my sister, Kory Wilson: What more can I say that has not been imparted between and among the pages of this book? To the degree I am able to speak the truth in this world, with whatever courage and dignity I can muster, it is because you showed the way. I have been so blessed.

To Heather Raybould and my late father-in-law, Vilven John Raybould: I appreciate your quiet but consistent support and opinions (and also the best newspaper clipping service one could ask for—thanks, Dad).

To my husband, Tim Raybould . . . for over a quarter of my life, you have been my constant companion and champion. Thank you for your fierce opinions; for reading, rereading, and editing successive drafts of this book; for challenging me to show more of myself in its words; and, above all else, for your love and support.

To our nieces and nephew, Kaija, Kaylene, Kadence, Jasmine, and Miles—collectively, you are my inspiration. The next generation.

In closing, as I have said in the past, "I express my thanks and pride for the generations of Indigenous peoples—past, present, and future—from coast to coast to coast—who have shown resilience, strength, and steadfast determination to build a more just Canada." I also want to express my deepest gratitude and pride to the residents of Vancouver Granville and the countless Canadians who have shared with me their vision for truth, love, and justice in this country, who stood up for what you believed, and who have and continue to contribute to making this country ever greater.

To my community of Cape Mudge. From the best friend and neighbour anyone could ask for (thank you, Howard Chickite) to everyone from one end of the village to the other . . . Gilakas'la. On all of my journey, including while writing, my community life—on our lands and territories, among our families, our cultures, our languages, and our traditions—is a unique and precious gift, a respite from all that is everywhere else. Cape Mudge is home, and always will be.

The reflection one sees of oneself in the mirror is the legacy that ultimately matters. I have strived to live a life of principle and values, to reflect the best of what I have been taught is important in life. I keep looking in the mirror as part of the striving, to make sure I am doing my part to honour the past, change the present, and build a stronger future. The journey continues.

Appendix:
Annex to Statement
Released on January 14, 2019

LEGISLATIVE ACHIEVEMENTS

As Minister of Justice, introduced 13 pieces of legislation:

Bill C-14—In conjunction with the Minister of Health, passed legislation that responded to the Supreme Court of Canada's *Carter* decision that gives Canadian adults with a grievous and irremediable medical condition the choice of a medically-assisted death.

Bill C-16—Groundbreaking human rights legislation that added gender identity and expression as a prohibited ground for discrimination under the Canadian Human Rights Act, and to the list of distinguishing characteristics of "identifiable group" protected by the hate speech provisions of the Criminal Code.

Bill C-45—In conjunction with the Ministers of Health and Public Safety, passed legislation to legalize, strictly regulate and restrict access to cannabis for adults.

Bill C-46—In conjunction with the Minister of Public Safety, passed the companion legislation to the Cannabis Act, which toughens laws on drug and alcohol impaired driving. Also authorized the use of the Draeger, the first roadside oral screening device regarding drug use.

Bill C-51—Legislated the first major update to sexual assault laws in over 25 years. It also legislated the requirement of Charter Statements to accompany each piece of government legislation, and repealed a number of redundant provisions of the Criminal Code.

Bill C-60—Passed the Miscellaneous Statute Law Amendment Act (the 12th of its kind), an Act to correct certain anomalies, inconsistencies and errors and to deal with other matters of a non-controversial and uncomplicated nature in the Statutes of Canada and to repeal certain Acts and provisions that have expired, lapsed or otherwise ceased to have effect.

Bill C-75 (currently before the Senate)—Our government's legislative response to the Supreme Court of Canada's decision in *Jordan*. It contains a comprehensive package of criminal justice system reforms and is the outcome of a review of the changes in our criminal justice system and sentencing reforms over the past decade. It also implements our platform commitments to toughen criminal laws and bail conditions in cases of domestic assault, in consultation with stakeholders and with the goal of keeping survivors and children safe.

As well, Bill C-75 reintroduces legislative amendments from the following four bills:

Bill C-28: An Act to amend the Criminal Code (victim surcharge);

Bill C-38: An Act to amend An Act to amend the Criminal Code (exploitation and trafficking in persons); and

Bill C-39: An Act to amend the Criminal Code (unconstitutional provisions) and to make consequential amendments to other Acts (this bill also included **Bill C-32**, An Act related to the repeal of section 159 (anal intercourse) of the Criminal Code).

Bill C-78 (currently before the Senate)—The first substantial update of Canada's federal family laws in over 20 years, which will put the best interests of children first, address family violence, reduce child poverty, and make Canada's family justice system more accessible and efficient.

Bill C-84 (currently in the House of Commons)—Strengthens the law on bestiality and animal cruelty, and responds to the Supreme Court of Canada's decision in *R v. D.L.W.*

For each piece of Justice legislation, as well as some other Government bills, introduced in the House of Commons an accompanying Charter Statement outlining how the bill potentially engages Canadians' Charter rights.

NON-LEGISLATIVE ACHIEVEMENTS

Overhauled the federal judicial appointments process, including the process of appointing Supreme Court Justices, to ensure that it is transparent, inclusive and accountable to Canadians.

As a result of that process, appointed 250 judges across Canada including a record number of 104 appointments in 2018. Of those, more than 56% are women, eight are Indigenous, twenty-two are members of visible minority communities, twelve identify as LGBTQ2S, and three identify as persons with disabilities. Created 75 new judicial positions across Canada responding to the needs of Canadians and the courts.

Expanded Unified Family Courts in Alberta, Ontario, Nova Scotia, and Newfoundland and Labrador.

Conducted a Criminal Justice System Review that included diverse consultations and round-tables across Canada.

Invested in victim's services and access to justice for victims and families through the Victims Fund.

Reviewed our government's litigation strategy, ending appeals, changing positions or settling cases where it was appropriate to do so.

Issued a prosecutorial directive on HIV non-disclosure cases to the Public Prosecution Service of Canada, to make our justice system fairer and to reduce the stigmatization of Canadians living with HIV.

Issued *Principles respecting the Government of Canada's relationship with Indigenous peoples.*

For the first time, published an annual *Litigation Year in Review* document in 2016, 2017 and 2018.

Issued a *Directive on Civil Litigation Involving Indigenous Peoples*, which will guide Canada's legal approaches, positions and decisions taken in civil litigation involving Aboriginal and treaty rights and the Crown's obligation towards Indigenous peoples.

Supported the Minister of Canadian Heritage in the restoration of a modern Court Challenges Program.

Led delegation to the United Nations Human Rights Council's third Universal Periodic Review in Geneva, a review of Canada's human rights record by United Nations member states. Was the first time Canada sent a cabinet-level head-of-delegation.

Initiated the first meetings of federal-provincial-territorial Ministers responsible for human rights in nearly 30 years.

Spoke to the UK House of Lords, with an introduction by the Rt. Hon. Kim Campbell.

Delivered the Annual Reconciliation Lecture at the Australian National University in 2016, the first non-Australian to do so.

Opened the 15th session of the United Nations Permanent Forum on Indigenous Issues in 2016, with a speech on Canada's relationship with Indigenous Peoples, the UN Declaration on the Rights of Indigenous Peoples, and the need for free, prior and informed consent.

Delivered the annual Campagnolo Lecture on Restorative Justice, 2018.

Note: All speeches, legislation and other documents referenced here can be found on the Department of Justice's website at: www.justice.gc.ca.

Sources

1:    **Robert Fife's front-page story:** Robert Fife, Steven Chase, and Sean Fine, "PMO Pressed Wilson-Raybould to Abandon Prosecution of SNC-Lavalin; Trudeau Denies His Office 'Directed' Her," *Globe and Mail*, February 7, 2019 (updated February 8, 2019), https://www.theglobeandmail.com/politics/article-pmo-pressed-justice-minister-to-abandon-prosecution-of-snc-lavalin.

1:    **The allegations in the *Globe* story:** Amanda Connolly, "Trudeau Says Report His Office Pressured Former Justice Minister to Drop SNC-Lavalin Prosecution 'False,'" Global News, February 7, 2019 (updated February 8, 2019), https://globalnews.ca/news/4934682/justin-trudea-pmo-snc-lavalin-jody-wilson-raybould.

10:    **In our system of government:** Canadian Press, "Jody Wilson-Raybould Resigns from Government," *Maclean's*, February 12, 2019, https://www.macleans.ca/news/canada/jody-wilson-raybould-resigns-from-cabinet.

37:    **The resurgence of Aboriginal governance:** Jody Wilson-Raybould, "Building a Stronger Canada Together: The Future of First Nations' Relations in Canada" (Keynote Speech, 2014 Liberal Biennial Convention, Montreal, QC, February 22, 2014).

52: **In my own experience serving:** Jody Wilson-Raybould, "Raising the Bar: Indigenous Women's Impact on the Law-Scape" (Public Policy Forum, Ottawa, ON, October 30, 2018).

63: **But, most of all, thanks to all of you:** Jody Wilson-Raybould, "Liberal Nomination Speech, VanGran" (nomination meeting, Vancouver, BC, July 31, 2014).

88: **I have two children in Vancouver Island:** *Dancing Around the Table, Part 1*, directed by Maurice Bulbulian (National Film Board, 1987).

95: **She's got the power:** Mark Burgess, "The Top 100 Most Powerful & Influential People in Government and Politics 2016," *Power & Influence* 5, no. 1 (Winter 2016): 33, https://www.hilltimes.com/wp-content/uploads/2016/02/012516_ht_sp.pdf.

96: **The justice minister without precedent:** Erin Anderssen, "Jody Wilson-Raybould: The Justice Minister without Precedent," *Globe and Mail*, April 1, 2016, https://www.theglobeandmail.com/news/politics/jody-wilson-raybould-the-justice-minister-without-precedent/article29491293.

144: **No relationship is more important to me:** Minister of Justice and Attorney General of Canada Mandate Letter, November 12, 2015, https://pm.gc.ca/en/mandate-letters/2015/11/12/archived-minister-justice-and-attorney-general-canada-mandate-letter.

146: **To support efforts to end the denial of Indigenous rights:** Canada, Department of Justice, "Principles Respecting the Government of Canada's Relationship with Indigenous Peoples," modified February 14, 2018, https://www.justice.gc.ca/eng/csj-sjc/principles-principes.html.

149: **I want to talk about the nation-to-nation relationship:** Jody Wilson-Raybould, "UNDRIP Is the Start Not the Finishing Line" (address to the 37th AGA of the Assembly of First Nations, Niagara Falls, ON, July 12, 2016).

166: **Consider the following articles:** "United Nations Declaration on the Rights of Indigenous Peoples" (resolution adopted by the General Assembly on September 13, 2007), https://www.un.org/development/desa/indigenouspeoples/wp-content/uploads/sites/19/2018/11/UNDRIP_E_web.pdf.

171: **This Framework gives us the opportunity:** "Remarks by the Prime Minister in the House of Commons on the Recognition and Implementation of Rights Framework" (Ottawa, ON, February 14, 2018), https://pm.gc.ca/en/news/speeches/2018/02/14/remarks-prime-minister-house-commons-recognition-and-implementation-rights.

173: **Litigation is by its nature an adversarial process:** Canada, Department of Justice, "The Attorney General of Canada's Directive on Civil Litigation Involving Indigenous Peoples," modified January 11, 2019, https://www.justice.gc.ca/eng/csj-sjc/ijr-dja/dclip-dlcpa/litigation-litiges.html.

174: **Words have meaning:** Jody Wilson-Raybould, "Recognition, Reconciliation, and Indigenous People's Disproportionate Interactions with the Justice System" (Inaugural Houston Lecture, Johnson Shoyama Graduate School of Public Policy, University of Saskatchewan, September 13, 2018).

195: **I can think of no world:** "Ministers Discuss New Roles Following Cabinet Shuffle," CPAC, January 14, 2019, https://www.cpac.ca/en/programs/headline-politics/episodes/65910900.

195: **I can't imagine where you have been hearing that:** Ibid.

196: **[We have been] hearing for months now:** Ibid.

197: **Several cabinet colleagues:** Peter Zimonjic, "After Being Removed as Justice Minister, Wilson-Reybould Defends Her Performance," CBC News, January 14, 2019, https://www.cbc.ca/news/politics/wilson-raybould-justice-veterans-1.4977782.

197: **Some who spoke on background:** Ibid.

197: **Her supporters said she wasn't hesitant to push back:** Ibid.

197: **Bizarre and incoherent removal of Jody Wilson-Raybould:** Merle Alexander, Leah George-Wilson, Mary Ellen Turpel-Lafond, Val Napoleon, Doug White, and Naiomi Metallic, "The Cabinet Shuffle Says Little about Jody Wilson-Raybould—and Plenty about the Government," *Globe and Mail*, January 16, 2019, https://www.theglobeandmail.com/opinion/article-the-cabinet-shuffle-says-little-about-jody-wilson-raybould-and.

207: **We gather due to a selfish man's injured pride:** Josiah Ryan, "Romney Calls Capitol Riot 'an Insurrection Incited by the President,'" CNN, January 7, 2021, https://www.cnn.com/politics/live-news/congress-electoral-college-vote-count-2021/h_3424b2b12690126f01c307ed50e3be52.

215: **If you think someone is trying to involve you in a crime:** Josh Gerstein, Twitter post, January 3, 2021, https://twitter.com/joshgerstein/status/1345804314128875524.

235: **Opposition Motion:** Canada, House of Commons Debates, February 20, 2019, https://www.ourcommons.ca/DocumentViewer/en/42-1/house/sitting-383/hansard.

241: **I will conclude by saying this:** Canada, Standing Committee on Justice and Human Rights, February 27, 2019, https://www.ourcommons.ca/DocumentViewer/en/42-1/just/meeting-135/evidence.

242: **For a period of approximately four months:** Ibid.

244: **Iqra Khalid (Mississauga—Erin Mills, Lib.):** Ibid.

250: **A significant part of the public dialogue:** Canada, Standing Committee on Justice and Human Rights, "Brief Submitted by: the Hon. Jody Wilson-Raybould, M.P. from Vancouver Granville," March 26, 2019, https://www.ourcommons.ca/DocumentViewer/en/42-1/JUST/related-document/10387710.

254: **We are stronger not in spite of our differences:** Robyn Urback, Twitter post, April 2, 2019, https://twitter.com/RobynUrback/status/1113221114447241216.

254: **Unconscionable:** Amanda Connolly, "Wilson-Raybould Defends Secret Recording That Led to Her Ouster, Says 'Something Very Dangerous' Loomed," Global News, April 3, 2019, https://globalnews.ca/news/5127098/jody-wilson-raybould-jane-philpott-snc-lavalin.

261: **Never going to be an absolute one side or another:** Amanda Connolly, "Trudeau, Scheer Shunned as Some Daughters of the Vote Attendees Turn Backs, Walk Out on Speeches," Global News, April 3, 2019, https://globalnews.ca/news/5126284/justin-trudeau-feminist-daughters-of-the-vote.

267: **After much reflection:** Jody Wilson-Raybould, announcement of decision to run as Independent (Vancouver, BC, May 27, 2019).

277: **It was a bittersweet mix of triumph and revenge:** Ted Cragg to Jody Wilson-Raybould, email, December 27, 2020.

290: **Data has shown that countries that use proportional voting:** Fairvote Canada, "A Look at the Evidence for Proportional Representation," October 24, 2018, https://www.fairvote.ca/2018/10/24/evidence.

290: **It has always been my view:** Canada, Standing Committee on Justice and Human Rights, February 27, 2019, https://www.ourcommons.ca/DocumentViewer/en/42-1/just/meeting-135/evidence.

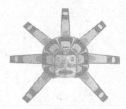

Illustration Credits

Granny and my great-uncle Billy, circa 1915–16: courtesy of the Wilson family

Auntie Donna, Granny, and Dad, circa 1948: courtesy of the Wilson family

Me as a baby with Dad, 1971: courtesy of the Wilson family

My sister, Kory, and me, in 1974, in Grandma's crocheted dresses: courtesy of the author

Me, at about four years old, sporting my favourite barrettes: courtesy of the author

Granny and me dancing at the Potlatch, Gilford Island, BC: courtesy of the author

Dad and me watching a soccer game in Kingcome, BC: courtesy of the author

My granny, Pugladee, circa 1980: courtesy of the Wilson family

Hemas Kla-Lee-Lee-Kla, K'ómoks Big House, Comox, BC: courtesy of the Wilson family

Pugladee, painted by Leonard Peltier, oil on canvas, circa 1990: courtesy of the Wilson family

Me, at age twenty-two, with Granny, at her kitchen table: courtesy of the author

Granny and Dad, sharing a moment: courtesy of the Wilson family

Kory and me, graduation day, UBC Law, 1999: courtesy of the author

With Tim, on our wedding day, Cape Mudge, BC: courtesy of Gary Feighan

Cape Mudge, on the southern tip of Quadra Island, BC: courtesy of the author

My nieces Kaija, Kaylene, and Kadence, in the summer of 2008: © Kory Wilson

Kadence, Kaylene, Kory, me, and Kaija, in Vancouver, June 2018: © Tim Raybould

One of many speeches as Regional Chief: © Tim Raybould

Kwakwaka'wakw Potlatch, 'Namgis Big House, Alert Bay: courtesy of the author

Tim and me, election night, October 19, 2015: © Kim Stallknecht/ Postmedia. Material republished with the express permission of Vancouver Sun, a division of Postmedia Network Inc.

Lea Nicholas-MacKenzie, Kory, and me, on Parliament Hill, 2015: courtesy of the author

That photograph, Rideau Hall, November 4, 2015: © Adrian Wyld/ Canadian Press

Cabinet room sign: courtesy of the author

Honouring ceremony at the Chief Joe Mathias Centre, North Vancouver, 2015: © Tim Raybould

Jane Philpott and me, upon the introduction of Bills C-45 and C-46: courtesy of the author

Mumma and me, Cape Mudge, BC, May 2017: © Tim Raybould

Me in the Cabinet room in Centre Block, December 12, 2018: courtesy of the author

Speaking at a Rideau Hall press conference, January 14, 2019: © The Hill Times photograph by Andrew Meade

INDEX